*'Heart attacks: Gone with the century?'*

*Nobel Prize Winners Brown and Goldstein*[1]

---

[1] *Brown MS, Goldstein JL. 1996. Heart attacks: Gone with the century?* Science; 272: 629.

# Acknowledgements

This report is the result of a National Heart Forum (NHF) initiative which included a 'Delphi-style' consultation survey, six Task Groups, and a national conference on *Coronary Heart Disease Prevention: Looking to the Future*, held in Cambridge in 1997.

The NHF would like to thank all those who helped in this initiative and in the production of this report. Particular thanks are due to:

**Principal sponsors**
British Heart Foundation
Department of Health

**Co-sponsors**
Health Education Authority
Northern Ireland Chest, Heart and Stroke Association

**Patrons**
Dr Keith Ball* OBE MD FRCP
Professor Sir Richard Doll CH MD FRCP FRS
Professor John Goodwin* MD FRCP
Sir Raymond Hoffenberg KBE MD FRCP FFDM
Professor Jerry Morris* FRCP

The National Heart Forum would also like to thank:
- The Task Group members whose papers form the basis of this report, and all those who commented on the papers (see Appendix 2)
- The conference Select Committee (see page vi)
- The conference participants (see Appendix 1)
- All those who participated in the Delphi-style consultation survey
- Dr Duncan Nicholson, of Cambridge Health Futures (Project Consultant)
- Ms Rosie Leyden for editorial work on the report
- Ms Gill Cawdron and Ms Jacquie Allix for conference administration
- Ms Samantha Church, Mr Adrian Field, Dr Alison Giles, Dr Rosemary Hunt, Ms Jane Landon, Ms Modi Mwatsama, Ms Kerry Price and Ms Tuesday Udell for their contributions to the report.

The opinions expressed in this report do not necessarily reflect the views of individual sponsors, patrons, Steering Group members or conference participants.

# Looking to the future

## Making coronary heart disease an epidemic of the past

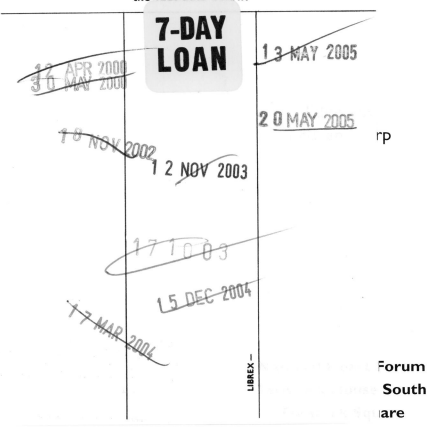
Forum
South
are
London WC1H 9LG

: The Stationery Office

ISBN 0 11 322093 6

**National Heart Forum**
Tavistock House South
Tavistock Square
London WC1H 9LG

Registered Company Number: 2487644
Registered Charity Number: 803286
VAT Number: 564 6088 18

Other publications by the National Heart Forum:

*At Least Five a Day: Strategies to Increase Vegetable and Fruit Consumption*
*Coronary Heart Disease Prevention in Undergraduate Medical Education*
*Coronary Heart Disease Prevention: A Catalogue of Key Resources*
*Coronary Heart Disease Prevention: Action in the UK 1984-1987*
*Coronary Heart Disease: Are Women Special?*
*Eat Your Words: Understanding Healthy Eating and Food Messages*
*Food for Children: Influencing Choice and Investing in Health*
*Physical Activity: An Agenda for Action*
*Preventing Coronary Heart Disease in Primary Care: The Way Forward*
*Preventing Coronary Heart Disease: The Role of Antioxidants, Vegetables and Fruit*
*School Meals Assessment Pack*
*Social Inequalities in Coronary Heart Disease: Opportunities for Action*

Published by The Stationery Office and available from:

**The Publications Centre**
(mail, telephone and fax orders only)
PO Box 276, London SW8 5DT
General enquiries 0171 873 0011
Telephone orders 0171 873 9090
Fax orders 0171 873 8200

**The Stationery Office Bookshops**
123 Kingsway, London WC2B 6PQ
0171 242 6393 Fax 0171 242 6394
68-69 Bull Street, Birmingham B4 6AD
0121 236 9696 Fax 0121 236 9699
33 Wine Street, Bristol BS1 2BQ
0117 926 4306 Fax 0117 929 4515
9-21 Princess Street, Manchester M60 8AS
0161 834 7201 Fax 0161 833 0634
16 Arthur Street, Belfast BT1 4GD
01232 238451 Fax 01232 235401
The Stationery Office Oriel Bookshop
18-19, High Street, Cardiff CF1 2BZ
01222 395548 Fax 01222 384347
71 Lothian Road, Edinburgh EH3 9AZ
0131 228 4181 Fax 0131 622 7017

**The Stationery Office's Accredited Agents**
(see Yellow Pages)

*and through good booksellers*

Printed in the United Kingdom for The Stationery Office by
J 74524 C12 3/99 9385

# Steering Group

| | |
|---|---|
| **Professor Desmond Julian** (Chair) | Chairman, National Heart Forum, 1993-98 |
| **Professor Godfrey Fowler*** | Department of Public Health and Primary Care, University of Oxford |
| **Mr Paul Lincoln** | Health Education Authority |
| **Professor Michael Marmot*** | International Centre for Health and Society, University College London |
| **Dr Alan Maryon Davis** | Royal Institute of Public Health and Hygiene |
| **Professor Klim McPherson*** | Cancer and Public Health Unit, London School of Hygiene and Tropical Medicine |
| **Dr Noel Olsen** | British Medical Association |
| **Professor Brian Pentecost** | British Heart Foundation |
| **Dr Mike Rayner*** | British Heart Foundation Health Promotion Research Group |
| **Lord Rea*** | Parliamentary Food and Health Forum |
| **Ms Maggie Sanderson** | British Dietetic Association |
| **Professor Gerry Shaper** | Vice-Chairman, National Heart Forum, 1995-98 |
| **Ms Imogen Sharp** | Director, National Heart Forum |
| **Professor Desmond Sheridan** | Royal College of Physicians of London |
| **Ms Martine Standish** | Society of Health Education and Health Promotion Specialists |
| **Dr Michael Wilkinson** | Coronary Prevention Group |
| **Ms Lynn Young** | Royal College of Nursing |

## Programme Group

| | |
|---|---|
| **Ms Imogen Sharp** (Project Director) | Director, National Heart Forum |
| **Mr Adrian Field** (Project Coordinator) | Policy Development Officer, National Heart Forum |
| **Ms Pauline Doyle** | Policy Communications Officer, National Heart Forum |

*\* Individual National Heart Forum member*

# Conference Select Committee

| | |
|---|---|
| **Professor Sir Michael Peckham** (Chair) | Director, School of Public Policy, University College London |
| **Dr Angela Coulter** | Executive Director of Policy and Development, King's Fund |
| **Professor Raanan Gillon** | Editor, Journal of Medical Ethics |
| **Dr Fiona Godlee** | Deputy Editor, British Medical Journal |
| **Ms Shirley Goodwin** | Associate Director of Commissioning, Hillingdon Health Authority |
| **Mr Alistair Robertson** | Director of Technical Operations, Safeway Stores PLC |
| **Professor Peter Sleight** | Professor Emeritus of Cardiovascular Medicine, Nuffield Department of Clinical Medicine |

# National Heart Forum

The National Heart Forum (formerly the National Forum for Coronary Heart Disease Prevention) is an alliance of over 40 national organisations concerned with the prevention of coronary heart disease. Members represent the health services, professional bodies, consumer groups and voluntary organisations.

The mission of the National Heart Forum is to work with and through its members to achieve a reduction in coronary heart disease mortality and morbidity rates throughout the UK. It has four main objectives:

- to keep under review the activities of member organisations and disseminate findings

- to identify areas of consensus, issues of controversy, and needs for action

- to facilitate the coordination of activities between interested organisations

- to make recommendations where appropriate.

**Member organisations**
ASH (Action on Smoking and Health)
ASH Scotland
Association of Facilitators in Primary Care
British Association for Cardiac Rehabilitation
British Cardiac Society
British Dietetic Association
British Heart Foundation
British Medical Association
British Nutrition Foundation
Chartered Institute of Environmental Health
Community Practitioners' and Health Visitors' Association
Consumers' Association
CORDA
Coronary Prevention Group
English Sports Council
Faculty of Public Health Medicine
Family Heart Association
Health Education Authority
Health Promotion Agency for Northern Ireland
Health Promotion Wales
King's Fund
National Association of Governors and Managers
National Association of Teachers of Home Economics and Technology (NATHE)
The NHS Confederation
Northern Ireland Chest, Heart and Stroke Association

Royal College of General Practitioners
Royal College of Nursing
Royal College of Paediatrics and Child Health
Royal College of Physicians of Edinburgh
Royal College of Physicians of London
Royal College of Psychiatrists
Royal College of Surgeons of England
Royal Institute of Public Health and Hygiene and the Society of Public Health
Royal Pharmaceutical Society of Great Britain
SHARP (Scottish Heart and Arterial disease Risk Prevention)
Society of Cardiothoracic Surgeons
Society of Health Education and Health Promotion Specialists
Society of Occupational Medicine
Trades Union Congress
The United Kingdom Public Health Association
The Wellcome Trust

**Observer organisations**
Department of Health
Department of Health and Social Services, Northern Ireland
Medical Research Council
Ministry of Agriculture, Fisheries and Food
National Consumer Council
Scottish Consumer Council
Scottish Office, Department of Health
Welsh Office

In addition, a number of distinguished experts in the field have individual membership.

# Preface

Coronary heart disease is not just the biggest killer of men and women in the UK, causing around 150,000 deaths a year, but a major cause of ill health and disability to many more people, often in the prime of life.

The government has made coronary heart disease a primary focus for action, not only in its proposed strategy for public health, but also in the delivery of service through a National Service Framework dedicated to coronary heart disease. Our commitment is to tackle the root causes of the disease, by involving key players in a national contract for health. The National Heart Forum, and its member organisations, will play an essential role.

The National Heart Forum brings together abundant expertise in coronary heart disease prevention and is ideally placed to consider the trends in heart disease, prevention strategies and policy development, and to determine future priorities for prevention. This is what this report does. It is the culmination of a substantial amount of work including an expert conference in July 1997, which I was pleased to launch. The result is a vision of heart disease prevention in the future based on a thorough and important body of research, policy assessment and recommendations for action. It will provide a vital impetus to all agencies, including government, responsible for and concerned with the prevention of coronary heart disease.

I commend this report and expect it to stimulate concerted action to reduce the incidence of the leading single, yet often preventable, cause of death in the UK.

**Tessa Jowell**
*Minister for Public Health*

# Contents

# Foreword

Coronary heart disease is the UK's leading single cause of death, including premature death. But it is largely preventable. The Canterbury conference in 1983 - *Coronary Heart Disease Prevention: Plans for Action* - from which the National Heart Forum derived, heralded a revolutionary approach to the prevention of coronary heart disease in the UK, and was highly influential in setting a new national agenda. Many of its recommendations - including national health strategies with targets and monitoring for coronary heart disease, and the structures, including cross-government Cabinet commitment, to achieve the goal of reducing coronary heart disease rates - are now in place. Since then, the National Heart Forum has influenced policy and practice through the united efforts of a broad range of agencies, using a public health approach based on a multifactorial model, incorporating both environmental and genetic causes. Preventive strategies have primarily focused on the classic risk factors for coronary heart disease - smoking, high blood cholesterol and high blood pressure - and the lifestyle factors, such as diet and physical inactivity, that cause them.

But the scenario has changed considerably since the early 1980s. While improvements in rates of coronary heart disease and its risk factors in the UK have not been as great they might, the context for prevention now is very different. Research has produced new evidence on risk factors and effective interventions, both in the population as a whole, and in high risk groups. At the end of the 20th century, the overall political, social and health climate differs greatly from that of the early 1980s. The need for a new approach to reducing coronary heart disease rates in the UK is apparent. The potential is great.

The goal of this National Heart Forum initiative, *Coronary Heart Disease Prevention: Looking to the Future*, is to set a new national agenda for further reducing rates of disability and death from coronary heart disease in the UK, in all social groups. The Cambridge conference, in 1997, from which this report derives, was the culmination of a series of initiatives to help shape a strategy for the next decade and beyond.

We would like to thank all those involved in *Looking to the Future*, including those who took part in the initial consultation survey; the conference participants; the Task Groups who produced the background papers and the commentators; the conference Select Committee; and of course the patrons. We are also grateful to the sponsors - the British Heart Foundation and the Department of Health - and the co-sponsors - the Health Education Authority and the Northern Ireland Chest, Heart and Stroke Association - for providing funding for the initiative.

Heart disease is now centre stage on the national public health agenda, and central to local health strategies. We hope that this report will shape strategies for coronary heart disease prevention - at both national and local levels - and act as a stimulus for action into the 21st century.

**Sir Alexander Macara**
*Chair, National Heart Forum*

**Professor Desmond Julian CBE**
*Chair, Looking to the Future*
*Chair, National Heart Forum 1993-98*

# Chapter 1

# Introduction

Coronary heart disease is the UK's leading single cause of death, killing some 150,000 people each year, including almost 21,000 before they reach the age of 65. The disease also causes illness and disability for many more: some 1.4 million people suffer from angina, a painful, debilitating disorder and, each year, an estimated 300,000 have a heart attack. The major economic consequences amount to annual costs of £10 billion to the UK economy: the costs of health care alone are £1.6 billion, and the costs of treatment and secondary prevention have been increasing substantially. The indirect costs of coronary heart disease, including lost production, amount to £8.5 billion. Over half the total cost to the economy is due to long-term illness among those of working age.

Death rates from coronary heart disease in the UK have been falling since the late 1970s. But the decline has not been as impressive as in other similar developed Western countries such as the United States and Australia, and rates in the UK are still among the highest in the world. The UK no longer tops the international league table for coronary heart disease death rates, but only because it has been overtaken by rising rates among Eastern European countries. Furthermore, levels of morbidity, particularly angina, do not seem to be falling and may even be rising, especially as the population ages. There are also now major social class, regional and ethnic differences in rates of coronary heart disease and risk factors. In particular, the falling rates are largely due to a decline among non-manual social groups; prevention strategies have been less successful among lower income groups. Efforts to tackle many of the risk factors and determinants of coronary heart disease have been only partially successful, for a number of reasons.

The National Heart Forum, founded at the Canterbury conference in 1983, has helped shape the public health policy agenda since the early 1980s. Many of the early recommendations, from Canterbury and since, have now been implemented - including the UK's first national public health strategies, which established coronary heart disease prevention as a priority, with targets; the establishment of a Cabinet committee on public health bringing together 11 government departments; a national monitoring system; a commitment to take health impact into account when policies are made; and a focus on wider alliances of agencies to improve health.

But many of the changes have been primarily structural. Although the UK has set a national agenda to prevent coronary heart disease, and has put in place public health structures, the direction of policy - on international, national and local levels - has often conflicted with the goal of health. Policy measures have been piecemeal rather than comprehensive - partly due to a lack of political will - and their impact on risk factors and coronary heart disease has been mixed.

So what has caused the reductions in coronary heart disease, and why have rates not fallen faster? What has been effective in changing risk factors and health behaviour, and what can be learnt? What should be done to ensure that policy and practice translates into a further reduction in coronary heart disease rates - across all social groups?

## Looking to the future

The National Heart Forum initiative - *Coronary Heart Disease Prevention: Looking to the Future* - aims to address these questions. The main aim of the initiative is:

• to generate a new national consensus agenda for further reducing rates of disability and death from heart disease in the UK, across all social groups.

The objectives are:

• to take stock of current patterns of heart disease and risk factors, prevention strategies and the policy context

• to explore new concepts and different visions of the future that will affect heart disease rates and strategies for prevention, and

• to set new priorities for prevention for the 21st century, and establish an agenda for action.

The initiative began with a Delphi-style consultation survey of some 300 national and international experts. Six Task Groups prepared background papers on trends in risk factors and heart disease; new concepts in heart disease causation; population policies to reduce heart disease risk; how to effect individual behaviour change; the role of medical interventions in reducing heart disease risk; and the social, political and economic trends that will affect coronary heart disease. The initiative culminated in a national conference in Cambridge in 1997, involving almost 100 health and policy experts. Conference workshops, involving all the participants, considered the implications of the evidence for different population groups - including children and young people, adults, and different socioeconomic, gender and ethnic groups - and generated many ideas and priorities. The conference Select Committee considered the evidence from the Task Groups, as well as the workshop conclusions, to offer clear directions for future policy action.

## The new context

*Looking to the Future* presents the opportunity to evaluate and assess in the light of trends and new evidence - to set a new agenda for national and local action. With a changing social and political context, and new national health strategies, come fresh expectations of what is possible and what can be achieved. The challenge now is to ensure that the evidence is translated into policy and practice, to make freedom from premature death from coronary heart disease an achievable goal in the 21st century.

# Chapter 2

# Select Committee report

**SELECT COMMITTEE**

**Professor Sir Michael Peckham** (Chair)
*Director, School of Public Policy, University College London*

**Dr Angela Coulter**
*Executive Director of Policy and Development, King's Fund*

**Professor Raanan Gillon**
*Editor, Journal of Medical Ethics*

**Dr Fiona Godlee**
*Deputy Editor, British Medical Journal*

**Ms Shirley Goodwin**
*Associate Director of Commissioning, Hillingdon Health Authority*

**Mr Alistair Robertson**
*Director of Technical Operations, Safeway Stores PLC*

**Professor Peter Sleight**
*Professor Emeritus of Cardiovascular Medicine, Nuffield Department of Clinical Medicine*

*This report was prepared by the Select Committee of the* **Looking to the Future** *conference, for the National Heart Forum.*

*The Select Committee considered the evidence from the Task Groups in the written background papers and the presentations, followed workshop discussions over the course of the conference, and took account of workshop conclusions and comments on the draft Select Committee report.*

*The Select Committee report is intended as a brief strategy paper, outlining priorities for coronary heart disease prevention for the next decade and beyond, and the means for their implementation. The Select Committee did not attempt to probe the validity of the evidence; their focus was on drawing conclusions and proposing policy action. The Committee also identified uncertainties and gaps in knowledge, and possible obstacles to the formation and implementation of policy.*

*The Select Committee report was prepared in 1997, at a time when several government initiatives were engaged in reviewing public health. Sir Donald Acheson was chairing a review committee to advise on means to reduce inequalities in health; the Chief Medical Officer was reviewing the public health function; and the government was promising a Green Paper on public health, development of a strategy and White Paper to tackle tobacco, and establishment of a Food Standards Agency. The government was also developing the concept of Health Action Zones, which focused on the need to establish links between health authorities and local authorities using urban regeneration funds. This Select Committee report offered guidance to those initiatives.*

# SELECT COMMITTEE REPORT: EXECUTIVE SUMMARY

1   Despite an encouraging decrease in incidence and mortality, coronary heart disease remains the single biggest cause of death in the UK. Morbidity is increasing as the proportion of elderly people rises, and there is widening divergence in coronary heart disease mortality between socioeconomic groups as well as geographical differences across the UK.

2   Policies and interventions designed to prevent coronary heart disease need to address anomalies in the structure of society as well as behavioural and other factors more obviously related to the condition. For this reason coronary heart disease is not only a major problem in its own right but also a test case for the effectiveness of strategies designed to correct inequalities related to class, income and opportunity.

3   To tackle the risk factors known to be associated with coronary heart disease, as well as the adverse influence of socioeconomic, ethnic and geographical inequalities, we make proposals for a new framework for public health through two complementary and interrelated developments: a Public Policy and Health Agency, and Local Health Action Teams.

4   The Public Policy and Health Agency would serve as a resource both for government and for initiatives at local level. Through its access to appropriate expertise it would propose new developments in policy relating to primary and secondary disease prevention and, through an understanding of the spectrum of public health problems, set the scene for a national strategy.

5   We propose that community-based initiatives devised and implemented by Local Health Action Teams involving lay people, should be piloted, funded and appropriately evaluated. The terms of reference should include the identification of priorities for improving health and preventing ill health, proposing mechanisms for delivery, as well as the identification of the criteria by which the success of initiatives will be judged.

6   To be effective such schemes need to be backed by appropriate government policies that shape the milieu in which local initiatives are developed. The policy framework needs to be coherent and broadly based, tackling multisector problems relating to urban development, natural environment, transport and other areas of activity that impinge on health.

7   We suggest that schemes developed by Local Health Action Teams should be put forward by local authorities and health authorities for support by public funds. Assessment of pilot schemes would provide the basis for national coverage aimed at reducing coronary heart disease but with wider significance for health.

8   We recommend that young people should be the focus of and be involved in a new public health initiative based on the framework we propose. Currently the economic, psychological and environmental circumstances of a third of children in the UK are likely to increase their risk of subsequent coronary heart disease. Actions through schools could and should play a substantial role, but the influence and environments to which children and adolescents are exposed outside school are also crucially important.

9   Physical risk factors for coronary heart disease include blood lipid levels, smoking, high blood pressure, diabetes, obesity and physical inactivity. Complementary and comprehensive strategies aimed at populations, individuals and high risk groups are likely to be most effective in reducing coronary heart disease mortality and morbidity. Coronary heart disease is a test case for welding such strategies into a coherent action plan. The approaches devised to achieve this will have wider relevance to health.

10  The problem of overweight and obesity needs serious attention. Evidence on adverse effects and on feasible action which individuals can take to avoid or correct overweight should be made known clearly to the public. A national food strategy is needed to bring together the large body of information on eating habits, coronary heart disease and health more generally and to translate this into policies and practical action. We support the establishment of the Food Standards Agency which has a powerful part to play in developing a cohesive strategy on changing dietary patterns across the UK.

11  More effort is needed to develop alternatives to foods particularly high in fat and salt that are of equal palatability to existing products. We recommend that government and the food industry jointly explore an appropriate framework to encourage industry to invest in the research and development necessary to achieve this.

12  The time is right to revise the Common Agricultural Policy to correct anomalies such as the financial incentives for higher fat content in milk, and seek to create a common food policy.

13  We welcome policy changes by government, including a ban on tobacco advertising. To back government action we recommend the creation of a Tobacco Forum. This would coordinate action against smoking and develop new proposals for policies and interventions.

14  We endorse the government policy of imposing real increases annually in tobacco taxes. Tobacco subsidies in the Common Agricultural Policy should be removed.

15  Despite evidence that moderate physical activity reduces coronary heart disease mortality and a sedentary lifestyle more than doubles the risk, there has been little impact on behaviour. We recommend the establishment of a Physical Activity Forum charged with developing and implementing a strategy for encouraging levels of activity that are beneficial and achievable.

16  Over the past decade there have been great advances in the medical and surgical treatment of coronary heart disease. Although effective primary prevention strategies to reduce coronary heart disease are the ideal, there is good evidence that secondary prevention interventions are effective and may have an important impact on overall mortality. It is important that they are applied in a cost-effective manner.

17  To ensure that policy formation and planning are aware of, and responsive to new developments, a dedicated effort is also needed to identify and monitor current and likely future trends in demography, science and technology, as well as in changes in society and in national and international policies.

# Introduction

Coronary heart disease is the single biggest cause of mortality in the UK with some 150,000 deaths in 1996, of which almost 21,000 were in those aged less than 65. While the incidence of and mortality from coronary heart disease are falling in both men and women, morbidity from angina and heart failure seems to be increasing as the population ages. In 1983, in response to the World Health Organization (WHO) recommendations for prevention of coronary heart disease, a conference was convened in Canterbury to explore means of rapidly implementing the WHO recommendations in the UK. The report from the 1983 conference led to structural changes, but the effect on policy has been less apparent. New evidence and a change in government have presented an opportunity to reassess strategies for prevention.

The appointment in 1997 of the Minister of Public Health, and the recognition by government of the need for cross-departmental initiatives directed at health, open up new opportunities for orientating public policy towards the prevention of ill health. Past experience has shown that policy initiatives designed to prevent disease have produced disappointing results, often due to a failure to implement. The challenge now is to match aspirations with well conceived and effective policies and actions.

This Select Committee Report is based on the documentation, presentations and discussions at the National Heart Forum conference, *Coronary Heart Disease Prevention: Looking to the Future,* held in Cambridge in July 1997. The coverage was wide, extending from national and international policy issues to the details of medical interventions.

## The context of coronary heart disease

Coronary heart disease is so common that population strategies are needed in addition to those that target high risk individuals. By reducing the coronary heart disease risk of the whole population, population strategies will help reduce morbidity from coronary heart disease or prevent deaths of a large number of people who die relatively suddenly before the possibility of arrival of medical or paramedical help. Seventy per cent of all coronary heart disease deaths occur outside hospital.

The risk of coronary heart disease depends on many factors including genetic constitution, diabetes, blood pressure and lifestyle factors such as smoking, lack of physical activity, and a diet high in animal (saturated) fat and low in fruit and vegetables.

Forms of behaviour that are associated with coronary heart disease also relate to health and ill health more widely. Thus smoking and diet are implicated in the cause of cancer, and high blood pressure and alcohol excess in the cause of stroke. Strategies to reduce coronary heart disease could have wider health gain implications.

But coronary heart disease is also a manifestation of the shortcomings of society. Social class, education, geography, income distribution, employment, and stress are elements that influence health. The interpretation of some epidemiological findings in relation to the multifactorial causation of coronary heart disease remains to be elucidated. Although socioeconomic disadvantage is associated with increased risk, the finding of a gradient of morbidity and mortality across the grades of the UK civil service indicates that other factors relating to position in a work hierarchy are also relevant.

The significance for the UK of societal dysfunction and inequalities, in terms of economic stability as well as health, must be better understood, and the correction of disadvantage and unfavourable factors viewed as an investment rather than a drain on resources. A strategy for coronary heart disease must therefore address not only problems specific to the disease and problems common to coronary heart disease and other conditions, but also issues of wider relevance.

## Tackling inequalities: coronary heart disease as a test case

In the 1990s there is widening divergence in coronary heart disease between different socioeconomic groups and the prospect of a growing burden of disability from coronary heart disease, particularly in the elderly. Over the past 30 years no real decline in coronary heart disease among the lowest social class is evident. These and other findings, including differences in coronary heart disease mortality in different parts of the UK, highlight the need to address social issues as well as the risk factors more specifically related to coronary heart disease.

Policies and interventions designed to prevent coronary heart disease need to address anomalies that are deeply rooted in the structure of society as well as behavioural and other factors more obviously related to the condition. For this reason coronary heart disease is not only a major problem in its own right but also a test case for the effectiveness of strategies designed to correct inequalities related to class, income and opportunity.

Tackling these fundamental issues means designing and successfully implementing policies that cut across the range of private and public sectors. This includes economic policies, particularly those that concern welfare (health, education and pensions).

## A fresh approach to public policy and health

Initiatives that are locally generated and embedded in the community offer a potentially powerful way of improving health and preventing ill health. To stand a chance of being effective, local schemes need to be developed in a milieu that favours their success, and backed by appropriate government policies. Such policies need to be coherent and broadly based, tackling problems relating to education, urban development, natural environment, transport, employment, crime and other issues that shape the health and vigour of society.

The development of integrated multisector policies, focusing on health, is a task for which the departmental structure of government is not well suited. Sources outside government have been insufficiently used and should be drawn on more systematically and more imaginatively to assist in this task. We make proposals for seeking to achieve this and to bridge the gap between community-led initiatives and central government through two complementary and interrelated developments: a Public Policy and Health Agency, and Local Health Action Teams.

### Public Policy and Health Agency

We identify the need for a body to take an overarching view of health determinants and that has the capacity and contacts necessary to inform policies and strategies designed to address them. To fulfil this role we propose the establishment of a Public Policy and Health Agency to spearhead the development of a national strategy for enhancing health and preventing disease. We have chosen to refer to the new agency in terms of 'public policy and health' rather than 'public health' to emphasise the need to address problems across government departments and across the range of sectors in society.

The Public Policy and Health Agency would play a role in the process of government while operating at arm's length from, but accountable to, Ministers. It would require a formal structure, clear responsibility delegated by government and sufficient funding to discharge its functions. It would serve as a resource both for government and for initiatives at local level. Through its access to appropriate expertise it would propose new developments in policy relating to primary and secondary disease prevention and through an understanding of the spectrum of public health problems set the scene for a national strategy.

The agency would seek to strengthen and harness the intellectual resource needed to tackle outstanding health problems. An important function would be to assess the health impact of public policies, including an assessment of the likely consequences for health of the policies of government departments, and an assessment of the effect of policies once they have been implemented.

The agency would draw on community-based skills, views and initiatives and facilitate and support innovative schemes generated and implemented locally. It would be a source of advice on their design and on appropriate methods of evaluation. It would assist in the identification of the most promising community-based approaches for wider application. The agency would seek to identify locally developed approaches that work and to determine whether they would be likely to work equally well in other localities.

We envisage the agency as the nerve centre or hub in a collaborative network involving a wide range of academic disciplines and sectoral interests. It would establish links not only with central government and community-led programmes but with the National Health Service (NHS), the science base, local authorities, industry and the voluntary sector. It would work closely with the Food Standards Agency. In conjunction with this and other relevant bodies, the Public Policy and Health Agency could be called upon to advise on European and wider international policies which impinge directly or indirectly on the health of UK citizens. To fulfil its role the Public Policy and Health Agency would need to be involved early in policy thinking and in government negotiations in Europe.

### Local Health Action Teams

The goal of a strategy aimed at reducing the burden of coronary heart disease and improving health more generally must be to encourage and support initiatives that capture the imagination and commitment of lay people, particularly in communities with the worst health. Local schemes should be backed by central policies, sustained with appropriately targeted resources and assisted by expert input as necessary. A prime task of local initiatives is to find ways of energising and gaining the input of the lowest quintile in society, particularly in inner cities. What is needed is a positive search for ways of reducing the current coronary heart disease burden and eliminating the discrepancies in coronary heart disease incidence and mortality, working towards this goal by addressing factors recognised by the community members as influencing their health.

We propose that local initiatives devised and implemented by Local Health Action Teams involving lay people should be piloted, funded and appropriately evaluated. The active participation of those most at risk, particularly from socioeconomically deprived groups, will be essential. The terms of reference of the teams should include the identification of priorities for improving health and preventing ill health in the local community, proposing mechanisms for delivery, and identifying the criteria by which the success of initiatives will be judged.

We suggest that community-led health promotion schemes should be put forward by local authorities and health authorities as pilot projects for support by public funds. Assessment of the outcome of pilot schemes over the next three to five years would provide information necessary for national coverage aimed at reducing coronary heart disease but with wider significance for health.

To be effective, local schemes will need to sustain their impact and adapt to changing circumstances and knowledge. Sustainability will depend on the structural framework in which they evolve. A major factor will be active cooperation between health and local authorities working towards the same goals. Links with primary care and the wider NHS as well as with industry and voluntary organisations should be developed, and there should be easy access to information and advice through the Public Policy and Health Agency. Consideration should be given to the way in which such schemes are assessed. It is likely to be difficult to apply conventional measures of effectiveness and thought should be given at an early stage to the criteria by which success could be judged.

Crucial to the success of local schemes will be a belief by those who participate that the actions and solutions they propose can be effective, as well as acceptance by government that innovation at local level can be a powerful mechanism for maintaining and improving health.

## Risk factors and their modification

Within this broader social context, physical risk factors for coronary heart disease include blood lipid levels, smoking, raised blood pressure, diabetes, obesity and physical inactivity. In addition, dietary factors, level of alcohol consumption and sedentary lifestyle are determinants or correlates of these primary risk factors. There is considerable interest in newer risk factors such as maternal nutrition and intrauterine environment, antioxidant vitamins, folic acid and homocysteine, and inflammation and infection, but the evidence for intervention on these factors is not yet clear.

Efforts to modify known risk factors have taken three approaches: attempts to reduce risk in the population as a whole; attempts to change individual behaviour;

and treatment of high risk groups. Experience suggests that interventions aimed at individuals that are not backed up by national policies are likely to be ineffective. A combination of complementary and comprehensive strategies aimed at populations, individuals, and high risk groups is likely to be most effective in reducing mortality and morbidity. Coronary heart disease is a test case for welding such strategies into a coherent action plan. The approaches devised to achieve this will have wider relevance to health.

The Select Committee focused on initiatives to change eating habits, reduce smoking, and increase physical activity. We recognised the need to use different approaches for different sectors of the community, and that policy should depend less on the relative contributions of the different risk factors and more on what can be modified.

### Dietary factors
There is now broad consensus and weight of evidence that dietary factors are one of the fundamental determinants of coronary heart disease. Dietary fat, and in particular saturated fatty acids, are widely accepted as being the factor most likely to increase blood cholesterol. While there has been a significant shift in the ratio of saturated to unsaturated fatty acids in the diet over time (which in part may explain the observed reduction in coronary heart disease), total fat intake has remained remarkably constant at approximately 40% of calorie intake.

To bring together the large body of information on eating habits, coronary heart disease and health more generally and to translate this knowledge into policies and practical action, a national food strategy is needed.

*Overweight and obesity*
Epidemiological evidence suggests that overweight and obesity are closely linked to the proportion of energy in the diet derived from fat. Fat is the most energy-dense food and is less satiating than carbohydrate or protein. Individuals exposed to a high fat diet tend to overeat, while low fat diets have been shown to produce spontaneous weight loss even in those eating without restriction.

Overweight/obesity is a risk factor for the development of high blood pressure, hyperlipidaemia and diabetes, which in turn are linked to coronary heart disease. The increase in the prevalence of obesity is a particular concern since this may be slowing the rate of decrease in coronary heart disease. Strategies to reduce the prevalence of overweight and obesity must consider both diet and physical activity. Obesity develops when energy intake exceeds energy expenditure for a prolonged period. Although low levels of physical activity may be an important factor contributing to the increased level of obesity, the fact still remains that individuals who become obese are overeating relative to a reduced energy requirement. The problem of overweight and obesity in the UK deserves more serious attention. The evidence on adverse effects and on feasible actions that individuals can take to avoid or correct overweight should be made known clearly to the public.

*Salt*
There is now consensus that dietary sodium is a factor in the development of high blood pressure, and therefore efforts should be directed at moderate lowering of salt in the whole population.

*Vegetables and fruit*
Emerging and increasing evidence on the relationships between vegetables, fruit, and antioxidants and coronary heart disease, combined with epidemiology on the benefits of a 'Mediterranean' diet, is sufficiently strong to drive national strategy on increasing fruit and vegetable consumption.

*Healthier food options*
Strategies aimed at changing dietary patterns of individuals have had a disappointing impact on the intake of healthy foods. More successful has been the availability of foods designed and developed to improve the intake of dietary elements advantageous to health, such as low fat milks and modified fatty acid spreads. We believe that efforts to develop alternatives to foods particularly high in fat and salt, should be encouraged, underpinned by food research and development. Currently much of the research and development effort of industry is directed towards food safety rather than the development of new products with lower salt and fat content. We recommend that government and the food industry should jointly explore the development of an appropriate framework to encourage the development of new products, promoting consumer uptake by ensuring that such alternatives are of equal palatability as existing products.

*Food messages*
We believe there is more to be done to ensure that the evidence is presented to the public in easy to understand terms. There is also substantial scope for providing advice on what individuals can and should do about their eating habits. The objectives of future initiatives should be to increase intake of fruit, vegetables and cereals, reduce the percentage of energy derived from fat, and reduce dietary salt.

*Food Standards Agency*
We support the establishment of a Food Standards Agency which, with a remit for diet and health, including nutrition, has a powerful part to play in developing a cohesive strategy on changing dietary patterns across the UK. This body should be instrumental in informing the development of policy and strategy on all factors relating to food, including dealing with the impact of international policies that are inconsistent on diet and health.

*Common Agricultural Policy*
A prime example is the European Common Agricultural Policy (CAP). With the review of the CAP, an opportunity exists to put health on the agenda of CAP reform. This opportunity should be taken to revise the CAP, to correct anomalies such as the financial incentives for higher fat content in milk, and seek to create a common food policy.

*Catering and education*
More attention should be paid to the standards of public catering (including hospital catering) where there is scope for setting standards in line with available evidence on healthy eating. School food should conform with national nutritional standards. There is also scope for providing instruction, in an attractive format, to children and adults on food buying and cooking skills.

*Choice and accessibility*
There is a need to draw a distinction between the failure of individuals to buy healthy foods when they have the opportunity to do so, and obstacles - economic,

access, and others - that prevent them from doing so. Cultural factors that lead to a division in terms of food-buying along lines of socioeconomic group regardless of access, need to be better documented and understood, and appropriate strategies developed to address them.

Strategies should be developed at the national and local level to improve access to healthy foods, especially fruit and vegetables, for all sections of the community, particularly for those who are socioeconomically deprived.

*Advertising and promotion*
Advertising and promotional strategies successful in attracting consumers to specific brands should be adopted to promote healthy eating. At the same time consideration should be given to tackling the issue of food advertising which is inconsistent with expert views on healthy eating, especially when aimed at children.

**Smoking**
Smoking is a major, potentially preventable, cause of coronary heart disease, with unassailable evidence underpinning the policy objective of reducing the use of tobacco. Since the recommendations of the Canterbury Conference in 1983 there has been an encouraging decline of smoking rates in adults, but the rate of decline is slowing. The decline has been less among women and people in socially disadvantaged groups, and there is an increase in teenagers, especially girls.

In view of the failure of many recent campaigns in a number of countries to achieve a decline in children's smoking, there is a need for innovative thinking and approaches about effective ways of preventing recruitment to smoking. At the same time every effort should be made to achieve this through government and European Union policies favourable to the abandonment of smoking, through alliances with the media, and through a better understanding of behavioural factors that encourage people to start smoking and prevent them from stopping.

A 'summit' on smoking was held under the auspices of the Department of Health in July 1997. Following this, proposed policy changes included legislation to ban tobacco advertising and promotion through sports and the arts, for example. The Select Committee greatly welcomed this. However, the lead set by government needs to be backed up by action to implement policies, to provide research and other inputs into new policies, and to monitor and evaluate the impact of policy.

*Tobacco Forum*
There is an urgent need for fresh approaches to tackle cigarette smoking in a sustainable manner. The smoking issue should be addressed through Local Health Action Teams backed by government policies and a resource to draw together knowledge, expertise and the lessons from national and international experience.

To fulfil this role we recommend the creation of a Tobacco Forum. The Tobacco Forum would form part of the Public Policy and Health Agency. The forum would establish links with relevant individuals and organisations in the public and private sectors in order to develop new proposals for policies and interventions and to coordinate actions against smoking across sectors.

*Strategies to reduce smoking*
We endorse current UK government policy of imposing real increases annually in tobacco tax, which should be maintained. However, we recommend that strategies to tackle smoking in low income groups need to be a priority. We also support a ban on advertising and advertising-based sponsorship and promotion of tobacco products and purveyors. We recommend that the Common Agricultural Policy be revised to remove the substantial tobacco subsidies.

Priority should be given to policies that are aimed particularly at the problem of smoking among children and socially disadvantaged groups. Emphasis is also needed on policies that restrict smoking in public places and workplaces, and that enforce the laws on not selling tobacco to under-16 year olds.

Subject to a continued scrutiny of impact, we support the continuation of individual and population-based approaches to smoking cessation including: general practitioner advice, nicotine replacement and smoking clinics; health education in schools; media advice and publicity; and quitlines.

## Physical activity
Moderate physical activity reduces coronary heart disease mortality and there is clear epidemiological evidence from many different populations that a sedentary lifestyle more than doubles the risk of the disease. Despite this, there is little evidence to suggest that this information has substantially influenced policy or the behaviour of the population. Currently it is estimated that almost a third of the population can be classified as sedentary, engaging in little or no physical activity. A major task is to integrate physical activity into everyday life and to see it as a normal function and indeed a reversal to habits that were once the norm.

*Physical Activity Forum*
We recommend the establishment of a Physical Activity Forum which would form part of the Public Policy and Health Agency. The prime task would be to develop and implement a coherent strategy for encouraging levels of physical activity that are beneficial and achievable. The Physical Activity Forum would maintain a broad overarching view of factors that might discourage or encourage physical activity. It would be charged with drawing together and clearly presenting information to government as well as to professional and other bodies and to the public.

Obstacles to physical activity should be clearly identified and the potential for correcting them explored by the Physical Activity Forum. Examples include the real and perceived dangers which prevent children walking or cycling to school, and patterns of transportation that encourage travel by car and discourage use of public transport.

To realise these objectives:

- Town and transport planning should take account of the need for an infrastructure that encourages cycling, and the need for well-lit streets, parks and easier access to recreation facilities as well as incentives and facilities which encourage cycling and walking.

- The balance of physical activity in the school curriculum should be reviewed.

### Ethnic groups

The risk factors discussed in this report apply to the range of ethnic groups in the UK. There are epidemiological differences between different ethnic groups, with those from South Asian groups in the UK at higher risk from coronary heart disease. The prevention strategies outlined here are applicable to ethnic minority groups although the way in which they are implemented must take account of cultural and other relevant factors.

## Focus on children and adolescents

Although coronary heart disease is a disease of adult life, we believe that young people should be involved in, and be a focus of, a new national public health initiative. At the threshold of a new millennium there should be appeal in the notion that we now know enough to prevent many of the premature deaths from coronary heart disease, as long as what we do know is effectively implemented.

The early years exert a major influence on subsequent behaviour patterns and on adult health. Children can also exert a positive influence on the behaviour of adults. Habits laid down in childhood can affect risk of coronary heart disease in later life. Some current trends put children at particular risk, including falling levels of physical activity and increased smoking. Currently the socioeconomic, psychosocial and environmental circumstances of a third of children are likely to increase their risk of subsequent coronary heart disease. The explanation for the increase in smoking in young children is unclear and in general there is a lack of knowledge on behavioural, psychological and sociological aspects of childhood and the teenage years.

Although actions on health through schools could and should play a substantial role, the influences and environments to which young people are exposed outside school are also crucially important. Young people should be the prime focus of some of the initiatives developed through Local Health Action Teams.

## Coronary heart disease patients, and high risk groups

Over the past decade there have been great advances in the medical and surgical treatment of coronary heart disease. Although effective primary prevention strategies to reduce coronary heart disease are the ideal, there is good evidence that secondary prevention interventions are effective and may have an important impact on overall mortality. It is important that they are applied in a cost-effective manner.

Between 70% and 75% of all people who die of coronary heart disease are recognised as having coronary heart disease or a major risk factor such as high blood pressure or diabetes, and treatment in these groups could have a major impact on mortality and morbidity in the population. Since the 1983 Canterbury Report there has been great progress in the medical and surgical treatment of established coronary disease. The challenge now is to apply available knowledge appropriately.

Epidemiological evidence on the role of cholesterol in coronary heart disease has been reinforced by large randomised trials of statin drugs which, with long-term use, lower cholesterol and reduce the need for angioplasty or surgery after a heart attack. No evidence of serious adverse effects has been demonstrated, particularly cancer or violent deaths or suicide. Recent trials have shown benefit whatever the initial level of cholesterol. The decision on how widely to use lipid-lowering drugs will depend on their current high cost, although some will soon be off patent.

Large randomised trials have produced clear evidence of benefit from aspirin and thrombolytic drugs if used promptly, with a reduction in mortality by about half if the combination was given within four hours of the onset of pain. The high proportion of deaths outside hospital, and the contraindications to treatment, limit the effectiveness of this therapy in population terms. Direct angioplasty without thrombolysis is a less well proven alternative, provided that experienced operators are available promptly, which is not the case for most of the UK.

Beta-blocking drugs particularly reduce the risk of a further heart attack (and also sudden death) by about 25%-30%, but are less used than they should be.

ACE inhibitors (angiotensin converting enzyme inhibitors) are effective in reducing mortality in patients who show heart failure or who have damage to the left heart muscle, both early and continued long-term. Heart failure is an increasing problem among the elderly, partly because of better survival after heart attacks.

Observational studies have suggested that hormone replacement therapy (HRT) substantially reduces the risk of coronary heart disease in both healthy pre-menopausal women and in those with coronary heart disease. The large trials needed to determine the effectiveness and safety of HRT are now in place.

Just as the emphasis for cholesterol reduction is now an individual's overall risk rather than cholesterol level alone, so the emphasis for blood pressure reduction should be greater and should start at lower blood pressure levels in patients with known coronary heart disease.

### Changes in lifestyle
Changes in lifestyle are especially important in people at high risk, and interventions to reduce smoking, alter eating habits, and increase physical activity should continue to be targeted at these individuals.

### Audit of patients with coronary heart disease
Overall, clearly proven targets now exist for reducing future risks in patients with identified coronary heart disease. This evidence also helps in formulating non-drug strategies for prevention in the normal population. However, uptake of these strategies is sub-optimal when such patients are audited after an event. We recommend that systematic audit of patients with documented coronary heart disease should be carried out regularly to ensure that available treatments are used appropriately. This would lead to further reduction in avoidable coronary deaths.

## Integrating primary prevention, secondary prevention and clinical care

The quest for solutions to problems relating to coronary heart disease causation and the management of established disease involves a huge range of tasks. These tasks are divided between many research disciplines, organisations, professional groups and interests, and they are distributed across government departments. The integration of initiatives designed to correct inequalities on the one hand and responses to advances in medicine and science and technology more generally is a particular challenge. The framework proposed in this report, based on a Public Policy and Health Agency and the development of an effective collaborative network, should be developed to assist government and those outside government to address this challenge.

Policies and strategies designed to enhance health and prevent disease will take time to exert an effect. In conjunction with these efforts, improved methods of treatment and secondary prevention of coronary heart disease as well as of rehabilitation and management of angina, heart failure and other disabilities associated with coronary heart disease, will need to be developed, tested and used appropriately. In addition, further research is needed to ensure the relevance of particular interventions across different cultural groups.

Achieving balance and coherence across this spectrum of activities will raise issues of resource allocation. This in turn will place emphasis on assessing the benefits secured through different approaches to coronary heart disease. In this context coronary heart disease could be a model of how an integrated approach might be developed, encompassing policies and interventions designed to tackle wider determinants of health as well as established disease.

## Ethical issues

The core ethical concerns of this Select Committee report were to recommend interventions likely to produce health benefits with minimal harm; that aim to respect the personal choices of the people affected; and that are developed in the context of social justice, including respect for people's rights and fair allocation of scarce resources. The Select Committee was particularly concerned by the adverse effects on coronary heart disease mortality of socioeconomic, ethnic, and geographical inequalities. Addressing the factors that give rise to these inequalities and to the ethical issues that they raise should be an explicit task for government policy assisted by the Public Policy and Health Agency.

## Gaps in knowledge, methodology and translation

The Select Committee became aware of substantial shortfalls in knowledge, in method of approach, in the translation of knowledge into policy and the translation of policy into action. Methods are needed for evaluating preventive interventions, and ways of implementing policies need to be reappraised and strengthened.

### Epidemiology
There is insufficient information on changes in the incidence and prevalence of coronary heart disease risk factors and on the growing burden of coronary heart

disease morbidity, particularly in the older age group. Not enough is known about the reasons for the decline in mortality rates, including international comparisons of changes in risk factor prevalence. Prospective data collection systems need to be established to correct these deficiencies. There are many gaps in knowledge of coronary heart disease aetiology and in our understanding of how individual risk factors contribute to causation.

### Evaluating effectiveness of prevention strategies

Psychological and behavioural factors are insufficiently understood, particularly those relating to childhood and adolescence. Little is known, for example, about how to prevent teenagers taking up smoking, including the effects of raising the legal age for buying cigarettes to 18, a proposal which we support but which must be carefully evaluated. Appropriate methods of evaluation need to be put in place to monitor the effects of a ban on tobacco advertising and sports sponsorship, including knock-on effects, for example, on smoking rates in the young, on the availability of sports facilities and hence on levels of physical activity.

Better methods are needed to document the effectiveness of population strategies to increase physical activity. For example, there is only limited evidence on the effect of curriculum changes on participation in sport and leisure time exercise among school leavers. Individual strategies, such as primary care referral schemes, also require more systematic evaluation. The impact of all these strategies on health outcomes must be evaluated.

The relative contributions of marketing strategies, access and availability, affordability, knowledge, and social and cultural factors on dietary patterns need to be teased out. Current research tends to be uni-disciplinary and ways should be explored of promoting and funding multidisciplinary research into policy implementation.

## Future trends

The development of policies and strategies for coronary heart disease, as for other causes of ill health, need to be set in the context of an understanding of current and likely future trends.

Of particular significance is the increasing proportion of elderly people and the concomitant increase in the burden of coronary heart disease morbidity. Individuals at high risk of coronary heart disease, and those who have or have had the disease will be exposed to a widening range of medical and surgical interventions, each of which should be identified at an early stage and appropriately assessed before general use.

At the same time there will be advances in social and behavioural science and knowledge derived from local initiatives. Over the next decade there is also likely to be a clearer understanding of the genetic contribution to coronary heart disease, providing a potential basis for targeting treatments and advice on the avoidance of risk factors.

These demographic and scientific trends will occur on a background of changes in society and national and international policies. Maintaining an overview requires a dedicated effort to identify and monitor such trends. This is a task in which the National Heart Forum and its members and partners could play a valuable role.

# Chapter 3

# Coronary heart disease and risk factors: current patterns and future trends

**TASK GROUP**

**Professor Klim McPherson** (Convenor)
*Cancer and Public Health Unit, London School of Hygiene and Tropical Medicine*

**Ms Karen Dunnell**
*Demography and Health Division, Office for National Statistics*

**Dr David Leon**
*Department of Epidemiology and Population Sciences, London School of Hygiene and Tropical Medicine*

**Dr Mike Rayner**
*British Heart Foundation Health Promotion Research Group*

**Professor Hugh Tunstall-Pedoe**
*Cardiovascular Epidemiology Unit, University of Dundee*

# Coronary heart disease and risk factors: current patterns and future trends

This chapter:

- assesses current and future trends in coronary heart disease mortality and morbidity, in relation to risk factor trends

- identifies the main problem issues in patterns of coronary heart disease and risk factors

- assesses the implications of current risk factor trends for future coronary heart disease rates, and

- considers the broad interventions which may be necessary to bend the trend.

**KEY THEMES**

1 Death rates from coronary heart disease in the UK are decreasing fairly uniformly, among both sexes at all ages, by around 4% a year.

2 Much of this change is consistent with observed trends in adult smoking and in population blood pressure levels. Limited long-term data on lipid levels and on levels of physical activity indicate much less change and less commensurate effect. Obesity changes might well be attenuating the observed decrease in death rates.

3 Evidence for a profound effect of secondary and tertiary care on mortality is not entirely convincing. The main determinant of coronary heart disease mortality rates is likely to be its incidence, much of which is explained by known risk factor prevalence.

4 Theoretical considerations combined with these observations indicate a potential for further improvement so that mortality from coronary heart disease among under-65 year olds could become rare, as it already has for those in non-manual occupations.

5 Greater understanding of the determinants of mass behavioural change and their health effects, and commitment to their policy implications, could still lead to great improvement. Or it could just occur, essentially consistent with current trends, but possibly more steeply, perhaps as a consequence of increasing awareness and personal control and more enlightened government policy.

# Introduction

Trends in mortality from what is now called coronary heart disease can be extrapolated back as far as the 1920s if certain assumptions are made about the now superseded terminology of cause of death and subsequent coding. The trend is clear: an increase among men at all ages up to 75 until the early 1970s, and then a decline which even appears to be getting more pronounced in the 1990s (see Figure 1). Among women there was an increase until the late 1930s and then a decline, quite marked among younger women, followed by an increase in the 1970s and then a decline very similar to that of men. This recent decline is predominantly a period effect[1] as opposed to an age or cohort effect - which means that the decline appears to be related most strongly with calendar time and not with a person's age nor with when they were born. The decline applies essentially to all age groups equally, implying *prima facie* that the changes in mortality from coronary heart disease are largely determined by contemporaneous changes in environmental factors, physical, social or health care, which involve the whole population.

**Figure I** *Age specific death rates for coronary heart disease, England and Wales, men and women, 1930-1997*

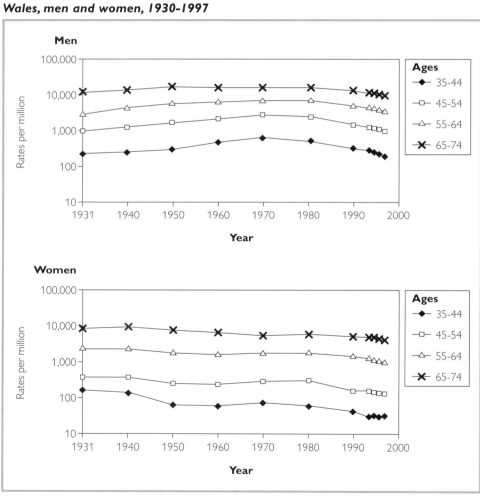

Source: See reference 2.

The ratio of mortality rates for men compared with women in the 1920s was around 50% excess for men at all ages. Subsequently this ratio increased, reaching a peak in the 1970s of nearly seven-fold among young people and three-fold at age 65-74. In the 1990s the ratio is around five-fold below age 55, and two-fold at age 65-74.

Interestingly, this is probably not a menopausal phenomenon, and not therefore a response to changing female hormone levels, since the sex ratio does not change markedly at around age 50.[3] The mortality rates for women and for men climb almost linearly with age on a log scale (more so for women than for men) between ages 30 and 90, and there is no departure from linearity at age 50.[4] However, the rates for women and men converge slowly over the entire age range.

To put these death rates in perspective, the annual mortality in the 1990s is around 1 per 10,000 per year at age 32 for men and age 40 for women, 1 per 1,000 at ages 44 and 55, and 1 per 100 at ages 70 and 80 for men and women respectively. The time trends are remarkable: among 45-54 year olds, the rates among men in 1921 were nearly four times as high (4 per 1,000) as they are in the 1990s, while for women they were the same as now (2 per 10,000). However, this disguises a doubling of death rates at around 1951 and again in 1971, and then a fall to current rates for women.

Coronary heart disease mortality rates in the UK, standardised for age, remain nearly twice as high in Northern Ireland, the west coast of Scotland and the Manchester/Liverpool conurbation than in the South East of England.[5] Moreover, the social class gradient in mortality from coronary heart disease, among men, in the early 1990s reached three-fold between unskilled (social class V) and professional classes (social class I) from a 25% excess in the early 70s (see Figure 2). This is the result of no change among social class V, but a massive reduction among the non-manual social classes (and in particular a halving among social class I) since the 70s.[6, 7]

**Figure 2** *European standardised death rates from coronary heart disease, men aged 20-64, by social class, at three time periods 1970-1993, England and Wales*

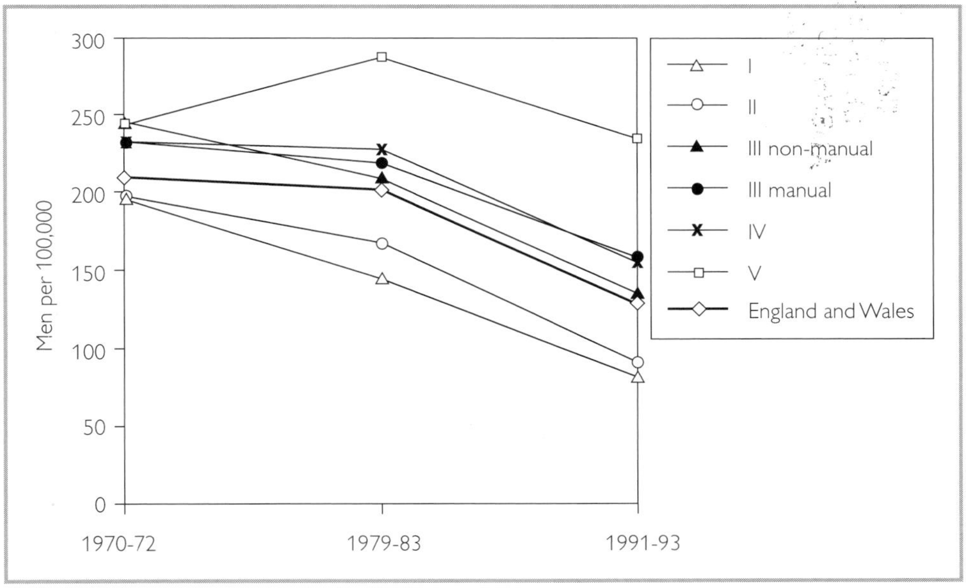

Source: See reference 7.

This recent overall decline in coronary heart disease mortality rates in the UK began later for both sexes relative to the decline seen in countries with markedly high rates in 1970, namely Finland, the United States and Australia, each of which underwent a dramatic public consciousness raising about coronary heart disease with commensurate public health changes of various kinds. However, the decline in the UK is similar in absolute terms to that seen in low mortality countries such as Japan and Italy, in spite of starting with at least double the rate. Interestingly, the increasing mortality rate in Eastern and Central Europe has recently caught up with and in some cases overtaken the mortality rate in the UK.

Coronary heart disease is clearly a complicated disease with a complicated multifactorial aetiology, which relies on an interaction between atheroma and a thrombotic event. Trends in mortality must depend on the combined trends in incidence, diagnosis, prognosis and efficacy of interventions. Incidence is not normally measured over time in a reliable way, although this has recently been attempted in the form of heart attack rates (myocardial infarction and coronary deaths) in the international WHO MONICA project, which in the UK involves centres in Glasgow and Belfast.[8] Hospitalisation was by no means uniformly indicated across the periods discussed and hence much coronary heart disease will be not be recognised or measured, particularly in the earlier periods. Recent advances in secondary prevention may arrest the mortality rates still further without necessarily reducing the overall burden of disease.

## Risk factors

The recent changes in coronary heart disease mortality rates are too large to be explained by changes in the disease coding, as the decline in deaths is carried through to all cause mortality and is not compensated for by increases for other causes. The most probable explanation is changing incidence related to changing risk factors because the majority of deaths still occur outside hospital and are hence relatively impervious to medical care. For example, in the WHO MONICA project 50% of coronary events were fatal within 28 days but, of these events, 35% died before reaching hospital, constituting 70% of all coronary deaths.[8]

Work in Finland[9] indicates that a high proportion of the changing mortality can be explained by changes in the prevalence of three risk factors: smoking, blood pressure and cholesterol levels. In the period 1972-92 in Finland, mortality among men decreased by 55% and among women by 68%. The weighted combination of these risk factors predicted a decline of 44% for men and 49% for women. However, the trend lines are remarkably close for both sexes until the late 1980s, after which treatment improvements could explain the more recent divergence. Similar explanations have been successful in Iceland[10] too, although the earlier Bethesda conference[11] on the decline in mortality in the United States was unable to attribute these changes to changing risk factors. Clearly these analyses are compromised by any unknown latent effects, unexplained aetiology such as genetic components and common factors with little individual effect,[12] changes in other risk factors such as vegetables and fruit and antioxidants,[13] and the profound problems of reliable measurement of known risk factors among populations.

The major unequivocal identified risk factors for coronary heart disease are cholesterol levels, smoking, blood pressure, diabetes and lack of physical activity. Diet, obesity and excessive alcohol may either help to determine levels of primary risk factors, or just be correlated with them, or they may induce mortality which emulates coronary disease. Social status itself might also be a strong risk factor after adjustment has been made for these other behavioural factors.[14] This might indicate general unspecific social factors which can be postulated and which might go some way to explaining the international differences.[15] It is clearly not social class itself because this relationship is inconsis'ent with time and place, but a strong relationship nonetheless exists between the social, cultural and economic features of society, possibly to do with personal control or autonomy.[16]

Factors operating in foetal life and infancy may affect the risk of coronary heart disease in adult life too.[17] There is increasing evidence from historical cohort studies conducted in Britain, Sweden and the United States that, as birthweight decreases, there is a progressive increase in the much later risk of coronary heart disease. This inverse association is most firmly established for men, although it has also been seen in two studies for women. Typically, studies have found a rate ratio of between 1.5 and 2.0 for death from coronary heart disease between those weighing less than 6lbs at birth and those weighing 9lbs and over. Initial concern that this association was due to confounding by socioeconomic circumstances has been largely allayed by studies that have been able to take simultaneous account of socioeconomic circumstances in early and later life. A number of studies have been able to look at the combined effects of conventional coronary risk factors with size at birth.[18] These suggest two important things: firstly, that obesity is at least one adult risk factor that acts to potentiate the effects of size at birth on coronary heart disease risk; and secondly, that conventional risk factors such as serum cholesterol levels and blood pressure do not appear to be important mediators of the association between size at birth and coronary heart disease.

Overall, these studies underline the fact that, whatever the influence of early-life factors on coronary heart disease risk, their impact can only be considered in combination with the influence of the conventional adult risk factors.

Moderate alcohol consumption is protective for coronary heart disease compared to abstention.[19] However, most of the epidemiological cohorts on which these conclusions have been based are unlikely to include those who indulge in binge drinking. Binge drinkers are thought to be at increased risk of sudden cardiac death from arrythmias (irregular heart rhythms) and cardiomyopathy (disease of the heart muscle).[20] The importance of this association on levels of disease is illustrated by increases in mortality from heart disease in Russia, where death from heart disease is thought to be associated with binge drinking in particular. It is possible that the current estimates of the impact of alcohol consumption on the health of populations underestimate the true effects, although binge drinking among those at risk of coronary heart disease is likely to be considerably less common than moderate drinking. Also, in cases in the UK where high alcohol levels are found at post mortem, forensic pathology is more likely to designate causes other than coronary heart disease for such deaths.

In the UK, the prevalence of these risk factors for coronary heart disease has been carefully measured in specific studies[21, 22] and measured repeatedly in the UK MONICA populations. However, only since 1991 have they been routinely measured over time by the *Health Survey for England* for monitoring *Health of the Nation* targets.[23] Similar surveys have been carried out in other parts of the UK. These data suggest that cholesterol is unchanging, blood pressure is decreasing independently of treatment, obesity is certainly increasing, and total smoking prevalence is decreasing. Smoking prevalence among adults has been showing a steady decline in both sexes since the 1970s, with a rather greater decline among men than women, and among adults than children.[5]

The change in cigarette consumption since the early 1970s, on conservative assumptions, could itself be responsible for between a quarter to a third of the observed reduction in mortality in the period. The reduction in diastolic blood pressure from 1991 to 1995 is also impressive and was foreshadowed by previous unstandardised survey results suggesting higher levels in previous decades.[24] Among men and women aged over 50, the reduction in the period 1991-95 seems to be of around 3mmHg. This is not a chance finding, nor is it attributable entirely to greater treatment levels.[25] If these data do represent a consistent trend that began in the 1980s, then another 30%-40% of the total reduction in mortality could be explained.

There are little data about population distribution of birthweight and foetal growth going much earlier than the 1950s. There are no data to show that there has been a progressive increase in size at birth during the course of this century. It cannot be assumed that the dramatic improvements in infant mortality that have been seen over the past century have gone hand in hand with improvements in foetal nutrition. The other problem in estimating the impact of foetal growth on current and future levels of coronary heart disease is that, as has been suggested above, the effect of impaired foetal growth on coronary heart disease risk is in part dependent upon circumstances in adult life, and in particular body mass index. The increase in obesity recorded since the 1980s and during the period of the *Health Survey for England* can be responsible for attenuating the observed decrease only if obesity itself is a primary cause of coronary heart disease in the absence of concomitant changes in other risk factors.[26]

Trends in rates of participation in exercise lack reliable data. However, an increase in leisure activity participation between 1987 and 1990, with no further change in 1993, has been observed in the *General Household Survey*. The implications for longer term trends in coronary heart disease mortality remain unclear.

Cholesterol levels, a potent determinant of risk, have apparently not changed in the period 1991-95, although household consumption of butter and whole milk have declined by at least 60% since the mid-1970s (see Figure 3). However, the consumption of total fat as a percentage of food energy has hardly changed, while that for saturated fatty acids has fallen by about a quarter since 1975. Since none of these household consumption indices have changed importantly since cholesterol has been reliably measured, the lack of change in cholesterol levels since 1991 may not be surprising. But if a downward trend in cholesterol since the 1970s is the predicted consequence of these dietary changes, then a considerable further proportion of the fall in coronary heart disease incidence and mortality could be explained. Of course, increased intake of vegetables and fruit and antioxidants could be protective too,[27] and there is evidence for an increase in the consumption of these foods, particularly fresh fruit and also fruit juice and fresh vegetables, since the mid 1970s.

**Figure 3** *Household consumption of fats, 1942-1995, Great Britain*

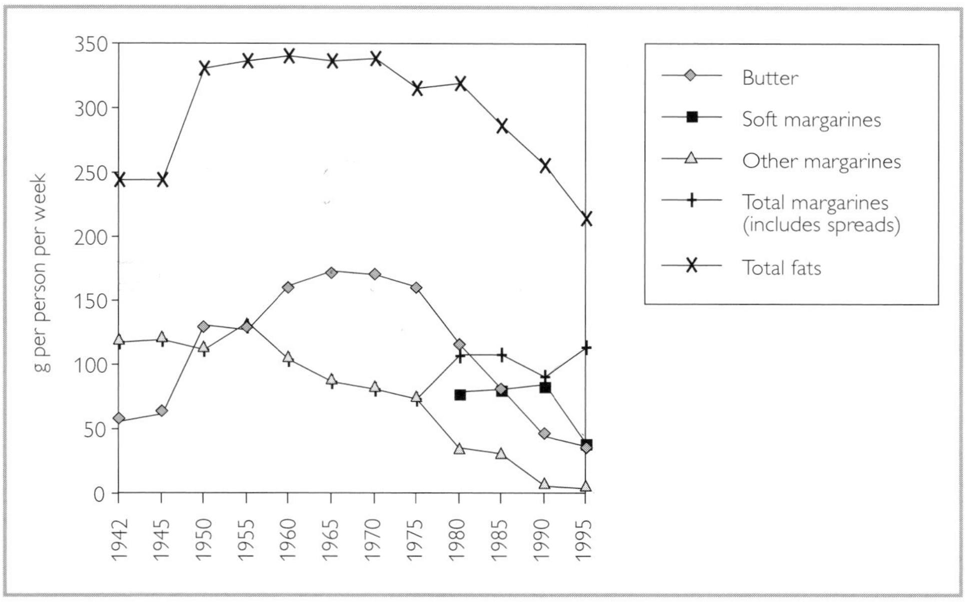

Source: See reference 5.

## Social class differences

In terms of social class trends, much of the latest difference in mortality among men under age 65 can be explained by differences in the prevalence of risk factors. In 1996, 12% of men in social class I smoked compared with 41% among men in social class V.[5] In the period since 1976, the excess prevalence of smoking between manual and non-manual men has remained fairly constant at around 14%: by 1996, 35% of men in manual groups smoked, compared with 21% in non-manual groups.[28] In contrast, over the same period, the difference in the smoking prevalence between manual and non-manual women has widened: in 1976, the percentage difference was 6%; by 1996 this had increased to 11%, and 33% of women in manual groups smoked, compared with 22% in non-manual groups. This is despite an overall decrease in the smoking prevalence over this period.

Likewise, there is a social class gradient for obesity, as well as for vegetable and fruit consumption, and blood pressure in the 1990s. There is, however, no clear social class gradient for consumption of fat and saturated fat, or for blood cholesterol levels or physical activity. The social class-specific trends in the period are more difficult to discern. However, while all of these factors would be expected to have varying amounts of time lag effects on coronary heart disease mortality, they can certainly explain the greater part of existing social class differences - except for the particularly high mortality in social class V. Possibly this is determined by largely unmeasured differences in levels of personal control or autonomy. It is also possible that a small proportion of the latter differences might be attributable to differences in access to health care.

## Morbidity and mortality

In the period since the 1970s, the other major change to affect mortality rates has been the effectiveness of interventions to reduce mortality among people with coronary heart disease. The trend in mortality rates appears to depart from those crudely predicted from changing prevalence of risk factors at the beginning of the 1980s - a trend which was also seen in data from North Karelia. It was in the early 1980s that surgical intervention for chronic angina rapidly became more common, and by 1994 it had increased more than four-fold. At about the same time, the routine use of aspirin after a heart attack also increased. It is difficult to calculate the precise effect that this will have on mortality rate trends, but it is entirely consistent with the hint of an increase in the steepness of the slope from the mid-1980s.

Moreover, the rapid increase in days of certified incapacity for coronary heart disease for men of all ages from 27 million in 1981-82 to 57 million in 1994-95 is also not inconsistent with mortality reductions happening at a faster rate than reductions in incidence in the period. The Minneapolis Heart Survey has also shown a reduction in the risk of death following heart attack of 25% for men and 16% for women since the mid-1980s.[29] However, the *Health Survey for England* covering the period 1991-94 shows little evidence of systematic changes in the prevalence of a history of angina nor of cardiovascular disorders in the short period of observation. There is a possibility of a downward trend in angina symptoms, therefore suggesting a lower prevalence now.

The WHO MONICA project has been examining trends in heart attack and coronary deaths (in particular 28-day mortality) over 10 years in 40 different populations. The original figure of 50% case fatality might be expected to change with the impact of better medication and interventions for acute coronary care over recent years. The 10-year findings suggest that change in case fatality accounts for around one-third of the population reduction in mortality rates.[30] In a number of MONICA populations, and in other population studies, the impact of drugs on case fatalities has been smaller than expected, or even negligible. The WHO MONICA project has paid great attention to standardisation of its diagnostic criteria. An apparently declining case fatality and greater population prevalence, which figure in some reports, could result from more sensitive diagnostic tests. The assumption that declining mortality and increased treatment are inevitably associated with increasing prevalence[31] may well be wrong. However, even if prevalence is constant at any given age, the ageing of the population in itself will produce an increase in the prevalence of coronary heart disease with time.

## Implications of these patterns

While mortality is decreasing, it is possible that incidence is decreasing less rapidly and that the burden of coronary heart disease might be transferring from a dominance of fatal events to a greater prevalence of serious morbidity. Current trends predict a continuing decrease in the total number of UK deaths from coronary heart disease among the age groups below age 80, between 1997 and 2020. Among adults aged over 80, the number will increase by only a few hundred over the same period, from a total of around 2,500 deaths a year among men in 1997 and 4,000 a year among women. The total number of deaths from coronary heart disease

**Figure 4**  *Numbers of deaths from coronary heart disease in the UK, 1980-1994, and predicted numbers up to 2025 based on current trends*

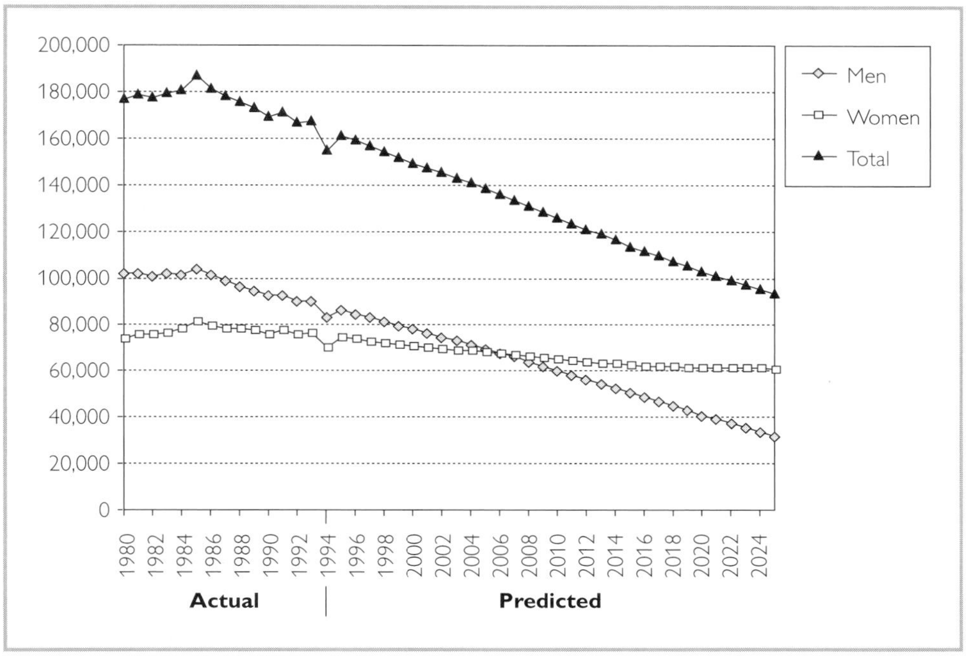

Source: See reference 32.

in the UK is predicted to fall from 155,000 in 1994 to just under 100,000 by 2025 (see Figure 4).[32]

However, more information is needed in order to analyse these trends with respect to potent risk factors and interventions as they change. This requires longer reliable time series for physiological measurements which might, or might not, respond to primary prevention strategies, such as blood pressure, birthweight and cholesterol. Such associations are being investigated for many different populations in the WHO MONICA project. The 10-year results show the relative contribution of changing event rates and changing survival or case fatality to trends in mortality.[30] The recent findings from the ARIC study[33] that incidence is unchanged and mortality rates fell through a fall in case fatality are unlikely to be replicated as the population are more heterogeneous in their behaviour. Data on changing incidence of coronary heart disease are essential in order to disentangle any differential effects from the routinely measured effect on mortality.

Examining the trends in mortality rates for both men and women under age 65 by age group does give an impression of little divergence from a constant slope since the mid-1980s. The decline for women might be slightly less steep, possibly reflecting a slower decline in cigarette smoking. It is also possible that the slope is steeper during the 1990s than the late 80s, although this is, as yet, just an impression. The opposite trend would now be expected as the mortality rates tended towards an unchanging level, determined by the current prevalence of genetic predisposition, diabetes mellitus and high blood cholesterol for example. This observation might imply therefore that the reduction being observed in the latter half of the 20th century in the mortality from coronary heart disease could have a long way to fall yet.

Mortality rates in Australia and the United States are already 30% lower than those of the UK (see Figure 5). Of course, such an observation would be consistent with what is observed in those cultures where dietary habits are such that fat intake is low and coronary heart disease is rare,[34] and in which cholesterol levels of 4.5mmol/l define high risk groups relative to local norms. In the UK and Australia, rates are not showing any signs of reaching a constant level, although in the United States the rate of decline may now be levelling off.

There is no reason to believe that coronary heart disease among healthy people aged less than 65 in the UK is not largely preventable, if acceptable means of reducing cholesterol levels to what might be a biologically normal level can be achieved. Since some 4,500 women and 16,250 men die each year in the UK by around this age,[5] the implications for our social and political life would be profound if we could come close to eliminating this major cause of premature mortality.

**Figure 5**   *Death rates from coronary heart disease, men and women aged 35-74, 1968-1994, selected countries*

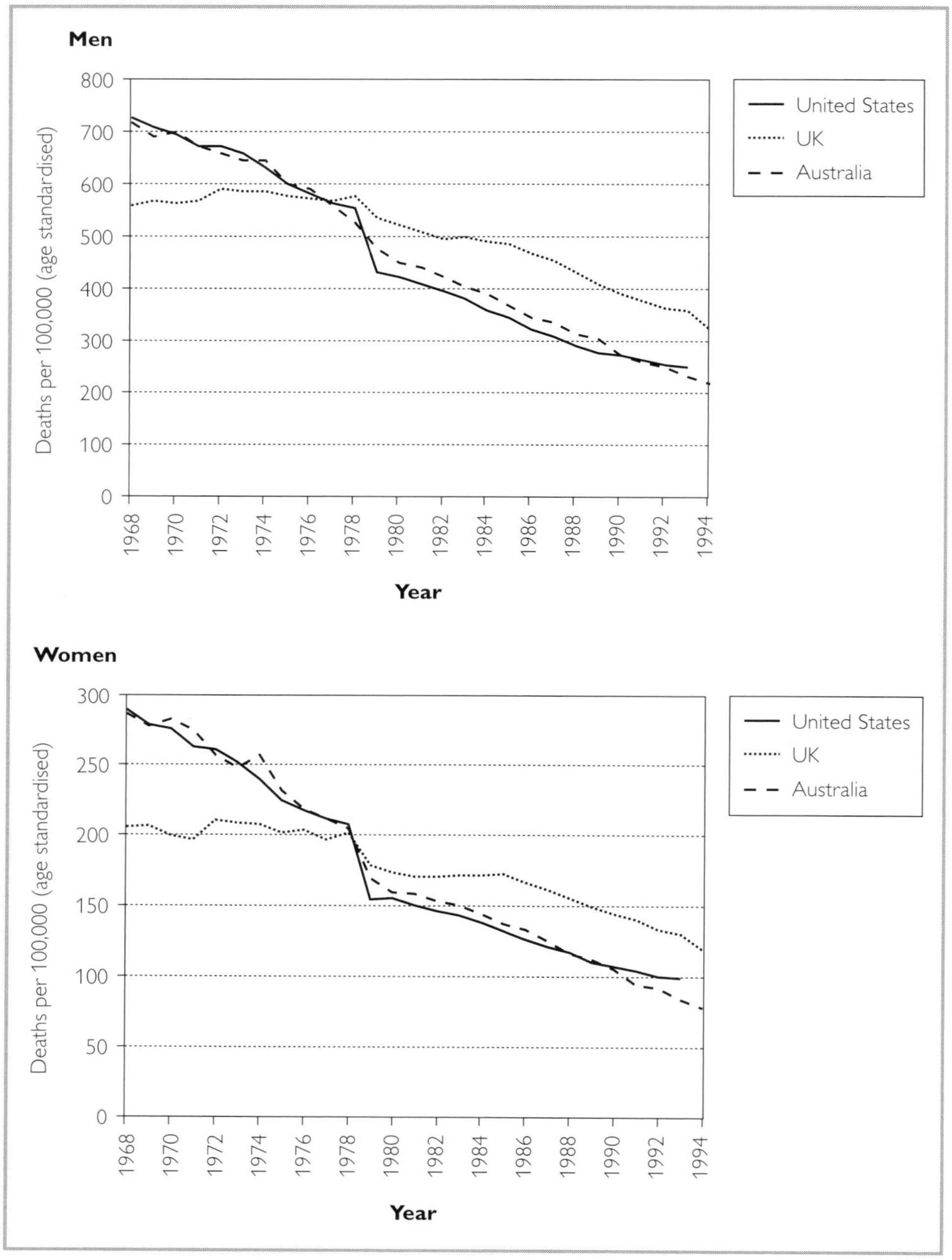

Source: See reference 5.

*Looking to the Future: Making Coronary Heart Disease an Epidemic of the Past*

## Broad interventions

The science of primary prevention is a relatively neglected area in public health policy,[35] particularly as it relates to mass behaviour change. Understanding of the complicated role of, and synergy between, public policy, health promotion strategy, individual behaviour and medical care on exposure to risk and changing disease patterns is very inadequate.[36] Too much effort goes into claiming and refuting benefit for particular key components of a highly complex interdependent reality. It seems that to gain credibility for one's main enthusiasm in prevention it is necessary to dismiss the alternatives, when the effect of one may interplay with another in quite complicated ways.

The transfer of a dominant biological tradition to enhance understanding about attributable effects in a social, political, economic and biological context may simply be inadequate. While health promotion appears to be discredited by some rigorous overviews,[37] the opportunity for contamination in control groups by generalised and specific social changes, whose aetiology is poorly understood, is often ignored.[38] Primary prevention strategies require a greater investment in research simply because to demonstrate a given benefit requires a far greater complexity of research design[39] than straightforward therapeutic interventions.

The clear indication here is that something is working, and possibly in principle these things could work better. If the Food Standards Agency is able to take on a clear public health role then the opportunities for proper prioritisation of food policy may well have a further impact on coronary heart disease. In general the requirements for a focus of a multidisciplinary public health science rather than a continuous professional competition could also have a dramatic effect. A better coordinated structure for public health practice across disciplines and sectors is an urgent requirement.[40]

Profits from selling tobacco is clearly a global problem over which national governments have little effective control. Is an agreed worldwide tobacco-specific fiscal trade policy on profits ever going to be feasible? What is required is international agreement and cooperation on primordial disease prevention, because profits from tobacco are much worse in terms of consequent global disease burden than any other overtly profit-making product used as recommended. Really serious in-roads into international commercial freedoms are sometimes necessary and in this instance such action is irresponsibly belated, essentially out of deference to the addicted. The World Trade Organization, established in 1995 after the Uruguay round of GATT negotiations, may be the body through which this might happen. If successful, all advertising and marketing to vulnerable groups by multinationals would no longer be sensible, and policing parochial bans would become unnecessary. Clearly tobacco cannot be banned, but it should be rendered non-profitable by international agreement on taxation of excess profit from its sale.

At this level of intervention important opportunities exist, for example with policy on national food supplies and marketing, with urban transport, and with determinants of patterns of physical activity. Such changes have also yet to be properly adopted, particularly the appropriate provision of sport and recreation facilities with national purpose, and an adequate response to malnutrition among the poor.[41] Appropriate policy is required to complement national transport policies, giving priority and safe opportunities for cycling and walking (and swimming).

Proper dietary strategies for school meals will have enormous consequences in the very long run. The opportunities for still further decreases in mortality from coronary heart disease in the UK remain largely untried since most of what has happened does not seem to be in response to any specific intervention or policy, just more appropriate general awareness of the personal strategies for avoiding premature cardiovascular death.

In the end, the resolution of these problems requires far better data systems from which reliable time trends in important risk factors can be related to changing incidence and mortality. These problems are important and coronary heart disease represents the most common preventable cause of premature death in Western communities. It also represents the most stark manifestation of social and gender inequalities in health status.

## References

1   Charlton J, Murphy M, Khaw K, Ebrahim S, Davey Smith G. 1997. Cardiovascular disease. In: *The Health of Adult Britain 1841-1994*; vol 1; Decennial Supplement no 13. London: The Stationery Office.

2   Office for National Statistics. *Health of Adult Britain*. London: The Stationery Office. With updates via personal communication with Karen Dunnell, Office for National Statistics.

3   Tunstall-Pedoe H. 1998. Myth and paradox of coronary risk and the menopause. *Lancet*; 351: 1425-1427.

4   Khaw K, Sharp I. The scale of the problem: should we be concerned? In: Sharp I (ed.) 1994. *Coronary Heart Disease: Are Women Special?* London: National Heart Forum.

5   Rayner M, Mockford C, Boaz A. 1998. *Coronary Heart Disease Statistics. 1998 Edition*. London: British Heart Foundation.

6   Drever F, Whitehead M, Roden M. 1996. Current patterns and trends in male mortality by social class (based on occupation). *Population Trends*; 86: 15-20.

7   Drever F, Whitehead M. 1997. *Health Inequalities: Decennial Supplement*. London: The Stationery Office.

8   Tunstall-Pedoe H, Kuulasmaa K, Amouyel P, Arveiler D, Rajakangas A-M, Pajak A, for the WHO MONICA Project. 1994. Myocardial infarction and coronary deaths in the WHO MONICA Project: registration procedures, event rates and case-fatality rates in 38 populations from 21 countries in four continents. *Circulation*; 90: 583-612.

9   Vartiainen E, Puska P, Pekkanen J, Tuomilehto J, Jousilahti P. 1994. Changes in risk factors explain changes in mortality from ischaemic heart disease in Finland. *British Medical Journal*; 309: 23-27.

10  Sigfusson N, Sigvaldason H, Steingrimsdottir L, Gudmundsdottir II, Stefansdottir I, Thorsteinsson T, Sigurdsson G. 1991. Decline in ischaemic heart disease in Iceland and change in risk factor levels. *British Medical Journal*; 302: 1371-1375.

11  Havlik RG, Feinleib M (eds.) 1979. *Proceedings of the Conference on the Decline in Coronary Heart Disease Mortality. National Heart, Lung and Blood Institute. October 24-25 1978. NIH Publication 79-1610*. Washington (USA): US Department of Health, Education and Welfare.

12  Rose G. 1992. *The Strategy of Prevention*. Oxford: Oxford University Press.

13  Gey KF, Puska P, Jordan P, Moser UK. WHO MONICA Project. 1991. Inverse correlation between plasma vitamin E and mortality from ischaemic heart disease in cross cultural epidemiology. *American Journal of Clinical Nutrition*; 53; 1: 326S-334S.

14  Rose G, Marmot M. 1981. Social class and coronary heart disease. *British Heart Journal*: 45; 1: 13-19.

15  Wilkinson R. 1996. *Unhealthy Societies*. London: Routledge.

16  Syme SL. To prevent disease: the need for a new approach. In: Blane D, Brunner E, Wilkinson R. 1997. *Health and Social Organisation*. London: Routledge.

17  Barker DJP (ed.) 1992. *Foetal and Infant Origins of Adult Disease*. London: British Medical Journal Books.

18  Leon DA, Ben-Shlomo Y. Pre-adult influences on cardiovascular disease and cancer. In: Kuh D, Ben Shlomo Y (eds.) 1997. *Life Course Influences on Adult Disease*. Oxford: Oxford University Press.

19  Doll R, Peto R, Hall E, Wheatley K, Gray R. 1994. Mortality in relation to consumption of alcohol: 13 years of observation on male British doctors. *British Medical Journal*; 309: 911-918.

20  Shanmugan M, Regan TJ. Alcohol and cardiac arrhythmias. In: Zakhari S, Wassef M (eds.) 1996. *Alcohol and the Cardiovascular System. Research Monograph 31:* 159-172. Bethesda, Maryland (USA): National Institute on Alcohol Abuse and Alcoholism.

21  Shaper AG, Pocock SJ, Walker M, Phillips AN, Whitehead TP, Macfarlane PW. 1985. Risk factors for ischaemic heart disease: the prospective phase of the British Regional Heart Study. *Journal of Epidemiology and Community Health*; 39: 197-209.

22  Tunstall-Pedoe H, Smith W, Crombie I, Tavendale R. 1989. Coronary risk factor and lifestyle variation across Scotland: results from the Scottish Heart Health Study. *Scottish Medical Journal*; 4: 556-560.

23  Department of Health. 1992. *The Health of the Nation. A Strategy for Health in England*. London: HMSO.

24  Tunstall-Pedoe H, Evans A, Martin I, Keil U, Kuulasmaa K. 1998. *WHO MONICA Project: Preliminary Analysis of Final Results*. Press Conference: European Congress of Cardiology, held in Vienna, August 1998.

25  Prescott-Clarke P, Primatesta P. 1997. *Health Survey for England 1995. Volume 1: Findings*. London: The Stationery Office.

26  Larsson B. Obesity and body fat distribution as predictors of coronary heart disease. In: Marmot M, Elliott P (eds.) 1992. *Coronary Heart Disease Epidemiology: From Aetiology to Public Health*. Oxford: Oxford University Press.

27  Sharp I (ed.) 1997. *Preventing Coronary Heart Disease: the Role of Antioxidants, Vegetables and Fruit*. London: The Stationery Office/National Heart Forum.

28  Office for National Statistics. 1998. *Living in Britain. Results from the 1996 General Household Survey*. London: The Stationery Office.

29  McGovern PG, Pankow JS, Shahar, Doliszny KM, Folsom AR, Blackburn H, Luepker RV. 1996. Recent trends in acute coronary heart disease - mortality, morbidity, medical care and risk factors. *New England Journal of Medicine*; 334: 884-890.

30  Tunstall-Pedoe H, Kuulasmaa K, Mahonen M, Amouyel P, Tolonen H, Ruokokoski E, for the WHO MONICA Project. How trends in survival and event rates relate to changing coronary heart disease mortality: ten-year results from 37 WHO MONICA Project populations. (Submitted for publication)

31  Hunink MG, Goldman L, Tosteson AN, Mittleman MA, Goldman PA, Williams LW, Tsevat J, Weinstein MC. 1997. The recent decline in mortality from coronary heart disease, 1980-1990; *Journal of the American Medical Association*; 277: 535-542.

32  Personal communication with Dr M Rayner.

33  Rosamond WD, Chambless LE, Folsom A, Cooper LS, Conwill DE, Clegg L, Wang C-H, Heiss G. 1998. Trends in the incidence of myocardial infarction and in mortality due to coronary heart disease, 1987 to 1994. *New England Journal of Medicine*; 339: 861-867.

34  Chen Z, Peto R, Collins R, MacMahon S, Lu J, Li W. 1991. Serum cholesterol concentrations and coronary heart disease in populations with low cholesterol concentrations. *British Medical Journal*; 303: 276-281.

35  Blane D, Brunner E, Wilkinson R. 1997. *Health and Social Organisation*. London: Routledge.

36  McKinlay JB. 1977. Paradigmic obstacles to improving the health of populations - implications for health policy. Presented to VII Congreso Nacional de Investigación en Salud Pública. Cuernavaca, Mexico, March 1977. Watertoen (United States): NERI.

37  Ebrahim S, Davey-Smith G. 1996. *Health Promotion in Older People for the Prevention of Coronary Heart Disease and Stroke*. London: Health Education Authority.

38   McPherson K. 1995. A population approach to interventions in primary care: assessing the evidence. In: Sharp I (ed.) 1995. *Preventing Coronary Heart Disease: The Way Forward*. London: HMSO/National Heart Forum.

39   McPherson K. 1994. Health promotion under fire. *Lancet;* 344: 890-891.

40   National Heart Forum. 1999. *Strengthening Public Health: Proposals for National Public Health Structures*. London: National Heart Forum.

41   Leather S. 1996. *The Making of Modern Malnutrition. The Caroline Walker Lecture*. London: The Caroline Walker Trust.

# Chapter 4

# Causes of coronary heart disease: new concepts

**TASK GROUP**

**Professor Gerry Shaper** (Convenor)
*Vice-Chairman, National Heart Forum, 1995-98*

**Professor Philip James**
*Rowett Research Institute*

**Professor Kay-Tee Khaw**
*Clinical Gerontology Unit, University of Cambridge*

**Professor George Davey Smith**
*Department of Social Medicine, University of Bristol*

**Professor Brian Pentecost**
*British Heart Foundation*

See also *Acknowledgements* on page 61.

# Causes of coronary heart disease: new concepts

This chapter:

*   identifies and examines new or controversial theories of coronary heart disease causation for their validity

*   assesses their implications for national coronary heart disease prevention strategies

*   considers their public health implications for the UK, and

*   considers the priorities of any new concepts for a future coronary heart disease prevention strategy.

## KEY THEMES

1   This review of 'new concepts' emphasises the predominance of behavioural factors - diet, smoking and physical activity - as the currently modifiable determinants of coronary heart disease.

2   There is an urgent need for new and more effective population strategies for the prevention of coronary heart disease.

3   A critical review of the precise nature of a 'healthy diet' is required.

4   New strategies are needed to lower average blood cholesterol levels and average body weight, and to encourage and facilitate regular, moderate physical activity at all ages.

5   The practical implications of the new work concerning intrauterine factors, childhood socioeconomic experiences and psychosocial stress are not yet well defined.

The aim of this chapter is to examine a number of 'new concepts' that add to or challenge the existing model of coronary heart disease causation, and to determine whether the available evidence supports changes in the existing model and thus changes in the current strategies towards the prevention of coronary heart disease. Most of these concepts are not 'new' and many have been investigated for decades. However, this chapter explores the new evidence and new interpretations regarding their role in coronary heart disease.

## Summary

The present public health approach to the prevention of coronary heart disease is based on a multifactorial model. Current interventions include: recommending a diet which is low in fat, and particularly saturated fat, and rich in fruit and vegetables; non-smoking; regular moderate physical activity; and the proper management of high blood pressure, high blood lipids and obesity. This review examines new concepts in coronary heart disease and asks whether they are sufficiently well based to warrant changing public health policy. New risk factors have been uncovered and new mechanisms elaborated. However, these continue to emphasise the predominance of behavioural factors such as diet, physical activity, smoking and obesity, as well as psychosocial factors, as the modifiable determinants of the physiological, biochemical and haematological abnormalities associated with coronary heart disease. Genetic variations may explain differences in individual susceptibility to coronary heart disease but are not regarded as primarily responsible for the high risk of the disease in the UK.

The review implies that new strategies are needed to modify the national diet in order to bring about a considerable decrease in average total blood cholesterol levels and to lower considerably the average body weight in the whole population, with a focus on the prevention of undue weight gain at all ages. This may require acceptance of and a stronger focus on the fundamental nature of the dietary background, and a critical review of the nature of a 'healthy' diet. New strategies are also needed to encourage and facilitate regular moderate physical activity at all ages.

While the identification of new mechanisms may lead to innovative treatments for established atherosclerosis and coronary heart disease, and for persistently high levels of certain risk factors, the new factors identified do not suggest that any dramatic changes should be made in current preventive strategies. Efforts to reduce cigarette smoking must continue unabated, particularly at the fiscal and legislative levels. Current strategies for the prevention of coronary heart disease, and which are certain to be of considerable benefit to the overall health of the nation, need to be reviewed in the light of new evidence of effectiveness.

## Introduction

In the UK, the present public health approach to reducing the risk of coronary heart disease is based on a model that views coronary heart disease as multifactorial, ie caused by many factors, both genetic and environmental. Of course, all diseases are multifactorial in the broadest sense, but in relation to coronary heart disease, the term implies that "no individual factor (is) strictly essential or sufficient for causation".[1] This is supported by the 1994 *Consensus Report* of the British Heart

Foundation on the causes and prevention of coronary heart disease,[2] which states that: "Coronary heart disease is not due to a single cause but is the result of the interplay of a number of factors". The major established risk factors cited in the *Consensus Report* are cigarette smoking, high blood cholesterol, high blood pressure, physical inactivity and family history. Prevention strategies are based on the reduction in the prevalence and incidence of these established risk factors. The *Consensus Report* further states that: "many other risk factors have been implicated with varying degrees of evidence. These include a relatively low birth weight, resistance to the effects of insulin, overweight, stress, clotting factors and low socioeconomic status. Some of these are undoubtedly of importance, but more research is needed to establish their influence in causing coronary heart disease".

To make sense of trends in coronary heart disease, to understand the role of changing risk factors and to plan strategies aimed at preventing coronary heart disease, it is necessary to agree on the theoretical model that is to form the background of any analyses. There is also a need to consider coronary heart disease as a 'multi-stage process', with initiating, promoting and precipitating factors, while recognising that some factors may be involved in more than one stage of the process. If there are new concepts that challenge the existing model, it will be necessary to examine the evidence supporting those concepts and to decide whether they should form part of or even replace the existing model. Such decisions could have a dramatic effect on the direction and emphasis of future preventive strategies.

## Diet and coronary heart disease[3-27]

There is considerable evidence that the sorts of foods and nutrients we consume, and how much of them we consume, are critical and possibly fundamental factors in the development of atherosclerosis and coronary heart disease. A statement from the American Heart Association (AHA) in 1993 concluded that results from animal and human studies, epidemiological surveys and clinical trials all provide highly consistent evidence that intake of saturated fats and cholesterol directly raises total and LDL (low density lipoprotein) blood cholesterol levels.[5] There is also consistent and convincing evidence that high blood levels of total and LDL cholesterol contribute directly to atherosclerosis and coronary heart disease. The conclusion that there is a direct link between diet and coronary heart disease - the 'diet-heart hypothesis' - is "almost inescapable", despite the difficulties encountered in directly linking diet and coronary heart disease within populations. Blood cholesterol appears to be the key intermediate marker between diet and coronary heart disease.

While the AHA statement does not go so far as to declare that a high blood cholesterol level is a necessary factor in coronary heart disease, it does say that "the other major cardiovascular risk factors appear to play an atherogenic role against a background of high cholesterol levels. Their impact is markedly reduced in populations in whom plasma total and LDL cholesterol levels are low. If LDL cholesterol blood levels can be reduced by dietary means, the risks (for coronary heart disease) attributable to other factors may be lessened significantly".

The AHA statement recommends a generalised diet change for all healthy Americans, together with a high risk approach that identifies and treats individual patients who have unusually high blood lipid levels or other risk factors. It states:

"A diet containing less total fat, saturated fatty acids, cholesterol, sodium chloride and alcohol is likely to lessen coronary heart disease risk ... and controlling intake of calories to achieve desirable weight is likely to have significant health benefits".

### The diet-heart hypothesis[5, 8, 9, 13, 22, 27]

The model underlying the above AHA statement is that a particular type of diet leads to high levels of blood cholesterol in individuals and populations and that this phenomenon is the *necessary* (essential) factor for increasing susceptibility to atherosclerosis and coronary heart disease *in populations*, although it may not usually be *sufficient* by itself to produce coronary heart disease.

In this model, high blood pressure, cigarette smoking, physical inactivity and diabetes mellitus are major aggravating factors. However, if there is not a high blood cholesterol level, these factors, however injurious to other systems and conditions, have a small impact on the absolute risk of coronary heart disease in a population. In this model, coronary heart disease is affected by a wide variety of genetic and environmental factors (ie it is multifactorial), but the dietary factors leading to a moderately high blood cholesterol level are *fundamental and necessary* for a high level of coronary heart disease in a population. There are, of course, conditions in which a high blood cholesterol in individuals is not dietary in origin - for example familial hypercholesterolaemia and chronic renal failure - but this does not negate the concept as applied to populations.

Epidemiological studies show that the average serum total cholesterol in a population is the determining factor for the risk level of coronary heart disease in that population. They also show that the population average total cholesterol level is determined mainly by the percentage of total calories (energy) provided by saturated fats. In studies comparing coronary heart disease rates in different countries, high blood pressure and cigarette smoking do not result in high levels of coronary heart disease in populations with low mean serum total cholesterol levels. For example, Japan has a high prevalence of high blood pressure and cigarette smoking, but low levels of coronary heart disease. This is not to deny that these risk factors increase the relative risk of coronary heart disease in individuals in Japan, but rather that the absolute risk of coronary heart disease in the population remains low *despite* high levels of smoking and high blood pressure. Similarly, diabetes mellitus is not a risk factor for coronary heart disease in many African countries with low average total cholesterol levels. Even age appears to be an important risk factor for coronary heart disease only in populations with a high average blood cholesterol level.

In many developing countries, such as India or Sri Lanka, coronary heart disease is a common cause for admission to hospital but the disease is not widely prevalent in the general population. In these countries, serum total cholesterol levels in coronary heart disease patients are much higher than in controls. South Asians in the UK have higher rates of coronary heart disease than the rest of the population but, contrary to popular thinking, their levels of serum total cholesterol are similar to those observed in the rest of the population.

The crux of the above arguments is that a population's susceptibility to coronary heart disease is dependent upon the average total blood cholesterol in the population, and that in turn is determined largely by the dietary pattern in the population.

*Looking to the Future: Making Coronary Heart Disease an Epidemic of the Past*

**The nature of the atherogenic diet**[3, 22, 27]

The dietary background to coronary heart disease is complex. The P:S ratio (the ratio of polyunsaturated to saturated fats, which is highly dependent upon the saturated fat content of the diet), specific fatty acids, dietary cholesterol, total calorie intake, fibre and antioxidants all play a role in both atherogenesis (the build-up of fatty deposits within the artery walls) and thrombogenesis (the formation of clots in the blood). Total blood cholesterol is made up of several distinct components, including the harmful LDL and VLDL (very low density lipoprotein fractions/ triglycerides), as well as the protective HDL (high density lipoprotein) component. Changes in the diet may affect any or all of these components and the effect on the risk of coronary heart disease will depend on which cholesterol component is altered and in which direction. Replacing saturated fats with unsaturated oils reduces mainly LDL. Low fat diets high in carbohydrates (sugars and starch) lower not only LDL but also HDL and also reduce intake of vitamin E and essential fatty acids. Replacing saturated fats with non-hydrogenated unsaturated oils improves the HDL to LDL ratio. The ratio of total cholesterol divided by HDL cholesterol probably provides the strongest predictor of risk of coronary heart disease. It is evident that total blood cholesterol or even the total cholesterol/HDL ratio does not represent the complete effects of blood lipids on the risk of coronary heart disease, although they are very good predictors.

It seems well established that the marked differences in serum total cholesterol *between populations* are almost wholly determined by dietary factors. *Within populations*, genetic and other factors play an important role in determining differences between the total cholesterol levels in individuals.

**Antioxidants**[7, 11, 16, 17, 23]

There is good evidence that a diet rich in a range of vegetables and fruit is associated with a lower risk of coronary heart disease and may be effective in lowering blood pressure. Current theory holds that it is the antioxidant content of this type of diet which offers protection. Cellular processes generate 'free radicals' in the process of oxidation. (A free radical is an atom or molecule with one or more unpaired electrons in their structure.) Free radicals are potentially damaging to fats, protein and DNA. They can be 'scavenged' by a number of systems including carotenoids, the alpha-tocopherol component of vitamin E, and vitamin C. The flavonoids in red wine and many plant foods, with structural similarities to vitamin E, may also aid scavenging. Oxidised LDL cholesterol plays a key role in atherosclerosis, and prospective epidemiological data indicate that a high intake of antioxidant vitamins, particularly vitamin E, is associated with a reduction in cardiovascular disease. However, the findings from randomised primary and secondary prevention trials regarding vitamin supplements are not convincingly supportive. Beta-carotene supplements cannot be recommended to prevent heart disease in the general population, and studies of vitamins C and E supplements do not provide conclusive evidence of benefit.

*The implications*

The implications are that the national and international recommendations to increase vegetable and fruit intakes form a sound basis for policy. However, there appears to be insufficient evidence at present to justify the prescription of specific antioxidant vitamin supplements to prevent coronary heart disease. While it is clear that beta-carotene should not be advocated, the outcome of major clinical trials, particularly in people at high risk, will determine attitudes to vitamins C and E.

### Lowering blood cholesterol[9]

Controlled clinical trials using diets low in saturated fats and dietary cholesterol have in general not been successful in the primary prevention of coronary heart disease. Trials which have considerably increased the P:S ratio by increasing polyunsaturated fats have been more successful, particularly in secondary prevention. However, a series of trials using the statin group of drugs - which reduce circulating cholesterol to a greater degree than previous dietary procedures or drugs - demonstrate reductions in all cause mortality as well as coronary heart disease mortality in the secondary prevention setting, and sizeable reductions in coronary heart disease incidence in primary prevention. In post-heart attack patients, cholesterol reduction with statins reduces the risk of further heart attack among those whose cholesterol levels are currently regarded as optimal by Western standards.

### Trans-fatty acids[4]

Trans-fatty acids are produced when liquid vegetable or seed oils are heated in the presence of hydrogen and a metal catalyst to form hardened vegetable fats or margarine (partial hydrogenation). Some of the isomers created are structurally similar to saturated fats and have adverse effects on plasma LDL and HDL cholesterol concentrations which are greater than those of saturated fatty acids. They may also compete with essential fatty acids but are only atherogenic when the intake of linoleic acid is very low.

Intakes of trans-fatty acids have increased since the 1950s and it has been suggested that they are associated with an increase in coronary heart disease. However, they contribute only about 2% of dietary energy intake and although some but not all epidemiological studies suggest that they are responsible for an increased risk of coronary heart disease, there is insufficient evidence to quantify any relationship with precision.

*The implications*

The implications are that the trans-fatty acids in the diet should be regarded as having at least the same effects on blood lipids and on the risk of coronary heart disease as saturated fatty acids and that it would be prudent not to let average intakes of trans-fatty acids rise.

### Postprandial lipaemia[14, 24]

After meals, particularly high fat meals, there is an increase in the fat content of the blood (triglycerides and cholesterol-rich remnant particles of chylomicron metabolism). Saturated fats produce the greatest and longest lasting increases; monounsaturated and polyunsaturated fats produce much less response. These lipoprotein particles increase atherosclerosis and also affect the clot-forming component of coronary heart disease through Factor VII coagulant activity. Factor VII is positively associated with long-term dietary fat intake and with plasma triglyceride concentration in the general population; people with high levels of long-term dietary fat intake and high levels of triglycerides are more likely to have high levels of Factor VII. It has been proposed that repeated episodes of high levels of blood fats after meals may hasten the progression of atherosclerosis. On the other hand, single episodes of moderate physical activity can reduce the magnitude of the postprandial lipaemia in healthy young adults and in middle-aged women.

*The implications*

The implication of these findings is that the patterns of food intake may influence the risk of atherosclerosis and coronary heart disease and that interventions to decrease high levels of blood fats after meals may be beneficial. These findings emphasise the current recommendations for the reduction of high intakes of fats and the protective role of regular physical activity in coronary heart disease prevention, particularly in those most at risk of thrombosis.

**Fish and omega-3 fatty acids**[6]

There is considerable interest in the possibility that eating fish may help protect against coronary heart disease. Omega-3 fatty acids, which are found in fish oils and oily fish such as herring and mackerel, have been the focus of attention. There is no doubt that these fatty acids have a wide range of effects likely to reduce the risk of coronary heart disease and in particular, sudden cardiac death. However, the evidence from epidemiological studies and clinical trials is conflicting, except in secondary prevention where the evidence seems more convincing.

**Dietary fibre**[5]

Certain types of fibre in the diet appear to have a beneficial effect on blood lipids and blood glucose levels and several epidemiological studies have reported an inverse relationship between fibre intake and the risk of coronary heart disease: the higher the level of fibre intake, the lower the risk of coronary heart disease. The protective effect has been attributed in particular to the insoluble fibre from grains, fruit and vegetables. Overall, the data suggest that some aspects of plant products may reduce the risk of coronary heart disease, although it is not clear whether it is a specific type of fibre or something other than the fibre.

**Coffee**[10, 15, 25, 26]

A number of studies support the hypothesis that heavy coffee drinking may affect coronary heart disease. Studies from Norway, where coffee is black, strong and boiled and not filtered, show a strong association between coffee consumption and coronary heart disease deaths. However, a meta-analysis, carried out in 1992, of all prospective studies conducted worldwide over the past 30 years has concluded that: "There is no association between coffee consumption and the occurrence of coronary heart disease".

What is clear is that coffee beans contain the diterpines cafestol and kahweol which can produce temporary increases in serum cholesterol levels and triglyceride levels. People at increased risk of coronary heart disease who drink large amounts of coffee should avoid boiled coffee (Scandinavian style), Turkish/Greek and plunger-pot coffee (cafetiere), and should instead drink instant (soluble), filtered or percolated coffee and moderate amounts of espresso or mocha coffee.

**Alcohol**[12, 18, 20, 21]

It has been shown consistently that non-drinkers have higher rates of coronary heart disease and total mortality than light or moderate drinkers. In addition, there are several mechanisms which support the widespread belief that light drinking is beneficial for coronary heart disease, particularly in middle-aged and older men and in post-menopausal women. Red wine has been singled out in particular as being protective, although the data suggest that the phenomenon is associated with all types of alcohol. However, another interpretation of the findings is that adverse characteristics of non-drinkers are responsible, to a considerable extent, for their increased risk of coronary heart disease and total mortality and thus for some of the apparent benefit seen in light to moderate drinkers, when non-drinkers are used as a baseline.

While alcohol does appear to have some protective effect at light to moderate intake levels, public health authorities are in almost universal agreement that people should not be encouraged to drink for their health. There is considerable evidence that moderate to heavy drinking can increase blood pressure and that heavy drinking, predominantly through this mechanism, can result in stroke. Heavy drinking, particularly 'binge drinking' can also result in abnormal heart rhythms and may increase the risk of sudden cardiac death. Heavy drinking is also a cause of chronic heart muscle damage (cardiomyopathy) with cardiac enlargement and heart failure.

**Note:** Cross-cultural analyses of 25-year mortality data from the Seven Countries Study show that antioxidants, vitamins, fish, fibre and alcohol do not explain population differences in coronary heart disease mortality, once cigarette smoking and intakes of saturated fatty acids and flavonoids have been taken into account.

### Overall implications of the diet-heart hypothesis[5, 22, 27]

If it is accepted that the population diet, and its effects on blood lipids and other biological factors, is an essential or necessary factor for a high level of coronary heart disease risk in a population, then the prime focus for prevention of the disease must be the population dietary pattern, with considerable emphasis on strategies leading towards a more desirable diet. It is likely that aspects of diet other than the quantity and type of fat may influence substantially the risks of coronary heart disease. These aspects may act by a variety of mechanisms, many unrelated to their effects on blood lipids. However, it is evident that a diet high in fruit, vegetables, cereals and both monounsaturated and polyunsaturated oils is to be preferred to a diet high in animal fat and hydrogenated vegetable products. It is important to convince the public and the responsible authorities that the national diet is not just another risk factor but that it is fundamental to the high risk of coronary heart disease in the population.

## Overweight and obesity[28-36]

There has been a tendency in the past for overweight/obesity to be underestimated as a risk factor for coronary heart disease, as many prospective studies showed that obesity was of little apparent significance once blood pressure and blood cholesterol levels had been taken into account. However, weight gain in most societies is strongly associated with the development of high blood pressure and hypercholesterolaemia as well as with the development of non-insulin dependent diabetes mellitus (NIDDM).

In recent years central (abdominal/visceral) obesity has been recognised as a risk factor for coronary heart disease independently of body mass index (BMI), and simple waist measurement as well as the waist-hip ratio is being promoted for use in risk assessment. Central obesity refers to the predominant accumulation of fat centrally in the abdomen rather than on the hips and elsewhere on the body.

Intentional weight loss has been shown to be beneficial in terms of coronary heart disease and total mortality in overweight women in the United States. In both the United States and the UK, it has been shown that the risk of cardiovascular mortality, heart attack and diabetes, as well as the levels of a wide range of cardiovascular risk factors, increase progressively from a BMI of about 20kg/m². A healthy BMI in middle-aged men and women appears to be about 22kg/m², rather than the current average of 25-26kg/m², suggesting that concern should be directed towards the average weight in the population rather than towards obesity, usually defined as a BMI of over 30kg/m².

In many countries, falling coronary heart disease mortality rates in the 1980s and 90s have been accompanied by considerably increased rates of obesity in men and women and even in young children. This apparent paradox raises the issue of the different dietary pathways which may lead to obesity, and in particular the fatty acid composition of the diet and its effects on blood lipids and on body fat deposition. In populations which become overweight or obese on diets which do not lead to raised average levels of total blood cholesterol and LDL cholesterol, the risk of coronary heart disease in that population is not increased, even in the presence of other risk factors such as high blood pressure and cigarette smoking. Obesity does however encourage the development of diabetes mellitus and other disorders associated with obesity.

There is a strong body of opinion which holds that the increasing rate of obesity in the UK is predominantly due to a decrease in the overall level of physical activity and not due to an increase in food or calorie intake. However, studies in the United States, which has seen a similar increase in the prevalence of obesity, suggest that the total mean energy intake may have increased, although it is generally under-reported in surveys. There is also increasing evidence that moderate physical activity, short of that which improves cardiovascular fitness, may have a beneficial effect on the risk of coronary heart disease and stroke, independent of its effect on obesity. Thus, any approach to the obesity problem needs to be closely linked to both the national diet and national patterns of physical activity.

*The implications*

The implication of present evidence is that the current focus on obesity (BMI of over 30kg/m²) may be misplaced and concern should be directed to the average weight in the whole population. It is necessary to find new ways of modifying the national diet and new ways of achieving increased regular moderate physical activity in the population. As weight reduction is extremely difficult to maintain, the focus must be on the prevention of undue weight gain at all ages.

## Insulin resistance[37-39]

Reaven has postulated that resistance to the uptake of glucose and other metabolic effects normally mediated by insulin (insulin resistance), and the resulting increase in levels of blood insulin hyperinsulinaemia affect the development and clinical course of non-insulin dependent diabetes (NIDDM), essential hypertension and coronary heart disease. Insulin resistance occurs in many aetiologically diverse conditions and, in many of these, the clinical significance of impaired insulin action is uncertain. The development of overweight/obesity is associated with acquired insulin resistance, with central (visceral) obesity in particular being closely associated with glucose intolerance and other features of the insulin resistance syndrome.

The obesity-insulin resistance hypothesis proposes that certain dietary factors, particularly fat and total calorie intake, in combination with physical inactivity, create total body obesity, with fat being deposited centrally. This in turn may present a powerful stimulus to increase insulin levels. At present, the nature of the association, if any, between insulin resistance and coronary heart disease remains uncertain. However, it has been argued that tissue insulin resistance is the primary initiating defect which leads to compensatory hyperinsulinaemia and atherogenic risk factors.

While the association between insulin, atherosclerosis and coronary heart disease remains controversial, it does appear that insulin resistance is implicated in the development of accelerated atherosclerosis in people with non-insulin dependent diabetes mellitus and impaired glucose tolerance. This mechanism is considered to be responsible for the high incidence of coronary heart disease among immigrants to the UK from the Indian subcontinent.

### The implications

Whatever the role of insulin in coronary heart disease, there is no doubt that overweight and obesity are commonly and closely associated with insulin resistance and that reduction of insulin resistance through weight reduction and the maintenance of desirable body weight is important in the prevention and management of non-insulin dependent diabetes mellitus, a major established risk factor for accelerated atherosclerosis and coronary heart disease. Insulin resistance is also improved by aerobic physical activity and stopping smoking, providing further support for the inclusion of these activities in policies to prevent coronary heart disease.

## Homocysteine metabolism[40-44]

Homocysteine is an amino acid produced by the breakdown of methionine in the body. A moderately high plasma level of homocysteine is common and is independently associated with a two-fold risk of cardiovascular disease in those with levels above the top quintile (12µmol/l or above). In patients whose coronary artery disease has been confirmed by angiography, plasma total homocysteine levels were a strong predictor of mortality. Homocysteine levels are determined by both genetic and nutritional factors, notably folic acid, and vitamins $B_6$ and $B_{12}$. Inadequate levels of any of these vitamins can increase blood homocysteine levels. It has been estimated that up to 30% of an elderly population in the United States are deficient in such vitamins. Diet can also influence the levels through higher intakes of the precursor methionine, a substance particularly abundant in meat and in dairy products. Plasma folic acid concentration in particular has been proposed as explaining the relationship between homocysteine and coronary heart disease risk. Questionnaire-based data from the Nurses' Health Study in the United States suggest that intakes of folate and vitamin $B_6$ at twice the recommended dietary allowance may help to prevent coronary heart disease among women. No randomised control trial of homocysteine reduction has yet been carried out, although homocysteine levels can readily be reduced by taking folic acid. Foods with high folic acid content include broccoli, brussels sprouts, spinach, green beans, spring greens and granary bread.

*The implications*
The implications are that inadequate intake of folic acid and/or possibly vitamins $B_6$ and $B_{12}$ might increase the risk of vascular disease, and that people who have inadequate amounts of these nutrients might need dietary advice about increasing their intake of folic acid (particularly with regard to fruit and vegetables), supplementation with folic acid (or other nutrients) for those at high risk, or a population food fortification policy. While enhancement of foods with folic acid may be justifiable for the prevention of neural tube defects, there is insufficient evidence as yet to recommend it for preventing coronary heart disease. Findings in patients with coronary heart disease provide a strong incentive for the initiation of intervention trials with homocysteine-lowering therapy.

## Foetal origins of coronary heart disease[45-47]

The association between low birthweight and coronary heart disease is now well established. The trends in coronary heart disease in relation to size at birth are paralleled by trends in five of its major risk factors: high blood pressure, non-insulin dependent diabetes, raised serum total cholesterol, high plasma fibrinogen concentrations and obesity. These associations are independent of adult lifestyle, including smoking, obesity and social class, and have led to the hypothesis that susceptibility to the disease is programmed *in utero*.

The foetal origins hypothesis proposes that the adaptations made by the foetus in response to undernutrition lead to persisting changes in metabolism and organ structure which predispose the individual to atherosclerosis and cardiovascular disease in later life. This hypothesis is supported by experimental evidence in which the offspring of undernourished pregnant animals show permanent changes including high blood pressure and abnormal glucose-insulin and lipid metabolism. Adult lifestyle interacts with the effects of intrauterine growth on some programmed processes that lead to coronary heart disease. Thus central obesity in adulthood amplifies any effects of foetal growth on blood pressure, insulin resistance and coronary heart disease incidence. Clinical studies and animal experiments are leading to an understanding of the mechanisms by which coronary heart disease may be programmed.

*The implications*
Foetal undernutrition may lead to small size and altered body proportions at birth and increase susceptibility to later coronary heart disease. It is not yet clear which nutritional influences act through the mother to programme the foetus and it is likely to be some time before the advice given to women before and during pregnancy can be improved.

## Life course influences on coronary heart disease[48-51]

Early life conditions other than programming *in utero* - such as postnatal growth, nutrition and health status - may have long-term influences on the risk of cardiovascular disease. Father's social class has been used as a proxy for childhood socioeconomic circumstances. It appears to make a particular contribution to coronary heart disease and stroke risk which is not due to the adverse social class destinations of those born into poor circumstances. Men with fathers in manual social occupations have a considerably higher risk of dying from coronary heart disease than those whose fathers were in non-manual occupations. Behavioural risk factors such as smoking and physical inactivity appear to be dependent on adult social position, and blood pressure and lung function are more strongly associated with current social class than parental social class. However, body mass index and blood triglycerides appear to be strongly conditioned by father's social class even when current social class has been taken into account.

A large Scottish study with 21 years' follow-up shows that mortality from cardiovascular disease appears to be more strongly related to *cumulative social disadvantage* than does mortality from cancer or non-cardiovascular non-cancer causes. Furthermore, whereas social class in adulthood is the more important socioeconomic indicator for differentiating groups with different risks of mortality from cancer and non-cardiovascular non-cancer causes, the socioeconomic environment in childhood appears to be particularly important with respect to mortality from cardiovascular disease. A review of the contribution of nutrition to inequalities in health proposes that the diet affects the health of socially disadvantaged people from the cradle to the grave and that there is enormous potential for health gains through improved diet.[51]

*The implications*
The focus of concern should be the accumulation of socially patterned adverse exposures over a lifetime. Nutrition in infancy and childhood may have long-term effects on the initiation of atherosclerosis, and infections acquired in childhood may underlie some of the associations observed. "There is scope for enormous health gains if a diet rich in vegetables, fruit, unrefined cereals, fish and small quantities of quality vegetable oils could be more accessible to poor people".[51] Psychosocial factors (patterns of child rearing, family disruption, disorganised and deprived neighbourhoods) must certainly affect children's behaviour (diet, smoking, exercise) and possibly their ability to fight off disease and infection.

Alternatively, all of these associations may be mainly or exclusively due to a common intrauterine influence which carries through to health, growth and nutritional status in adulthood. The information at present does not indicate any specific actions beyond those already regarded as optimal for childhood health.

## Psychosocial factors and stress[52-54]

Psychosocial factors and stress ('worry and strain') have long been considered to be implicated in coronary heart disease. A psychosocial factor is defined as one which relates psychological phenomena to the social environment and to changes in body systems. Psychosocial factors may influence coronary heart disease through behaviours such as smoking, diet, alcohol intake or physical activity and access to medical care. They may also have direct effects on the body systems, for example short-lived stressor effects on endothelial function and platelet behaviour. Thus psychosocial factors may act as triggers for acute events or exert chronic cumulative effects ('ever-agitating') on atherosclerotic disease initiation and progression.

Large prospective studies examining specific hypotheses about psychosocial effects suggest the importance of psychosocial factors in relation to coronary heart disease aetiology and prognosis. Further evidence of a causal role is provided by human and other primate evidence of biological and behavioural pathways mediating these effects. Observational studies suggest that it is low control in the workplace which is most closely linked to coronary heart disease. Lack of social supports, as well as depression and anxiety, have been identified as factors which increase the risk of coronary heart disease, and social supports and depression may have an effect on the prognosis for patients with coronary heart disease. Psychosocial interventions may reduce mortality after heart attacks.

*The implications*
At the individual level, counselling and stress techniques have some effect on cardiovascular risk, but the evidence is not entirely consistent. At the population level, social inequalities in health require attention to childcare, employment opportunities and the work environment.

## Thrombosis and fibrinolysis[55]

Virtually all cases of major heart attacks and deaths from coronary heart disease involve thrombosis in the coronary arteries. This rarely occurs in the absence of atheroma, which is a necessary but not always sufficient cause of heart attack and coronary heart disease death. Platelet activity contributes to the tendency to thrombosis, and there is no doubt as to the value of platelet-active agents such as aspirin and dipyridamole in the secondary prevention of coronary heart disease and stroke. Fibrinogen levels are strongly and independently associated with all forms of cardiovascular disease and may be the common pathway for a variety of exposures, including psychosocial factors. They may also be a marker for existing vascular disease. Fibrinogen levels are determined by both genetic and environmental factors, particularly smoking (which increases the fibrinogen level) and exercise and alcohol (which lower it). Factor VII is positively associated with long-term dietary fat intake and with plasma triglyceride concentration in the general population. Impaired fibrinolytic activity has been shown to be associated with an increased risk of coronary heart disease and stroke. At present there are no validated pharmacological approaches to the modification of fibrinolytic activity, although lifestyle factors (diet, physical activity and not smoking) have been shown to be effective.

*The implications*
The available evidence shows that the characteristics affecting the clotting system and fibrinolytic activity are similar to those affecting lipid and blood pressure levels, ie age, diet, smoking, obesity and physical activity. Thus the uncovering of these mechanisms has no new implications for the prevention of coronary heart disease or other cardiovascular disease through changes in lifestyle. However, the implications of a 'hypercoagulable' state (increased risk of clot formation) may be considerable in terms of pharmacological approaches.

## Inflammation and infection[56-61]

It has been suggested, for more than a century, that inflammation may be a factor in the development of atheroma, and it has been recognised that the most powerful inflammatory agent regularly present in the walls of the arteries is cholesterol. More recently it has been proposed that *Helicobacter pylori* and *Chlamydia pneumoniae* may be specifically linked to atherosclerosis and coronary heart disease and even the herpes simplex virus and poor dental hygiene have been implicated. The association between *Helicobacter pylori* and *Chlamydia pneumoniae* and increased risk of coronary heart disease is heavily confounded by the relationships between these common infections and adult social class and other major cardiovascular risk factors. The decline in coronary heart disease in recent decades has been attributed in part to the introduction of the broad-spectrum antibiotics, and regional variations in coronary heart disease in the UK have also been related to infection with these organisms. However, there is no comprehensive information on regional variations in the seroprevalence of either organism within the UK, nor on changes in their prevalence over time.

As atherosclerosis is in essence a chronic inflammatory disease, it is possible that recurrent infections may aggravate atherosclerosis, particularly in people with high blood cholesterol levels. Macrophages (large white cells capable of engulfing bacteria and other harmful particles) play a key role in the increase in plaque lipid content by engulfing lipids from the bloodstream. Increased rates of coronary heart disease mortality in the winter months could be explained by increased risk of infections. A wide range of mechanisms have been incriminated in the infection hypothesis, including high levels of plasma fibrinogen and C-reactive protein and adhesion of leukocytes (white cells) to endothelial cells lining the blood vessels. Most of these are non-specific but sensitive markers of the acute-phase response to infectious agents, immunologic stimuli and tissue damage.

In the Physicians' Health Study in the United States, it has been shown that, among healthy men, baseline serum levels of C-reactive protein are predictive of heart attack and stroke, even when the values are within the normal range. The increased risk associated with increasing levels of C-reactive protein was independent of lipid-related and other cardiovascular risk factors and was reduced by treatment with aspirin in direct proportion to the baseline C-reactive protein level.

*The implications*
The implications are that certain infections may aggravate the inflammatory process already present in the arterial walls. It is unlikely that they initiate the inflammatory response. There is no evidence at present to support the use of antibiotics at any stages of the atherosclerotic process. However, it would be of interest to establish trials to examine the effect of prophylactic antibiotic cover - for example anti-chlamydial antibiotics such as azithromycin, and/or anti-inflammatory agents such as aspirin - in subjects at high risk of major coronary heart disease events, particularly during the winter months.

# Nitric oxide[62]

Vascular endothelial cells (the inner lining of blood vessels) generate nitric oxide from a substrate L-arginine. Nitric oxide helps to dilate the arteries, thus helping to lower blood pressure. It also inhibits platelet and white cell adhesion and aggregation and may slow down smooth muscle cell growth. Defects in the L-arginine-nitric oxide pathway have been described in patients with high blood pressure, hypercholesterolaemia, diabetes mellitus, or overt atheroma, in those who smoke, and in those with a family history of cardiovascular disease. Animal models suggest that a small defect in the ability to generate nitric oxide increases the risk of atherogenesis, possibly through the mechanisms listed above. There are reports that the amino acid arginine prevents the onset of atheroma in experimental models and restores certain aspects of endothelial function in humans, although the mechanisms are far from clear. Endothelial function is inversely related to LDL cholesterol concentrations: the greater the endothelial function, the lower the LDL concentration. Reduction of LDL levels by statins restores endothelial function.

*The implications*

The implications are that dietary changes may affect the levels of nitric oxide, although this is not established. Arginine is present in relatively large amounts in nuts (brazil nuts and almonds), shellfish and meats including beef, bacon and game. However, the effects of arginine supplementation on vascular responses and blood pressure remain to be determined.

# Environmental factors[63-72]

There is evidence relating a number of environmental factors to cardiovascular disease, including climate, outdoor and indoor air pollution, environmental tobacco smoke and water quality.

## Climate

There are considerable seasonal variations in mortality in the UK with death rates about 14% higher in the winter, and a large proportion of those deaths are from cardiovascular disease. The excess winter mortality is higher in the poorer sections of the community and has not fallen substantially even though use of central heating has become widespread over the past three decades. A number of mechanisms, including blood pressure, viscosity of the blood, platelet and red cell counts, have been incriminated. It is unclear whether the winter excess is specific to those who are already severely affected by cardiovascular disease ('winter harvesting'). A study in eight European regions shows that, in the regions with a mild winter, the percentage increases in coronary heart disease and cardiovascular mortality were greater than in countries with a colder winter, possibly because protective measures (warm clothing, physical activity) against a given degree of cold were fewer in milder climates than in regions with more severe winters.

## Air pollution

Studies suggest that increases in 'particulate air pollution' (black smoke or particles smaller than 10μm in diameter) are associated with increased cardiovascular mortality. However, a large British study did not support this suggestion, as it found that a high ozone concentration was associated with a higher cardiovascular death rate. (Ozone is a condensed form of oxygen, $O_3$.) A study of almost 400,000 admissions to London hospitals in the period 1987-94 showed a strong association between outdoor air pollutants (except ozone) and acute myocardial infarction (heart attack), even after allowing for weather and other risk factors. The study concluded that "one in 50 heart attacks ... may be triggered by outdoor air pollution" and that carbon monoxide emissions were a particular cause of concern. "Biologically plausible mechanisms have been advanced by which emissions, mainly from motor vehicles, might trigger circulatory disorders." Studies in the United States link outdoor particulate pollution with all cause mortality, and particularly with cardiopulmonary causes. However, the excess risk could be due to residual confounding by socioeconomic status and past exposure to pollution.

Indoor air pollution with carbon monoxide occurs in association with faulty combustion appliances and/or inadequate ventilation and may be added to by cigarette smoking. A small rise in the concentration of carboxyhaemoglobin induced by exposure to environmental carbon monoxide may aggravate angina in susceptible people.

### Environmental tobacco smoke

The American Heart Association has concluded that passive smoking is an important risk factor for coronary heart disease. A study of 32,000 women in the United States who had never smoked suggests that regular exposure to passive smoking at home or work doubles their risk of coronary heart disease, although no absolute rates are provided to allow a proper assessment of the impact compared with active smoking. A meta-analysis of 19 epidemiological studies provides almost incontrovertible evidence that exposure to environmental tobacco smoke is a cause of coronary heart disease. It has determined that environmental tobacco smoke caused an increase of 23% in risk after adjustment for dietary confounders. The dose-response relationship was not linear: at low level doses the risk increased rapidly, while at high doses it increased more slowly.

### Water quality

Areas of the UK with hard water supplies have lower age-standardised rates for cardiovascular mortality than soft water areas. This association remains significant even after allowing for climate and socioeconomic conditions. However, the magnitude of effect is relatively small compared with other risk factors for cardiovascular disease and is no greater than the effects of temperature or rainfall. Studies in areas where there have been changes of water quality show a weak negative association between the hardness of drinking water and mortality from cardiovascular disease. No argument relating to cardiovascular disease is made for widespread hardening of soft water supplies.

*The implications*

At present there is no clear evidence that improvement in indoor heating in winter will remove the excess winter death rate. There are suggestions that better use of protective clothing and increased physical activity outdoors may reduce outdoor cold stress and reduce cardiovascular mortality. There is at present no clear evidence that reduction in outdoor particulate air pollution will affect cardiovascular mortality rates. The effect of environmental tobacco smoke (passive smoking) would seem to be firmly established. No argument relating to cardiovascular disease is made for widespread hardening of soft water supplies.

## Genetics and coronary heart disease[73-75]

Individual susceptibility to coronary heart disease, particularly in younger age groups, is strongly influenced by genetic factors. However, coronary heart disease is clearly not inherited through a single gene. Atherosclerosis and its complications are manifestations of a complex multifactorial disease, in which a gradient of disease susceptibility arises from multiple common genetic variants interacting with each other and with multiple environmental factors. Many common genetic variants affecting lipid metabolism have been identified, but the relative risks ascribed to specific individual variants are low. It is unlikely that genes modulating lipid metabolism account for all the genetic risks of coronary heart disease. Genetic variations in the formation and breakdown of clotting have been implicated and there may also be genetic variations in the proteins which control the structure of blood vessels.

## The implications

Currently, the cumulative impact of an individual's inherited susceptibility to coronary heart disease can best be determined by a careful family history. Even when more detailed genetic information relating to the prognostic implications of specific gene variants becomes available, it will still be difficult to predict individual, rather than cohort, risk given the complexity of factors and the lack of knowledge of how they interact. It may well be that the main reason for pursuing genetic studies is not to provide new markers of risk but to better understand the disease process. Genetic studies may also allow targeting of specific treatments to specific groups and may identify novel biological processes suitable for pharmaceutical intervention.

## References

1    Kannel WB, Wilson PWF. 1995. An update on coronary risk factors. *Medical Clinics of North America;* 79: 951-971.

2    British Heart Foundation. 1994. *The Causes and Prevention of Coronary Heart Disease. The Consensus Report from the British Heart Foundation.* London: British Heart Foundation.

*Diet and coronary heart disease*

3    Appel LJ, Moore TJ, Obarzanek E, Vollmer WM, Svetkey LP et al. 1997. A clinical trial of the effects of dietary patterns on blood pressure. *New England Journal of Medicine;* 336: 1117-1124.

4    British Nutrition Foundation. 1995. *Trans Fatty Acids.* London: British Nutrition Foundation.

5    Chait A, Brunzell JD, Denke MA, Eisenberg D, Ernst ND, Franklin FA et al. 1993. Rationale of the Diet-Heart Statement of the American Heart Association. Report of the Nutrition Committee. *Circulation;* 88: 3008-3029.

6    Daviglus ML, Stamler J, Orencia AJ et al. 1997. Fish consumption and the 30-year risk of fatal myocardial infarction. *New England Journal of Medicine;* 336: 1046-1053.

7    Diaz MN, Frei B, Vita JA, Keaney JF. 1997. Antioxidants and atherosclerotic heart disease. *New England Journal of Medicine;* 337: 408-416.

8    Ebrahim S, Smith GD. 1997. Systematic review of randomised controlled trials of multiple risk factor interventions for preventing coronary heart disease. *British Medical Journal;* 314: 1666-1674.

9    Fey R, Pearson N. 1996. Statins and coronary heart disease (editorial). *Lancet;* 347: 1389-1390.

10   Greenland S. 1993. A meta-analysis of coffee, myocardial infarction, and coronary death. *Epidemiology;* 4: 366-374.

11   Jha P, Flather M, Lonn E, Farkouh M, Yusuf S. 1995. The antioxidant vitamins and cardiovascular disease: a critical review of epidemiologic and clinical trial data. *Annals of Internal Medicine;* 123: 860-872.

12   Kromhout D, Bloemberg BPM, Feskens EJM, Hertog MGL, Menotti A, Blackburn H. 1996. Alcohol, fish, fibre and antioxidant vitamins intake do not explain population differences in coronary heart disease mortality. *International Journal of Epidemiology;* 25: 753-759.

13   Lewis B, Watts GF. 1997. Paradise regained: insights into coronary heart disease prevention from recent clinical trials and basic research. *Journal of the Royal College of Physicians of London;* 31: 263-275.

14   Miller GJ, Stirling Y, Howarth DJ et al. 1995. Dietary fat intake and plasma factor VII antigen concentration. *Thrombosis and Haemostasis;* 73: 893-897.

15   Myers MB, Basinski A. 1992. Coffee and coronary heart disease. *Archives of Internal Medicine;* 152: 1767-1772.

16   Rogers L, Sharp I (eds.) 1997. *Preventing Coronary Heart Disease. The Role of Antioxidants, Vegetables and Fruit.* London: The Stationery Office/National Heart Forum.

17   Ness AR, Powles JW. 1997. Fruit and vegetables, and cardiovascular disease: a review. *International Journal of Epidemiology;* 26: 1-13.

18   Chadwick DJ, Goode J (eds). 1988. *Novartis Foundation Symposium No. 216. Alcohol and Cardiovascular Diseases.* Chichester: Wiley.

19   Oliver MF. 1996. Which changes in diet prevent coronary heart disease? A review of clinical trials of dietary fats and antioxidants. *Acta Cardiologica;* 51: 467-490.

20   Rimm EB, Giovannucci EL, Willett WC, Colditz GA, Ascherio A, Rosner B et al. 1991. Prospective study of alcohol consumption and risk of coronary heart disease in men. *Lancet;* 338: 464-468.

21   Shaper AG. 1995. Alcohol and coronary heart disease. *European Heart Journal;* 16: 1760-1764.

22   Stamler J. Established major coronary risk factors. In: Marmot M, Elliott P. 1992. *Coronary Heart Disease Epidemiology. From Aetiology to Public Health:* pages 35-66. Oxford: Oxford University Press.

23   Stephens NG, Parsons A, Schofield PM et al. 1996. A randomised controlled trial of vitamin E in patients with coronary disease: The Cambridge Heart Antioxidant Study (CHAOS). *Lancet;* 347: 781-786.

24   Tsetsonis NV, Hardman AE, Mastana SS. 1997. Acute effects of exercise on postprandial lipaemia: a comparative study in trained and untrained middle-aged women. *American Journal of Clinical Nutrition;* 65: 525-533.

25   Tverdal A, Stensvold I, Solvoll K et al. 1990. Coffee consumption and death from coronary heart disease in middle-aged Norwegian men and women. *British Medical Journal;* 300: 566-569.

26   Urgert R, Katan MB. 1996. The cholesterol-raising factor from coffee beans. *Journal of the Royal Society of Medicine;* 89: 618-623.

27   Willett WC. Diet and coronary heart disease. In: Willett WC (ed.) 1998. *Nutritional Epidemiology.* Second edition. Oxford: Oxford University Press.

*Overweight and obesity*

28   American Health Foundation. 1996. Roundtable on healthy weight. *American Journal of Clinical Nutrition;* 63 (suppl): 409-477.

29   Chadwick DJ, Cardew G (eds.) 1996. *The Origins and Consequences of Obesity. Ciba Foundation Symposium 201.* Chichester: John Wiley.

30   Egger G, Swinburn B. 1997. An 'ecological' approach to the obesity pandemic. *British Medical Journal;* 315: 477-480.

31   Ernst ND, Obarzanek E, Clark MB, Briefel RR, Brown CD, Donato K. 1997. Cardiovascular health risks related to overweight (Review). *Journal of the American Dietetic Association;* 97 (suppl): S47-51.

32   Prentice AM, Jebb SA. 1995. Obesity in Britain: gluttony or sloth? *British Medical Journal;* 311: 437-439.

33   Rosenbaum M, Leibel RL, Hirsch J. 1997. Obesity (Review). *New England Journal of Medicine;* 337: 396-407.

34   Shaper AG, Wannamethee SG, Walker M. 1997. Defining a healthy body weight for middle-aged men: implications for the prevention of coronary heart disease, stroke and diabetes mellitus. *British Medical Journal;* 314: 1311-1317.

35   Willett WC. 1997. Is dietary fat a major determinant of body fat? *American Journal of Clinical Nutrition;* 56: 373-378.

36   Williamson DF, Pamuk E, Thun M, Flanders B, Byers T, Heath C. 1995. Prospective study of intentional weight loss and mortality in never-smoking overweight US white women aged 40-64 years. *American Journal of Epidemiology;* 141: 1128-1141.

## Insulin resistance

37  Krentz AJ. 1996. Insulin resistance. *British Medical Journal;* 313: 1385-1389.

38  Laws A, Reaven GM. 1993. Insulin resistance and risk factors for coronary heart disease. *Bailliere's Clinical Endocrinology and Metabolism;* 7: 1063-1078.

39  Landsberg L, Krieger DR, Parker D et al. 1991. Obesity, blood pressure and the sympathetic nervous system. *Annals of Epidemiology;* 1: 295-303.

## Homocysteine metabolism

40  Graham IM, Meleady R. 1996. Heart attack and homocysteine (editorial). *British Medical Journal;* 313: 1419-1420.

41  Nygard D, Nordrehaug JE, Refsum H, Ueland PM, Farstad M, Vollset SE. 1997. Plasma homocysteine levels and mortality in patients with coronary artery disease. *New England Journal of Medicine;* 337: 230-236.

42  Rimm EB, Willett WC, Hu FB, Sampson L, Colditz GA, Manson JE, Hennekens C, Stampfer MJ. 1998. Folate and vitamin $B_6$ from diet and supplements in relation to risk of coronary heart disease among women. *Journal of the American Medical Association;* 279: 359-364.

43  Scott JM, Weir DG. 1996. Homocysteine and cardiovascular disease. *Quarterly Journal of Medicine;* 90: 561-563.

44  Tucker KL, Selhub J, Wilson PWF, Rosenberg IH. 1996. Dietary intake pattern relates to plasma folate and homocysteine concentrations in the Framingham heart study. *Journal of Nutrition;* 126: 3025-3031.

## Foetal origins of coronary heart disease

45  Barker DJP. 1995. Foetal origins of coronary heart disease. *British Medical Journal;* 311: 171-174.

46  Joseph KSD, Kramer MS. 1996. Review of the evidence on foetal and early childhood antecedents of adult chronic disease. *Epidemiologic Reviews;* 18: 158-173.

47  Scrimshaw NS. 1997. The relation between fetal malnutrition and chronic disease in later life. *British Medical Journal;* 315: 825-826.

## Life course influences on coronary heart disease

48  Bartley M, Blane D, Montgomery S. 1997. Health and the life course: why safety nets matter. *British Medical Journal;* 314: 1194-1196.

49  Black D. 1996. Deprivation and health. *Journal of the Royal College of Physicians of London;* 30: 466-471.

50  Davey Smith G, Hart C, Blane D, Gillis C, Hawthorne V. 1997. Lifetime socioeconomic position and mortality: prospective observational study. *British Medical Journal;* 314: 547-552.

51  James WPT, Nelson M, Ralph A, Leather S. 1997. The contribution of nutrition to inequalities in health. *British Medical Journal;* 314: 1545-1549.

## Psychosocial factors and stress

52  Brunner E. 1997. Stress and the biology of inequality. *British Medical Journal;* 314: 1472-1476.

53  Hemingway H, Marmot M. Psychosocial factors in the primary and secondary prevention of coronary heart disease: a systematic review. In: Yusuf S, Cairns JA, Fallen E, Gersch BJ, Camm AJ (eds.) 1997. *Evidenced Based Cardiology.* London: British Medical Journal Publishing.

54  Michie S, Cockcroft A. 1996. Overwork can kill (editorial). *British Medical Journal;* 312: 921-922.

## Thrombosis and fibrinolysis

55  Meade TW. The epidemiology of atheroma, thrombosis and ischaemic heart disease. In: Bloom AL, Forbes CD, Thomas DP, Tuddenham EGD (eds.) 1994. *Haemostasis and Thrombosis.* Edinburgh: Churchill Livingstone; chapter 53: 1199-1227.

## Inflammation and infection

56  Grimble R. 1996. Interaction between nutrients, pro-inflammatory cytokines and inflammation. *Clinical Science;* 91: 121-30.

57    Gupta S, Camm AJ. 1997. *Chlamydia pneumoniae* and coronary heart disease. Coincidence, association or causation. *British Medical Journal;* 314: 1778-1779.

58    Khaw K-T, Woodhouse P. 1995. Interaction of vitamin C, infection, haemostasis and cardiovascular disease. *British Medical Journal;* 310: 1559-1563.

59    Laurila A, Bloigu A, Nayha S, Hassi J, Leinonen M, Saikku P. 1997. *Chlamydia pneumonia* antibodies and serum lipids in Finnish men: cross sectional study. *British Medical Journal;* 314: 1456-1457.

60    Whincup PH, Mendall MA, Perry IJ, Strachan DP, Walker M. 1996. Prospective relations between *Helicobacter pylori* infection, coronary heart disease and stroke in middle-aged men. *Heart;* 75: 568-575.

61    Ridker PM, Cushman M, Stampfer MJ, Tracy RP, Hennekens CH. 1997. Inflammation, aspirin, and the risk of cardiovascular disease in apparently healthy men. *New England Journal of Medicine;* 336, 973-979.

## Nitric oxide

62    Vallance P. 1997. Exploring vascular nitric oxide in health and disease. *Journal of the Royal College of Physicians of London;* 31: 321-327.

## Environmental factors

63    Curwen M. 1990. Excess winter mortality: a British phenomenon? *Health Trends;* 22: 169-175.

64    Anderson HR, Ponce de Leon A, Bland JM, Bowers JS, Strachan DP. 1996. Air pollution and daily mortality in London 1987-92. *British Medical Journal;* 312: 665-669.

65    Curwen M, Donaldson GC, Tcherjavskii VE, Ermakov SP, Bucher K, Keatinge WR. 1998. Winter mortality and cold stress in Yekaterinburg, Russia: interview survey. *British Medical Journal;* 316: 514-518.

66    Katsouyanni K, Touloumi G, Schwartz J et al. 1997. Short term effects of ambient sulphur dioxide and particulate matter on mortality in 12 European cities: results from time series data from the APHEA project. *British Medical Journal;* 314: 1658-1663.

67    Kawachi I, Colditz GA, Speizer FE, Manson JE, Stampfer MJ, Willett WC, Hennekens CH. 1997. A prospective study of passive smoking and coronary heart disease. *Circulation;* 95: 2374-2379.

68    Law MR, Hackshaw AK. 1996. Environmental tobacco smoke. *British Medical Bulletin;* 52: 22-34.

69    Law MR, Morris JK, Wald NJ. 1997. Environmental tobacco smoke exposure and ischaemic heart disease: an evaluation of the evidence. *British Medical Journal;* 315: 973-980.

70    Poloniecki JD, Atkinson RW, Ponce de Leon A, Anderson HR. 1997. Daily time series for cardiovascular hospital admissions and previous day's air pollution in London, UK. *Occupational and Environmental Medicine;* 54: 535-540.

71    Shaper AG. Water-hardness and coronary heart disease. In: Golding AMB, Noah N, Stanwell-Smith R (eds.) 1994. *Water and Public Health:* pages 155-170. London: Smith-Gordon/ Nishimura.

72    The Eurowinter Group. 1997. Cold exposure and winter mortality from ischaemic heart disease, cerebrovascular disease, respiratory disease, and all causes in warm and cold regions of Europe. *Lancet;* 349: 1341-1346.

## Genetics and coronary heart disease

73    Hamsten A. 1996. Molecular genetics as the route to understanding prevention and treatment. *Lancet;* 348 (suppl) 1; 17-19.

74    Marenberg ME, Risch N, Berkman LF, Floderus B, de Faire U. 1994. Genetic susceptibility to death from coronary heart disease in a study of twins. *New England Journal of Medicine;* 330: 1041-1046.

75    Ye S, Eriksson P, Hamsten A, Kurkinen M, Humphries SE, Henney AM. 1996. Progression of coronary atherosclerosis is associated with a common variant of the human stromelysin-1 promoter which results in reduced gene expression. *Journal of Biological Chemistry;* 271: 13055-13060.

# Acknowledgements

*The Task Group is grateful to the following people who made contributions to individual sections of this chapter.*

### Diet and coronary heart disease
*Professor Gerry Shaper, Vice-Chairman, National Heart Forum, 1995-98*

### Antioxidants
*Professor Stephen Ball, Institute for Cardiovascular Research, University of Leeds*

### Postprandial lipaemia
*Dr George Miller, MRC Epidemiology and Medical Care Unit, St Bartholomew's Medical College, London*

### Overweight and obesity
*Professor Philip James, Director, Rowett Research Institute, Aberdeen*

### Insulin resistance
*Professor George Alberti, Royal College of Physicians*

### Homocysteine metabolism
*Professor Ian Graham, Department of Cardiology, Adelaide Hospital, Dublin*
*Dr Raymond Meleady, Department of Cardiology, Adelaide Hospital, Dublin*

### Foetal origins of coronary heart disease
*Professor David Barker, MRC Environmental Epidemiology Unit, University of Southampton*

### Life course influences on coronary heart disease
*Dr Yoav Ben-Shlomo, Department of Social Medicine, University of Bristol*
*Professor George Davey Smith, Department of Social Medicine, University of Bristol*

### Psychosocial factors and stress
*Professor Michael Marmot, International Centre for Health and Society, Department of Epidemiology and Public Health, University College London*

### Thrombosis and fibrinolysis
*Professor Tom Meade, MRC Epidemiology and Medical Care Unit, St Bartholomew's Medical College, London*

### Inflammation and infection
*Professor Tom Sanders, Department of Nutrition and Dietetics, King's College London*

### Nitric oxide
*Professor Patrick Vallance, Department of Medicine, University College London*

### Environmental factors
*Dr David Strachan, Department of Public Health Sciences, St George's Hospital Medical School, London*

# Genetics and coronary heart disease

*Dr Adriano Henney, Department of Cardiovascular Medicine, John Radcliffe Hospital, Oxford*

*Professor Hugh Watkins, Department of Cardiovascular Medicine, John Radcliffe Hospital, Oxford*

# Chapter 5

# Preventing coronary heart disease: population policies

**TASK GROUP**

**Ms Imogen Sharp** (Convenor)
*National Heart Forum*

**Dr Alan Maryon Davis**
*Lambeth, Southwark and Lewisham Health Authority*

**Ms Christine Godfrey**
*Centre for Health Economics, University of York*

**Mr Donald Reid**
*The United Kingdom Public Health Association*

**Ms Maggie Sanderson**
*School of Health and Sports Science, University of North London*

# Preventing coronary heart disease: population policies

This chapter:

- reviews major policy proposals over the last decade

- reviews the effectiveness of prevention policies in the UK and internationally

- assesses which policies are likely to have most impact

- considers the factors affecting implementation of policy proposals, and

- considers policy proposals for the future.

**KEY THEMES**

1   Population policies are needed which focus on structural and environmental factors. While health education is important, it is unlikely that a large proportion of the population will make individual behaviour changes which are discouraged by the environment and existing social norms.

2   Comprehensive strategies are needed to tackle each coronary risk factor, including smoking, physical activity and nutrition. Single, piecemeal interventions, which have been the norm, have a limited impact on their own.

3   A priority must be policies which help reduce risk among low income groups, and reduce the increasing health divide. There is a need for innovation, involving new agencies and social policies, starting with children, and supported by evaluation.

4   Investment is needed in research into effective population policies.

5   With a Minister for Public Health, government has an important opportunity to introduce public policies which genuinely improve public health. Token responses will call real commitment into question.

# Introduction

The World Health Organization noted in relation to coronary heart disease in 1982:

> "... with regard to several key preventive measures, the balance of evidence indicates sufficient assurance of safety and a sufficient level of probability of major benefits to warrant action at the population level. The evidence is similar in nature and strength to that governing past policy decisions on air pollution control, sanitary improvements, and the formulation of dietary requirements."[1]

It is well accepted that there are complementary population and high risk strategies, with population strategies focusing on reducing risk factors in the population as a whole, and the latter aiming to reduce the risk in individuals identified as being at particularly high risk. Geoffrey Rose wrote:

> "...potentially far more effective, and ultimately the only acceptable answer, is the mass strategy, whose aim is to shift the whole population's distribution of the mass variable."[2]

The evidence favouring a multifactorial and a population approach is overwhelming. The large majority of premature cardiovascular deaths in the UK occur among people who have relatively low levels of a few risk factors only. The events which occur among people with high levels of acknowledged risk factors are a minority. The question is, which population strategies are worthwhile?

## The place of population policies

Since the 1970s, and even before, a number of population policies have been advocated to improve public health in general and in particular to reduce the UK's high rates of coronary heart disease. The Labour government document *Prevention and Health: Everybody's Business*[3], published in 1976, acknowledged the impact of population interventions on public health, but nevertheless concluded that the health problems of the 1970s were concerned mainly with individual human behaviour and lifestyle.

> "Many of the current major problems in prevention are related less to man's outside environment than to his own personal behaviour; what might be termed our lifestyle ... (which) raises the question of whether man should be protected from himself (sic) either by legislation or by heavier taxation, for example of drink or tobacco."[3]

In the early 1980s the Canterbury Report,[1] based on World Health Organization recommendations, marked a sea-change in the UK towards a recognition of the importance of public policy in prevention strategies. Almost a decade later, the publication of *The Health of the Nation*, and equivalent health strategies in Scotland, Northern Ireland and Wales, represented perhaps the most significant step forward in public health since the establishment of the NHS. They set out government structures, including a Cabinet Committee with representatives of 11 government departments, that acknowledged the importance of wider policy influences on health. More recently, the Labour government has extended this approach in *Our Healthier Nation* by explicitly acknowledging the wider determinants of health - including social, economic and environmental factors – and committing itself to undertake health impact assessments of its relevant key policies, as they are being developed and implemented.[5]

*Our Healthier Nation* also recognises, by setting out a national 'contract for health', and a 'contract' for heart disease, the role that different agencies can play in reducing heart disease risk, at national, local and community, and individual levels. In this, and in its strategies on tobacco, transport and social exclusion, as well as the development of a Food Standards Agency, for example, the government acknowledges the place of population policies in improving health, and pledges to deliver key economic and social policies.[6-9] Coronary heart disease is identified as a key priority area, in this and the health strategies for other parts of the UK.[10, 11]

At a local level, a range of policies on health, transport, environment and education will be important for public health. Health authorities have been given a key role in leading local alliances to develop Health Improvement Programmes and Health Action Zones, to translate the national contract into action and implement the National Service Framework for coronary heart disease. Local authorities have a new duty to promote the economic, social and environmental well-being of their area. A wide range of agencies will need to be involved, with a focus on implementing effective population policies.

**Inequalities in health**
However, whether *The Health of the Nation*,[4] and strategies for other parts of the UK, actually effected change has yet to be assessed. Moreover, they gave no priority to tackling the underlying causes of ill health, and addressing the inequalities in rates of disease, including coronary heart disease; tackling 'social variations' was largely confined to what the NHS could achieve, rather than dealing with more deep-seated, intrinsic structural measures.[12]

By contrast, the new national public health strategies[5, 10, 11] make tackling health inequalities a priority: *Our Healthier Nation*, for example, has a specific goal "to improve the health of the worst off in society and to narrow the health gap".[5] The government-commissioned Acheson *Independent Inquiry into Inequalities in Health* also makes comprehensive and broad-based recommendations to tackle the underlying determinants of ill health.[13]

Coronary heart disease has increasingly become associated with disadvantage, and the social class gap is widening. To tackle it effectively will demand strategies that address social inequalities first and foremost and from a young age. The widening gap is largely due to faster declines in coronary heart disease among non-manual social groups (see chapter 3), and there is a need to ensure that effective policies also work for the lower income groups. An advantage of population policies is their potentially universal coverage, and the ability to use a range of levers for change. Although there are social inequalities in many of the risk factors, these explain only a proportion of the social class gap in disease. Thus it is also important to tackle the root causes of health inequalities, through education and an anti-poverty strategy, for example, as well as by introducing population policies which address classic risk factors for disease perhaps, for example, through the Social Exclusion Unit. This is an increasingly urgent task as the gap widens.

**Review of policy proposals**
This chapter takes as its starting point the major policy proposals made by the National Heart Forum, and other bodies, since the inception of the National Heart Forum at the Canterbury Conference in 1983. A 'major' policy proposal is defined

as one which requires a significant policy shift and resource input to make it happen.

Inevitably some division was necessary, and the policy proposals are divided by the three lifestyle factors: smoking, nutrition and physical activity. While this does not take into account the potential multiplicative effect of risk factors addressed by the multifactorial community cardiovascular disease programmes in the 1970s and 1980s (see chapter 6), it takes the reality of the UK policy context as a starting point. Inequalities in health cut across these risk factors, but are only explained in part by them.

The chapter uses several tools to analyse existing policy proposals and their population impact. The Task Group looked for evidence of effectiveness, where it exists. However, population policies are notoriously difficult to assess by conventional research. It is not possible, for example, to use the randomised controlled trial in the same way as for clinical interventions. McPherson[14] has pointed out the problems: health promotion interventions are not specific, are often poorly measured, and are sometimes based on poorly understood, complex psychological and social phenomena. The populations are usually large, very heterogeneous, and often poorly defined. End-points are rare, and it is often decades before hard outcomes are observed. In free-living healthy populations, contamination of controls is often not avoided, as it is difficult to maintain separate intervention groups and controls. As a result, population policy interventions are often not the subject of research attention, or indeed of research funding.

Furthermore, it is clear that policy is not made simply on the basis of effectiveness. Thus judgements on costs and cost-effectiveness have been made, considering the costs and consequences of different policies from a societal and population perspective, rather than simply an NHS perspective. Evidence is used where available, but formal research on the costs or cost-effectiveness of population strategies is limited: there is a paucity of economic evidence.

The context, and the strengths and weaknesses of policies, have also been assessed, and best judgements made by the Task Group on whether the policy is essential, an important reinforcing policy, or a useful support policy.

# TOBACCO

## The problem

Smoking is one of the main preventable causes of coronary heart disease. It is estimated that 24% of deaths from coronary heart disease among men, and 11% of deaths from coronary heart disease among women are due to smoking.[15] Over 120,000 people in the UK are killed by smoking each year.[6]

While smoking rates are declining in the UK, they are still high. The rate of decline among adults in the UK has levelled off, and a small rise has already occurred in the United States. The gap in rates between men and women has also essentially disappeared. In 1996, 29% of men, and 28% of women were smokers.[16]

Smoking is increasingly associated with disadvantage. The social class gap has widened. While smoking has declined in high income groups, for those on the very lowest incomes, smoking has not declined at all. In 1996, among unskilled manual workers (social class V), 41% of men and 36% of women were smokers, compared to 12% of men and 11% of women in professional groups (social class I).[16] These figures mask bigger divides. For example, the 4% of the population who are bringing up young children in council housing now constitute 10% of all smokers.[17]

Among young people, smoking rates have not fallen in the past decade, and indeed the latest figures show an increase. Prevalence rates among young adults may have stopped declining, and in teenagers appear to be rising, particularly among girls. In 1996, about 13% of children aged 11-15 were regular smokers. Notably, one in three 15-year-old girls smoke regularly - an increase from one in five in 1988.[6] There are also signs of a similar increase in other English-speaking countries. Importantly, 82% of smokers take up the habit as teenagers.[6]

The successes are mainly due to cessation. Although teenage smoking is common among all social classes, middle class smokers are more likely to give up by the age of 30.[17] Seven out of ten adult smokers say that they want to give up.[18]

| POLICY MEASURE | EVIDENCE OF EFFECTIVENESS | COSTS AND COST-EFFECTIVENESS |
|---|---|---|
| **FISCAL** | | |
| **Real increases in tobacco tax annually**<br><br><br>Canterbury Report,[1] Royal College of Physicians[19] | Price elasticity about -0.5 for consumption. Also associated with substantial falls in prevalence.[20]<br><br>Available evidence suggests the poor, children and the young are at least as price sensitive as average, although specific UK research is limited. | Direct effects borne by smokers and industry. High cost-effectiveness. |
| **LEGAL / REGULATORY** | | |
| **Ban tobacco advertising, sponsorship and promotion**<br><br><br><br>Canterbury Report[1] | Probable effects on adult consumption and teenage prevalence.[21, 22] | Some direct costs in preparing and implementing legislation. May have some indirect costs if average prices fall. Overall cost-effectiveness dependent on realised fall in consumption. |
| **Restrict smoking in workplaces**<br><br><br>Royal College of Physicians[24] | Up to 10% fall in consumption may occur; long-term decline in prevalence also possible.[25] | Direct costs dependent on type of policy. Potential for savings to industry in longer term from increased productivity and lower sickness absences. Cost-effectiveness of different programmes in UK requires further research. |
| **Restrict smoking in public places eg restaurants, pubs and trains**<br><br><br><br>Royal College of Physicians[19, 24] | Associated with reduced smoking in some US states, but direction of causality uncertain.[26]<br><br>In the UK, 42% of people now take the availability of a non-smokng area into account when choosing a restaurant; one in five people do so when choosing a pub.[6] | Implementation varies across sectors. Provision of separate smoking sections involves costs but in non-smoking areas or where there are complete bans, the costs of cleaning and fire insurance fall. Other 'non-health' benefits to non-smokers. Cost-effectiveness dependent on effects. |
| **Stop sales to under-16 year olds**<br><br><br>Royal College of Physicians[19] | Vigorous local activity can reduce sales locally; if so, it may have a small delaying effect on children's recruitment to smoking.[27] | Direct costs can be considerable. Population impact is unknown, but may have additional effects on community. Cost-effectiveness needs to be demonstrated. |
| **Social policies to address low income smokers**<br><br>National Heart Forum[28] | Relatively slow decline in smoking among disadvantaged groups suggests that broader policies to combat inequality are required.[17, 29] | Direct costs could be substantial but so could benefits. Likely to have wider benefits than just health gain. Directed at equity rather than cost-effectiveness per se. |
| **Product modification: reducing tar and nicotine levels of cigarettes**<br><br><br>Royal College of Physicians[24] | Limited contribution to fall in smoking-related disease; trivial compared to cessation.[25] | Direct costs fall mainly on manufacturers. |

| STRENGTHS AND OPPORTUNITIES | WEAKNESSES AND THREATS | TASK GROUP VERDICT |
|---|---|---|
| • Strong evidence: effective policy. Well rehearsed and simple policy, well accepted by professional groups and generates government revenue.<br>• Opportunities include: annual budget, potential new supporters of policy, more research on effectiveness among children, and potential for upward harmonisation of tax across the European Union (EU). | • Diminishing returns as prevalence falls, ultimately limited by smuggling incidence; organised industry response.<br>• Increasing social divide may make tax less acceptable as policy. | ESSENTIAL |
| • Simple message, with high professional, public and parliamentary support.<br>• Symbolic: sets example, indicates government commitment to reducing smoking.<br>• Affects all population simultaneously.<br>• UK government commitment, and EU Directive. | • One-off policy; would be best as part of overall strategy.<br>• Ban on advertising without promotion would lead to increased sponsorship.<br>• Should be accompanied by a requirement for generic packaging.[23]<br>• Media and sports dependence can lead to opposition.<br>• Undermining by industry through new avenues, eg films, brand-stretching and Internet. | ESSENTIAL |
| • Widely accepted in larger places of work, especially among office workers.<br>• Introduction of restrictions may stimulate increased quitting activity and provision of cessation advice by employers.<br>• Health and Safety Commission Approved Code of Practice on smoking in the workplace, for implementation of health and safety legislation.[6] | • Less widely accepted in smaller workplaces employing manual workers. | IMPORTANT REINFORCING POLICY |
| • Majority agreement that smoking should be restricted in public places.[6]<br>• Increasingly acceptable in public transport; further evidence of effects of passive smoking may promote additional restrictions.<br>• Public Places Charter agreed by hospitality trade, and national industry-led scheme, in the White Paper on tobacco.[6] | • Complete bans less acceptable in pubs; portrayed as 'health fascism' by tobacco industry apologists. | USEFUL SUPPORT POLICY |
| • Can generate valuable publicity; popular with national politicians.<br>• Requires a licensing scheme for tobacconists, funded by the tobacco industry.[27] | • High level of enforcement difficult to achieve nationally; also requires removal of vending machines.[27]<br>• Increasing tendency of children to purchase from older friends; also possibility of creating 'forbidden fruit' effect.[27] | IMPORTANT REINFORCING POLICY |
| • Disadvantaged groups are especially susceptible to smoking-related disease.<br>• National health strategies, and the White Paper on tobacco, focus on reducing inequalities.[5, 6]<br>• Social Exclusion Unit provides opportunity. | • Requires cross-government commitment to reducing income inequality. | ESSENTIAL |
| • A weak option for those who cannot give up. Consideration needs to be given to greater use of nicotine replacement products as substitutes. | • Value limited owing to compensatory behaviour of smokers and low acceptability of safer products.[30]<br>• Low tar cigarettes may be perceived as a 'safe' alternative to quitting, and may be especially attractive to children. | USEFUL SUPORT POLICY |

| POLICY MEASURE | EVIDENCE OF EFFECTIVENESS | COSTS AND COST-EFFECTIVENESS |
|---|---|---|
| **EDUCATION/INFORMATION** | | |
| **Paid and unpaid mass communications - preventing teenage smoking**<br><br><br><br>Royal College of Physicians[19] | Controlled trials overseas have had mixed results.[24] | High direct cost; effectiveness not guaranteed. |
| **Mass communications - cessation campaigns**<br><br><br>Royal College of Physicians[19, 24] | Can enhance natural quit rate by up to 5%.[25] | High direct costs but high reach. Not fully evaluated but could produce similar cost per life year saved as individually directed cessation programmes. |
| **Mass communications - media advocacy and unpaid publicity** | Elasticity of -0.5 for consumption; linked with major declines in prevalence. Major effect is on public opinion.[25] | Direct costs in terms of professional time can be high. Benefits could include enhancing the benefits of other policies. Generally thought to be cost-effective. |
| **Health education in schools**<br><br><br>Royal College of Physicians[19] | Sophisticated programmes can delay recruitment to smoking for several years but not indefinitely.[27] | Cost-effectiveness dependent on benefits of delayed onset. |
| **Pack information, including health warnings and tar and nicotine content**<br><br>Royal College of Physicians[24] | Possibly some influence with adolescents;[25] support from smokers.[33] | Cost borne by manufacturers and smokers. |
| **SERVICE PROVISION** | | |
| **Nicotine replacement therapy (NRT)** | Significantly enhances effectiveness of GP advice, especially with more addicted smokers.[34] | Direct costs to those attempting to give up or to the NHS. Cost-effectiveness in the range of £600 to £2,000 per life year saved. Patches less cost-effective than brief advice, both to GP and smoker.[32] |
| **Smoking cessation advice in NHS, primary care and clinics**<br><br><br><br>Royal College of Physicians[24] | Brief advice from GP leads to up to 5% quit rate;[35, 36] advice clinics achieve 10%-25% in one year.[25] | High cost-effectiveness compared to most other health service interventions - in the range of £14 to £100 per life year saved. Longer and more elaborate GP interventions achieve higher quit rate, but are less cost-effective.[32] |
| **Telephone 'quitline' services and advice**<br><br><br>Royal College of Physicians[24] | Quit rate of 19% at six months in Scotland with mass campaign.[37] | Cost-effectiveness not yet evaluated. |

| STRENGTHS AND OPPORTUNITIES | WEAKNESSES AND THREATS | TASK GROUP VERDICT |
| --- | --- | --- |
| • Can reach large numbers of teenagers very rapidly.[27]<br>• Acceptable to policy makers and professionals: government funding commitment.<br>• Controlled trials needed. | • High cost; effectiveness not guaranteed.[27] Successful approaches in overseas campaigns may not be effective in the UK.<br>• High saturation of health message already; maintenance and new messages needed. | IMPORTANT REINFORCING POLICY |
| • Can reach 90% of smokers within three months and can work well with other interventions such as tax increases.<br>• Support with local cessation services.<br>• Can target low income smokers.<br>• Government commitment. | • Costly. | ESSENTIAL |
| • High reach, with direct influence on climate of public opinion, and provides strong basis for other initiatives.<br>• Potential of many agencies: existing motivation; government's White Paper on tobacco, with specific policy measures, provides a focus. [6] | • Can demand substantial resources for creation of 'peg'.<br>• Dependent on priority of agencies; media support and coverage depend on new messages.<br>• Tobacco industry lobbying of media industry. | ESSENTIAL |
| • Highly acceptable to parents, politicians and press; might be more effective in combination with mass media campaigns.[27] | • Effective programmes are difficult to implement on a large scale, so effectiveness is limited in practice.[27]<br>• Tobacco is rarely perceived as a high priority in schools. | USEFUL SUPPORT POLICY |
| • Essential for ethical reasons; gives clear message and has existing support.<br>• Need for increased prominence and size. | • Size and familiarity of message are limiting factors.<br>• Industry resistance to increasing size of warnings. | USEFUL SUPPORT POLICY |
| • Simple 'medical' intervention which tackles cessation and addiction among individuals.<br>• Seven out of ten smokers want to give up. [6]<br>• Support by manufacturers and pharmacists: sales motive.<br>• NHS to bear costs for short prescriptions for low income groups: government commitment in White Paper.[6] | • Tackles cessation only, and requires individual desire to quit.<br>• Best as part of overall strategy.<br>• NHS cost concerns. | IMPORTANT REINFORCING POLICY |
| • Politically acceptable, and potentially high reach through NHS.<br>• NRT focus, and private profit-making clinics provide opportunities.<br>• White Paper priority. | • Limited by low reach in practice: less than half of smokers report receiving advice from their GP;[18] smokers' advice clinics not popular with smokers. | IMPORTANT REINFORCING POLICY |
| • High demand and potentially high reach: depends on cost to smoker and advertisement of number; complements mass campaign.<br>• New communications technology may provide opportunities. | • Dependent on individual initiative, and on advertising; effectiveness depends on mass campaign. | IMPORTANT REINFORCING POLICY |

# Conclusions

There is no single cause of smoking, and no one-shot solution; and none are likely to exist in the future. International experience indicates that comprehensive packages of measures can lead to significant reductions in smoking. [6]

To reduce smoking rates in the UK, a comprehensive and sustained strategy, with a wide range of components to tackle all levels of influence, is needed. It will need to include wide national policies, personal and local community interventions, and the media. For all interventions, there is evidence of greater effectiveness when initiatives are multi-faceted rather than stand-alone, and in the context of concerted action on all fronts. Thus, while some policies may have a limited impact alone, they nevertheless form an important component. Mass media advocacy provides an important foundation. Working within an international context of tobacco control will be vital.

The government's White Paper on tobacco[6] provides a new strategy with a comprehensive package of measures: its successful implementation, at all levels, is essential to its effectiveness.

In particular, there is a need to focus on targeted approaches, innovation and evaluation, and to refine policies to tackle the high smoking rates among low income groups and the young, particularly girls. New community-based initiatives will be needed, particularly for low income groups. Achieving continued reductions in smoking among adults is crucial to reducing smoking among the young. Tackling addiction will also be important.

Innovation at this time is crucial. The evidence of diminishing returns on some policies also needs to be addressed: there is evidence that those countries which have stuck to the same policies over many years are now seeing limited returns.

Continual evaluation needs to be built into any strategy to assess which components are working. Evaluation is needed particularly to assess whether current policies are simply insufficiently targeted or the solutions are not yet available. Funding for experimental interventions and assessing effectiveness will be vital.

One longer term policy is a programme to control the supply of the drug nicotine, since smokers smoke mainly to obtain nicotine. This might involve setting up a nicotine control agency to regulate the supply of products containing nicotine, including cigarettes. Its functions might include: regulating the manufacture and sale of all such products; encouraging the development of safer and more acceptable forms of nicotine products; and working towards the long-term weaning of the population from nicotine, but with the medium-term goal of reducing harm.

# NUTRITION

## The problem

Diet and nutrition are key factors in the development of coronary heart disease and other forms of cardiovascular disease.

In order to help reduce the high rates of cardiovascular disease in the UK, the Committee on Medical Aspects of Food Policy (COMA)[38] recommends reductions in fat and particularly saturated fat, a reduction in salt intake and an increase in carbohydrates. COMA also recommends that the consumption of vegetables, fruit, potatoes and bread should be increased by at least 50%.

Although the absolute amount of fat consumed over the past 20 years has fallen, there has been little change in the percentage of food energy derived from total fat, from about 42% in 1975 to about 40% in 1996 (compared to the COMA recommendation of a maximum of 35% of dietary energy). There have, however, been shifts in the type of fat consumed: the percentage of food energy derived from saturated fat has fallen from about 20% to about 15.5% in the same period, although it is still far from the COMA recommended maximum of 10% of dietary energy.[15, 38]

Although there have been gradual increases in the intake of vegetables and fruit since the late 1950s, average consumption in the UK is very low at only 250g a day, compared with the recommended 400g (five portions).[39] The average masks wide social class differences, with lowest consumption levels among poorest groups, mirroring social class differences in rates of coronary heart disease. In 1995-97, people in the lowest income group ate less than half the amount of vegetables and fruit eaten by those in the highest income group (1,567 grams per person per week, compared to 3,295 grams *)[40, 41] - a gap that has shown no sign of abating. Consumption levels are also particularly low in Scotland, and among young people.[39]

Children's diets give particular cause for concern.

The UK is also facing a growing problem of overweight and obesity. In England between 1980 and 1996, the proportion of overweight or obese adults (with a BMI above 25) increased from 39% to 59% of men, and from 32% to 48% of women. Obesity rose to 16% of men and 17% of women, and is linked both to excessive energy intake, including intake of dietary fat, and to insufficient energy expenditure.[15]

---

* These data are from the National Food Survey. Figures for fruit and vegetables include the weights of peel, core and outside leaves which are not eaten. Actual intakes are estimated to be around 20% lower.

| POLICY MEASURE | EVIDENCE OF EFFECTIVENESS | COSTS AND COST-EFFECTIVENESS |
|---|---|---|
| **FISCAL** | | |
| **Revise Common Agricultural Policy (CAP) to promote health and subsidise healthy foods**<br><br><br><br>Canterbury Report[1] | The CAP has facilitated the switch from butter to margarine by maintaining price differentials.[42]<br><br>CAP policies have had a negative effect on fruit and vegetable consumption.[43] | Involves considerable administrative resources to negotiate. Revising subsidies may involve changes in transfers rather than a net increase in resources. Given the market distortions created by the CAP, revision may be important to ensure cost-effectiveness of other policies. |
| **Grading and payment systems to encourage production of leaner meat**<br><br><br><br><br><br>Canterbury Report[1] | Small but significant reductions in fat content of meat in last 12 years.[44] Financial incentives have reduced the subcutaneous fat in pig meat by 30% in the last 10 years. The fat content of carcass beef and sheep has also been reduced during this period but not so dramatically.[45] | Costs - which are uncertain - fall on taxpayer and possibly meat consumers. The majority of meat consumers may be willing to pay. If not priced competitively, may lead to an increase in imports which would reduce the effectiveness and hence cost-effectiveness of policy. |
| **Competitive pricing for 'healthier' foods**<br><br><br><br><br><br>Canterbury Report[1] | In Norway, a combination of fiscal and regulatory strategies designed to affect relative prices of preferred 'healthy' foods has contributed to a 30% increase in consumption of vegetables, a 17% increase in fruit consumption, and a 13% decrease in total fat intake, between 1970 and 1993.[46] | Costs depend on consumer reaction. If demand is strong, it may reduce the need for subsidy over time. Cost-effectiveness of policy unknown. |
| **LEGAL / REGULATORY** | | |
| **Minimum nutritional standards for catering, including school meals**<br><br><br><br><br><br><br><br><br><br>National Heart Forum[47, 48] | Positive effect on food choice and nutrient composition possible in the short term. Passive intervention to reduce fat in school meals resulted in decrease in saturated fat content in total diet of 3% of energy over one year.[49, 50]<br><br>Promotion of healthy items at point of sale leads to increased sales of 2% to 12% of total sales.[51] However, in catering, changes in food accessibility or price have substantial short-term effects, but these are not sustained beyond the intervention.[51] | Likely to be cost-effective. |
| **Regulations on food advertising to children**<br><br><br><br><br><br>National Heart Forum[48] | Food advertising has an effect on purchase requests made by children to parents.[52] Artificial 'view then choose' experiments demonstrate the effect of food advertising on choice.[52] | For a voluntary code, the major costs fall on industry. Overall impact on health behaviour is uncertain but some non-health benefits arise from consumers gaining more accurate information. |
| **Clear, comprehensive and meaningful nutrition labelling**<br><br><br><br><br><br><br><br>Canterbury Report[1] | Non-numeric labelling is better understood than numeric. Verbal is the most readily understood and most effective.[54] US research indicates that although consumers prefer verbal labelling, they perform better when nutrients are expressed as a percentage of RDAs (recommended daily amounts).[55] | Costs mainly borne by food manufacturers and retailers. To be effective and cost-effective, there may be a need for additional information campaigns on how to use labels to improve health. |

| STRENGTHS AND OPPORTUNITIES | WEAKNESSES AND THREATS | TASK GROUP VERDICT |
|---|---|---|
| • Structural, universal access, long-term and pan-European, so avoids local negotiations.<br>• Opportunities include: growing food awareness and concerns in Europe; CAP negotiations; Article 152 in the Amsterdam Treaty on public health competence; and EU food standards agency. | • Long-term policy goal: need to negotiate European bureaucracy, and convince other EU member states.<br>• Globalisation of food trade, and vested interests, including farmers and manufacturers, are threats to change. | ESSENTIAL |
| • Structural: widens availability of 'recommended' products, with normative effect.<br>• Industry experience, and existing breeding programmes: small but significant reductions already achieved.<br>• Opportunities include consumer and retailer influence and demand, and establishment of Food Standards Agency. | • Production costs, including technology and longer term breeding programme, and maintenance of eating quality of leaner meat. Reductions limited by biological feasibility and production economics.<br>• Public resistance to new technologies and genetic manipulation, and consumer confidence in meat safety, are threats. | IMPORTANT REINFORCING POLICY |
| • Removes cost considerations from healthy food choice (important for low income groups), to facilitate positive shifts and experimentation in choice; 'mainstreams' products.<br>• Concentration of UK food industry, and Food Standards Agency, are opportunities. | • Impact may only be for the time of the intervention, with limited long-term change.<br>• Lack of short-term financial incentive, and risk of reduced short-term profits, and possible effects on quality.<br>• Food retailing siting trends may lead to increased price disparities. | ESSENTIAL |
| • Well-rehearsed policy measure; national nutritional guidelines for catering exist, and can be monitored.<br>• Passive and active interventions possible, with local flexibility of implementation.<br>• Importance increases with increases in eating outside the home.<br>• Government proposals for compulsory school meals standards is an opportunity. | • Nutritional standards need to be compulsory and monitored.<br>• Training of caterers needed in preparation and presentation: needs inclusion in catering courses, eg NVQs.<br>• Threats include competitive tendering with financial focus; perceived costs of healthier meals; cash cafeterias and breadth of choice; centralisation of catering supplies; and lack of training. | ESSENTIAL |
| • Wide reach; important symbolic policy.<br>• Could lead to more balanced advertising to children, with new advertisers.<br>• National Food Guide as guide: recommends that fatty and sugary foods should make up only about 8% of a healthy, balanced diet; on children's TV, 60% of adverts are for such foods.[53]<br>• Overseas models of restrictions on food advertising are opportunities. | • Extent of advertising 'hidden' from majority of adults as much of it is shown on children's TV.<br>• Industry resistance.<br>• Lack of regulatory power. | IMPORTANT REINFORCING POLICY |
| • Well rehearsed and accepted policy, with wide potential reach, enabling consumers to make an informed choice; can improve public nutrition education.<br>• Important with increased emphasis on pre-prepared foods.[53]<br>• Can be used by retailers to promote products. | • Consumer interest in calories not nutrients, and difficulty in interpretation of labels. Needs support by education or leaflets to simplify.<br>• Effective labelling format not implemented: continued focus on numeric rather than graphic labelling obscures message.<br>• Need for regulation of nutrient and health claims.<br>• Manufacturers' resistance. | USEFUL SUPPORT POLICY |

| POLICY MEASURE | EVIDENCE OF EFFECTIVENESS | COSTS AND COST-EFFECTIVENESS |
| --- | --- | --- |
| **Healthy changes to content of processed and prepared foods** | Salt content of selected standard products reduced by 14%-24% since 1986, undetected by consumers.[56]<br><br>In North Karelia, Finland, collaboration with food manufacturers and caterers, including food processing and new product development, to help people buy healthier products at competitive prices, contributed to positive changes in dietary intakes.[57] | May increase costs to the consumer, but ingredients are only one of the cost components of processed foods. Costs also fall on manufacturers to change products. Implementation costs and unknown effectiveness without enforcement. However, cooperation in health schemes may bring commercial benefits to retailer or manufacturer. |

## EDUCATION/INFORMATION

| POLICY MEASURE | EVIDENCE OF EFFECTIVENESS | COSTS AND COST-EFFECTIVENESS |
| --- | --- | --- |
| **Strategy to increase vegetable and fruit consumption, including increased promotion**<br><br>National Heart Forum[39] | Doubling of reported vegetable consumption since 1979 achieved in North Karelia, Finland, using a combination of measures, including free salad with catered meals, and improved availability of vegetables.[57]<br><br>Intensive intervention, including promotion, led to 65% of the intervention group eating more than five portions of vegetables and fruit a day, sustained over six months.[58]<br><br>In the United States, the *5 A Day* programme, including mass media and local community interventions, achieved high message awareness, and contributed to an increase in average adult intake from 3.9 to 4.4 portions a day, in five years.[39] | Pilot programmes to examine the cost-effectiveness of different strategies could be usefully pursued. |
| **School nutrition education programmes, including cooking skills**<br><br>Canterbury Report[1] | Positive effect of schools healthy eating interventions, using educational approach in classroom: achieved reduced fat intake of 2% to 6% of total energy and reduction in blood cholesterol of 5% to 11%.[51]<br><br>Effective in a range of social groups. The most effective schools interventions focused on diet alone, or diet and exercise.[51] More frequent interventions over a longer time period were associated with more sustained effect.[59] | Educational opportunity costs attached to any school. Benefits are long-term and therefore difficult to measure. Cost-effectiveness depends on the programme's individual effectiveness. |

## SERVICE PROVISION

| POLICY MEASURE | EVIDENCE OF EFFECTIVENESS | COSTS AND COST-EFFECTIVENESS |
| --- | --- | --- |
| **Dietary advice in primary care**<br><br>Canterbury Report[1] | Individual dietary interventions can achieve modest improvements in diet (including fat intake) and cardiovascular risk status (including blood cholesterol), sustained for up to three years, with personal counselling plus written educational material. Increasing intensity of intervention may have a small positive impact. Higher perceived level of risk, or evidence of disease, may motivate greater reduction in fat intake.[51, 61] | Requires more intensive interventions than some other lifestyle changes and effectiveness may be more uncertain. Wider implementation of more intensive primary care interventions needs to be researched for cost-effectiveness, including the elements of future health care costs savings from healthier diets. Considerably cheaper than cholesterol drug therapy. Cost-effective as part of a stepped programme for groups at high risk of coronary heart disease.[63] |

| STRENGTHS AND OPPORTUNITIES | WEAKNESSES AND THREATS | TASK GROUP VERDICT |
|---|---|---|
| • 'Passive' changes possible: healthy changes without need for choice. Useful in developing tastes for healthier food. As eating habits change, consumers may be more likely to try new products.<br>• Developments in food preservation enable changes in ingredients, leading to potentially healthy products.<br>• Important with changing eating patterns, and increased dependence on pre-prepared foods. | • Consumer taste preferences important. Potential price premium may reduce availability to low income groups.<br>• Producer/manufacturer resistance; seen as 'cannibalisation' of standard product. | ESSENTIAL |
| • New, positive nutrition message with wide potential appeal and benefits - for consumers as well as food industry.<br>• Support from different sectors of fruit and vegetable industry, eg fresh, frozen, canned.<br>• Potentially large health benefits for a variety of diseases; public awareness of general health benefits of vegetables and fruit; specific benefits need promotion.<br>• Food Standards Agency may present opportunity. | • Generic promotion unappealing to producers.<br>• Consumer perception of fruit as expensive and vegetables as boring, unappetising and difficult to prepare; lack of perceived need to increase personal consumption.<br>• Need for sustained and coordinated, multisector strategy to achieve change.<br>• Low consumption among low income groups, children and in Scotland; need to address availability and price. | ESSENTIAL |
| • Childhood focus for life skills.<br>• Provides consistent messages and practical skills: enables messages to be put into practice, and encourages informed choice and flexibility.<br>• Studies indicate that involvement of children, emphasis on whole school environment including food provision, and family involvement are important.[51, 59, 60]<br>• National healthy schools initiative, curricular reform and school standards review are opportunities. | • Competing priorities in schools, and limitations of curriculum: lack of time, and lack of agreed structure to provide practical skills.<br>• School budget cuts and commercial pressures: space and resource constraints for home economics and cooking skills, and increased dependence on commercial resources.<br>• Lack of nutrition training for teachers (reduced content in BEd degrees). | ESSENTIAL |
| • Potentially high reach through NHS, and individuals can be targeted.<br>• Advice can be individually tailored, with skills training, enhancing effectiveness.<br>• National Service Framework on coronary heart disease, Primary Care Groups and Healthy Living Centres provide opportunities. | • Effective interventions relatively intense, requiring substantial resources (cost-effective if changes are sustained for five years).<br>• Dependent on NHS contact, and individual motivation; follow-up needed.<br>• Need for training of primary care and other health professionals in nutrition knowledge and dietary counselling.<br>• Public perception that experts disagree on diet messages may reduce receptivity. | IMPORTANT REINFORCING POLICY |

## Conclusions

Although there have been some successes in changing the population's diet, there are also important failures. Many of the successes in changing diet are visible, and controllable by consumers at no extra cost - such as the switches from full-fat to skimmed milks and from white to wholemeal bread.

For further dietary changes, there is a need to assess the changing nature of eating patterns. An increasing emphasis on pre-prepared and processed foods increases consumer dependence on food manufacturers making products healthier, on pricing policies, and on effective and accurate nutritional labelling and claims. An estimated 65%-85% of salt, for example, comes from manufactured foods.[38]

The need for population-wide strategies to tackle nutrition is emphasised by the need in particular to improve the diets of low income groups, and tackle issues such as availability and price. A strategy to tackle poverty as it affects diet should be a main priority including, for example, improved quality of and widened eligibility for free school meals.

The dietary disparity between social groups is most marked in vegetable and fruit consumption - a gap that is not decreasing.[40] The new and positive messages on the role of fruit and vegetables in protecting against chronic diseases demand a coordinated and sustained strategy which is not only promotional, but also ensures availability and access.

Accessibility is a particular problem in light of current retailing trends, with supermarkets increasingly sited outside town centres. This demands a town planning policy response that tackles both nutrition and physical activity - and therefore obesity.

Preserving the population's ability to prepare and cook foods will also need to be a priority. This means an important emphasis on education of children in nutrition and food skills, including cooking. Interventions in natural community settings such as schools or workplaces, focusing on diet only, or on diet and one related risk factor such as exercise, are found to be effective.[51]

The Food Standards Agency could provide the focus for a much needed comprehensive nutrition strategy. Nutrition policy in the UK has largely been concerned with surveillance and an emphasis on education to inform choice. But to tackle diet-related public health problems demands more. Norway and Finland have introduced wide-ranging nutrition strategies, including legislation (on fat and on maximum salt content of specific foods, for example), and regulations on labelling and claims. They have also negotiated changes with the food manufacturers and catering industry to increase availability of vegetables and fruit, implemented minimum nutritional standards for school meals, and introduced widespread nutrition education.

The time is ripe to introduce a real national food and nutrition strategy in the UK.

# PHYSICAL ACTIVITY

## The problem

Two-thirds (64%) of men, and three-quarters (75%) of women in the UK are either sedentary or moderately active on an irregular basis.[64]

Activity is more likely to be continued in adulthood if it is established as a regular habit in childhood: active children are 10 times more likely than inactive children to be active adults.[65] However, studies consistently point to low levels of physical activity among children. Girls are less active than boys. There are also sharp declines in physical activity with age, with a 50%-75% decline between ages 6 and 18, and a continued decline during adulthood.[66] Over half of adults aged 65-75 are sedentary and fail to report any moderate physical activity. Girls and women have particularly low levels of physical activity.

Social class differences in physical activity levels are small. Although there is lower participation in leisure time physical activity with lower social class, this is balanced by higher physical activity levels in manual groups in work time.[64, 67]

Although there is evidence of increased participation in sports and leisure activities,[67] both adults and children are becoming less active in their daily life. There has been a progressive elimination of physical activity from normal living - with growing mechanisation of work and transport for example - contributing to the rise in obesity levels.

Although the relative risk of coronary heart disease associated with inactivity is similar to that of other factors,[68] the prevalence of inadequate physical activity in the UK is greater than, for example, the prevalence of smoking, hypertension (high blood pressure) or raised blood cholesterol.[64] It has been estimated that if half of those people taking some moderate activity increased it to moderate activity at least five times a week, there would be a 7% reduction in deaths from coronary heart disease.[65]

The relatively new evidence on the health benefits of moderate intensity activity, and the graded relationship between physical activity and the incidence of coronary heart disease - more activity, in terms of time and intensity, confers more benefit[69] - has not fully filtered through into policy and practice, and so is not yet sufficiently informing action.

| POLICY MEASURE | EVIDENCE OF EFFECTIVENESS | COSTS AND COST-EFFECTIVENESS |
|---|---|---|
| **FISCAL** | | |
| **Fiscal and tax incentives to encourage a switch from cars to bicycles and public transport**<br><br><br><br><br><br><br><br><br>National Heart Forum[69] | Cost and availability of car parking is an important influence on the decision to commute by car, and reduction aids a shift to cycling.[70,71] Company cars receiving free fuel do on average 20% more commuting miles than company cars that do not.[70] The import tariff on cars in Denmark, where no significant domestic car manufacturing exists, contributes to the high rates of cycling. | Costs borne by those not gaining health benefits from policy. Some costs to those switching to less preferred transport. Environmental benefits. Health benefits and hence cost-effectiveness uncertain. |
| **Local pricing policies for local facilities: subsidised access**<br><br><br><br><br><br><br><br><br><br><br><br><br><br><br>National Heart Forum[69] | Reducing access costs to facilities has a significant impact on overall visits; but main impact is more frequent use by existing users, rather than encouraging new participants. Pricing is a relative rather than an absolute barrier.[72]<br><br>For swimming, removal of prices led to reduced age profile of pool users, an increase in women attending, and a shift towards lower socioeconomic groups among women. No impact on retired and unemployed participant numbers.[73] | Direct costs administering and targeting the scheme. Net costs may be low if there is an overall increase in use of facilities. May be cost-effective if the numbers undertaking physical activity increase. |
| **LEGAL / REGULATORY** | | |
| **National physical activity strategy, with Cabinet commitment**<br><br><br><br><br><br>National Heart Forum[69] | Comprehensive strategies that target environmental and social factors influencing physical activity, as well as individual strategies, will be most effective.[74,75] Australian strategy with targets was launched in 1994; process evaluation currently being undertaken.[76] | Direct costs involve administrative input and continued support from politicians and civil servants. The impact on the effectiveness of other national policies is likely to ensure cost-effectiveness. |
| **National targets for physical activity**<br><br><br><br><br><br><br>National Heart Forum[69] | No specific evidence of effectiveness; however, targets with set dates are considered important to clarify goals, focus efforts, provide yardstick and judge effectiveness.[4] People want quantified goals for measurement of individual achievement.[77] | Cost-effectiveness of target-setting unproven. |
| **Transport policies to support traffic calming, and safe environments for walking and cycling**<br><br><br><br><br><br><br><br><br><br><br><br><br>National Heart Forum,[69]<br>British Medical Association[78] | With York city council's cycling and pedestrian strategy, journeys by bike fell only from 22.1% in 1981 to 20.3% in 1991, compared to a national fall from 4.0% to 3.2%; pedestrian journeys rose from 22.9% to 24.1%.[79]<br><br>Transport policies can create safer environments. Road accidents involving children fell by an average of 67% in 200 20mph schemes.[80] Revision of traffic law in Denmark in the late 1970s, including speed limits and street layout changes in residential streets, with priority for pedestrians, led to a 78% fall in serious injuries.[81,82] | Involves costs. Health benefits from accident prevention as well as potential to increase physical activity. Transport policies have been found to be cost-effective compared with most health care interventions in the United States.[83] |

| STRENGTHS AND OPPORTUNITIES | WEAKNESSES AND THREATS | TASK GROUP VERDICT |
|---|---|---|
| • Structural, universal measure, giving a clear message. Has environmental as well as health gains, and support from environment and transport groups. Generates revenue.<br>• Traffic reduction targets, and national cycling and walking strategies are opportunities. | • Conflicts with car culture and manufacturers' interests; tax increases unpopular. | USEFUL SUPPORT POLICY |
| • Existing policies of subsidised access; well-rehearsed. Implementation flexible and easy; can be tailored to target specific groups and activities.<br>• Healthy Living Centres and lottery funding provide opportunities. | • Relatively low prices of local authority facilities already; sport perceived as relatively cheap.<br>• Indoor facilities recover less than half their costs already.[72] Potential loss of revenue may be a barrier, particularly for commercial interests.<br>• Needs sustained publicity to support; uncertain attraction to new groups. | IMPORTANT REINFORCING POLICY |
| • Provides national leadership and demonstrates commitment; has a potentially wide impact on policies at all levels.<br>• Development work on UK strategies done.<br>• Opportunities include Minister for Public Health, national health strategies and the White Paper on an integrated transport policy with sustainable development focus.[7] | • Competing policy priorities, need for resource commitment, and lack of Cabinet status for public health are threats, particularly as the goal runs counter to trends.<br>• Transport focus rather than health focus for strategy may be a threat. | ESSENTIAL |
| • Targets provide a common goal, are motivational, and a means to monitor progress; monitoring tools available.<br>• New health strategy is an opportunity.<br>• Existing target to double cycling by year 2002 and double again by 2012.<br>• Local walking and cycling targets promoted in the White Paper on transport.[7] | • Variable quality of data on trends, particularly among children, and costs of data collection for monitoring. | IMPORTANT REINFORCING POLICY |
| • Long-term; Policy Planning Guidance 13 in place, supporting current initiatives. Local Agenda 21 initiatives and local regeneration programmes, and lottery funding, provide opportunities.<br>• White Paper on transport, local transport plans, and national cycling strategy provide framework.[7] | • Long-term planning process, involving negotiation and costs, may be a barrier. | ESSENTIAL |

| POLICY MEASURE | EVIDENCE OF EFFECTIVENESS | COSTS AND COST-EFFECTIVENESS |
| --- | --- | --- |
| **Town planning to encourage physical activity, including facilities for walking and cycling**<br><br>National Heart Forum,[69]<br>British Medical Association[78] | Observational studies show an increase in habitual physical activity associated with positive environmental changes in a community, eg cycle paths, well-lit streets, parks, easier access to recreational facilities.[84, 85]<br><br>Evidence shows that, where cycling facilities are provided, people use them. In Groningen, town planning included installation of cycle station with safe facilities, hire and repair, car-free central area, plus car parking fees. Journeys by bike increased by 20% to 57% in seven years.[86] | Cost-effectiveness depends on effectiveness, but could be similar to traffic calming measures. |
| **EDUCATION / INFORMATION** | | |
| **Mass media campaign** | Significant increases in awareness of health message and high campaign awareness, but limited if any effect on behaviour, particularly among younger people.[89, 90] Australian campaign found increases in reported walking prevalence among older people, but there was a decline in effectiveness with repeated campaigns.[91, 92]<br><br>Mass media effective for awareness raising, reinforcing lifestyle changes, and supporting community and individual interventions. Participation is higher if the campaign event is linked to a traditional structure or community event.[84, 93] | High cost if undertaken on a large enough scale to have population impact. Could generate wider benefits in terms of effectiveness of other activities. Need to explore cost-effectiveness of different approaches, given the complex messages. |
| **Minimum time for physical activity in school curriculum**<br><br>National Heart Forum[69] | Activity experiences and/or physical fitness during childhood influence adult activity habits; physical activity levels track from childhood to adolescence and into adulthood. Studies also indicate a link between sporting participation during childhood and adult physical activity levels.[66]<br><br>Focus on enjoyment and on activity which can be continued in later life and which is popular with adults is important. Different preferences for boys (games-based) and girls (individual-type activities).[94, 95] | Potential costs in terms of opportunity costs of a drop in other educational activities. Benefits are difficult to estimate. |

| STRENGTHS AND OPPORTUNITIES | WEAKNESSES AND THREATS | TASK GROUP VERDICT |
|---|---|---|
| • Benefits to trade: 49% of pedestrianised areas report improvements in trade, 2% report worsening; retail turnover increases by an average of 25%.[87]<br>• Scope for improvement: only 2.3% of all trips are by cycle in the UK, compared with 11% in Germany, and 18% in Denmark.[88]<br>• White Paper on transport provides opportunity.[7] | • Current retailing trends may be a barrier. | ESSENTIAL |
| • Well tried health education technique with mass reach; could build on previous national campaign. Important support for other interventions.<br>• 'New' message on moderate physical activity needs to be conveyed; need to target messages for clarity.<br>• New media, including Internet, may provide novelty value. | • Broad, complex physical activity message: less effective, needs targeting. Difficult to capture public's attention on physical activity.[90]<br>• Paid advertising costly, with limited duration of effect; needs support by local interventions.<br>• Growth of multiple media channels reduces audience. | IMPORTANT REINFORCING POLICY |
| • National statutory policy which would receive wide support.<br>• Combine with active schools policies to cover teaching and hidden curriculum, to promote consistent messages, and address attitudes and knowledge.<br>• National government healthy schools initiative provides an opportunity and framework. | • Competing priorities in the school curriculum, particularly with academic league tables: over 50% of children have less than two hours' PE each week.<br>• Need a focus on choice and sustainable activities; sharp decline in physical activity levels on leaving school.<br>• Threats include lack of follow-through beyond school, and limited resources (including staff time for coordination, and loss of school playing fields). | IMPORTANT REINFORCING POLICY |

| POLICY MEASURE | EVIDENCE OF EFFECTIVENESS | COSTS AND COST-EFFECTIVENESS |
|---|---|---|
| **Advice on physical activity by primary care team (including referral schemes)**<br><br><br><br><br><br><br><br><br><br><br><br><br><br><br><br><br>Canterbury Report,[1]<br>Royal College of Physicians[96] | Evidence does not seem to support 'prescription for exercise' schemes which refer patients to a leisure centre; facility-based interventions are not necessarily effective.[97] Less than 1% of a practice list are referred to such schemes.[98]<br><br>Home and community strategies may be more effective. A review of trials finds it is possible to increase activity among sedentary people, and maintain the increase at sufficient frequency and intensity to achieve long-term health gain. Sustained high levels of participation are possible if the intervention: is a home-based programme; is unsupervised, informal exercise; involves frequent professional contact; involves moderate intensity exercise; or if walking is the promoted exercise.[98] Interventions that encourage walking but do not require attendance at a facility are most likely to lead to sustainable increases in overall physical activity. | As for smoking advice, if it results in some change in activity, it would be very cost-effective despite low individual effectiveness. More involved schemes including exercise prescriptions can involve more direct costs. |
| **Information on local facilities provided for example by local authorities, health authorities and primary care**<br><br><br>Canterbury Report[1] | The Minnesota Heart Health Program found highest participation and cost-effectiveness were achieved by maximising the use of existing community facilities in combination with information leaflets.[93] | Likely to be highly cost-effective. |

## SERVICE PROVISION

| | | |
|---|---|---|
| **Increase provision of accessible and affordable, multi-use exercise facilities**<br><br><br><br><br><br><br><br><br><br><br><br>National Heart Forum[69] | Accessibility, convenience and safety of facilities and locations in the community affect physical activity levels; geographical and time constraints are important.[100] Improved provision of and access to facilities can lead to increased participation rates.[101]<br><br>High provision of accessible facilities, plus low prices, may also reduce social class differences in participation.[102]<br><br>Convenience particularly influential on children's activity levels.[66, 103] | Some changes in accessibility can be brought about by low cost interventions, eg better use of existing facilities. New investment more costly to procure. |
| **Workplace facilities and financial incentives**<br><br><br><br><br><br><br><br><br><br><br><br><br><br><br><br><br><br><br><br><br>National Heart Forum,[69]<br>British Medical Association[78] | Workplace physical activity programmes can enhance fitness, reduce absenteeism, increase productivity, and reduce employers' health care costs.[67, 104]<br><br>The Minnesota Heart Health Program found increases in self-reported physical activity levels in the intervention group: existing community settings where people spend much of the day, such as workplaces and schools, were most effective, and most cost-effective.[93, 105]<br><br>Few workplace schemes to promote travel to work by cycling.[106] A combination of financial incentives and facilities led to a 60% increase in cycling, increases in walking, and 700 fewer cars on site, at Southampton University Hospital Trust.[107] | A US review estimated that the total financial benefit of exercise programmes to companies was $513 per worker per year.[108] Benefits to employers may be lower in the UK than the United States because employers in the UK do not carry the burden of health care. However, such initiatives are likely to be cost-effective from society perspective. |

*Looking to the Future: Making Coronary Heart Disease an Epidemic of the Past*

| STRENGTHS AND OPPORTUNITIES | WEAKNESSES AND THREATS | TASK GROUP VERDICT |
|---|---|---|
| • Build on current enthusiasm for 'prescriptions for exercise', but focus on unsupervised, informal exercise of moderate intensity, with frequent professional contact. Regular follow-up improves maintenance of initial increases.[99]<br>• Advice can be individualised; computerised health registers allow targeting of high risk groups, including cardiac patients.<br>• Behavioural techniques such as signing contracts, may be effective.[90]<br>• National Service Framework, Primary Care Groups and Healthy Living Centres provide opportunities.<br>• Provides symbolic message about the health benefits of physical activity. | • Competing priorities at practice and locality level.<br>• Many health professionals do not have adequate training on (nor interest in) the benefits of physical activity, or advice-giving. | USEFUL SUPPORT POLICY |
| • Wide coverage for low cost; can be targeted and updated; and promotes choice and local variety. Can link with local campaigns and events.<br>• Greater market-driven approach, lottery funding, and the Internet and other new media provide opportunities. | • Information cannot be individually tailored, but take-up depends on stage of change. | ESSENTIAL |
| • 'Traditional' provision, which can be combined with subsidies and information, and can promote variety and choice.<br>• Swimming very popular, with consistent increases (across age and social groups) after local investment in pools.<br>• Lottery funding provides opportunity. | • Provision of facilities is costly, and is affected by local government cuts.<br>• Sports facilities are of limited appeal to non-exercisers; increased emphasis on play rather than exercise in pools. | ESSENTIAL |
| • Has symbolic benefits, and benefits both employees and employer.<br>• 'Captive audience': can tailor, sustain, and combine with other interventions.<br>• Scope for employers, including health authorities and trusts, to include cycling provisions and incentives.<br>• New government emphasis on healthy workplaces may provide stimulus. | • Only reaches the employed, with further self-selection of the physically active. Low popularity in the UK: 6% of workplaces in England (mainly large companies); low participation and high drop-out.[106]<br>• Perceived resource costs - time and money; short-term contracts and insurance liabilities may be threats. | IMPORTANT REINFORCING POLICY |

| POLICY MEASURE | EVIDENCE OF EFFECTIVENESS | COSTS AND COST-EFFECTIVENESS |
|---|---|---|
| **School sports facilities, including fields and pools, available for wider community use, outside school hours**<br><br>National Heart Forum[69] | Extra-curricular activities, and suitable community facilities, are important for physical activity participation.[66] Use of existing community settings, such as schools, is effective.[93] | Involves costs but at a community level may be more cost-effective than investment in new facilities.[93] |
| **Safe routes to schools schemes**<br><br><br><br><br><br><br><br><br><br><br>National Heart Forum[69] | A Danish scheme led to an 85% fall in child pedestrian and cyclist accidents, and nearly two-thirds of children cycle to school.[109]<br><br>A survey of 10,000 UK children found that 30%-40% wanted to cycle to school, but less than 10% were able to do so.[80] Traffic calming eases parental fears: those saying they would allow their children to travel independently to school rose from 22% before traffic calming to 33%; those allowed to visit a local shop rose from 27% to 43%.[110]<br><br>Evidence suggests a strong link between restrictions on children's mobility and physical activity outside home at weekends.[111] | Environmental and health benefits. Likely to be cost-effective. |

| STRENGTHS AND OPPORTUNITIES | WEAKNESSES AND THREATS | TASK GROUP VERDICT |
|---|---|---|
| • Uses existing facilities, and enhances community involvement and local ownership.<br>• National healthy schools initiative provides an opportunity. | • Staff costs, and sales of school playing fields, are barriers. | IMPORTANT REINFORCING POLICY |
| • New but growing UK initiative: popular appeal and government and local authority support. Useful for community involvement, including children, and awareness-raising.<br>• Integrated transport strategy, with schools travel advisory group;[7] national healthy schools initiative;[5] regeneration programmes, and improved security surveillance equipment provide opportunities.<br>• Widened cycling proficiency scheme for younger ages is important: well-established and encourages early positive attitudes. Proficiency classes show better results when on-road training is provided.[112] | • Slow development phase: funding, planning and consultation.<br>• Reversing major declines in independent travel to school (from 80% of 8-9 year olds walking to school in 1971, to less than 20% in 1990).<br>• Resource and training implications of wider cycling proficiency scheme; local authority cuts reduce cycle training. | ESSENTIAL |

## Conclusions

The shift, with relatively recent evidence, to a recognition of the cardiovascular health benefits of moderate intensity activity coincides with the progressive elimination of activity in daily life. The focus now needs to be on promoting lifelong moderate intensity physical activity in the context of everyday life.

Because physical activity has been relatively neglected as a risk factor for coronary heart disease, research and theory on interventions to increase activity is in its infancy in relation to that for other risk factors. There is relatively little evaluation of the effectiveness of interventions, particularly for young people. Furthermore, the majority of interventions that have been evaluated have focused primarily on leisure time activity, rather than activity as part of daily life.

However it is increasingly clear that, to achieve a significant impact on the population activity levels as a whole, strategies that target the environmental and structural forces influencing physical activity, such as transport policy and town planning, need far greater attention.[74, 113] Any strategy to increase activity levels will need sustained and coordinated investment. It is clear from evidence that a comprehensive approach with a variety of measures is needed, and that isolated measures by themselves have a limited impact.[114]

A focus on children is also needed, as there is evidence that activity levels in childhood are predictive of activity in later life. While there is a relative paucity of evidence on children's fitness and activity, there is clear evidence that children are becoming less mobile in their daily lives.[111, 115]

In line with the goal of increasing activity in daily life are several strands of evidence indicating that focusing on individual pursuits may be most fruitful. For example, among children, these are most likely to transfer to out-of-school participation, and are most likely to be continued into adult life; interventions among adults achieve sustained high levels of physical activity if the intervention focuses on unsupervised and informal exercise, such as walking. Furthermore, the sedentary population, at highest risk of coronary heart disease, is least likely to join exercise classes.[74]

In terms of general awareness-raising, because of the relative complexity of the message, targeting, with specific focused messages, is important.

A serious and sustained focus in public health towards policies to increase physical activity in daily life would tie in with the integrated transport policy,[7] and trends in transport policy towards more environment-friendly policies, encouraging walking and cycling. If current trends continue, a major increase in traffic is forecast, with an increase in cars from 20 million to 35 million between 1988 and 2025. However, it has been estimated that, with a shift from cars to cycling for 20% to 50% of non-walk trips, there are potential total savings of £1.3 billion to £4.6 billion, and a possible reduction in coronary heart disease of 4.7% to 17.1%.[116]

# References

1 Rose G, Ball K, Catford J, James P, Lambert D, Maryon Davis A, Oliver M, Player D, Robbins C, Smith A. 1984. *Coronary Heart Disease Prevention: Plans for Action.* ('The Canterbury Report'.) London: Pitman.

2 Rose G. 1981. Strategy of prevention: Lessons from cardiovascular disease. *British Medical Journal;* 282: 1847-1851.

3 Department of Health and Social Security. 1976. *Prevention and Health: Everybody's Business. A Reassessment of Public and Personal Health.* London: HMSO.

4 Department of Health, 1992. *The Health of the Nation. A Strategy for Health in England.* London: HMSO.

5 Department of Health. 1998. *Our Healthier Nation: A Contract for Health. A Consultation Paper.* London: The Stationery Office.

6 Department of Health. 1998. *Smoking Kills: A White Paper on Tobacco.* London: The Stationery Office.

7 Department of the Environment, Transport and the Regions. 1998. *A New Deal for Transport.* London: The Stationery Office.

8 Ministry of Agriculture, Fisheries and Food. 1998. *The Food Standards Agency: A Force for Change.* London: The Stationery Office.

9 Department of Health. 1997. *The New NHS: Modern, Dependable.* London: The Stationery Office.

10 The Scottish Office Department of Health. 1999. *Towards a Healthier Scotland: A White Paper on Health.* Edinburgh: The Stationery Office.

11 Welsh Office. 1998. *Strategic Framework: Better Health - Better Wales.* Cardiff: Welsh Office.

12 Department of Health. 1995. *Variations in Health: What Can the Department of Health and the NHS Do?* London: The Stationery Office.

13 Acheson D. 1998. *Independent Inquiry into Inequalities in Health.* London: The Stationery Office.

14 McPherson K. 1995. A population approach to interventions in primary care: assessing the evidence. In: Sharp I (ed.) *Preventing Coronary Heart Disease in Primary Care: The Way Forward.* London: National Heart Forum/HMSO.

15 Boaz A, Kaduskar S, Rayner M. 1996. *Coronary Heart Disease Statistics.* London: British Heart Foundation.

16 Office for National Statistics. 1998. *Living in Britain. Results from the 1996 General Household Survey.* London: The Stationery Office.

17 Marsh A, McKay S. 1994. *Poor Smokers.* London: Policy Studies Institute.

18 Freeth S. 1998. *Smoking-related Behaviour and Attitudes 1997: A report on Research Using the ONS Omnibus Survey. Produced on behalf of the Department of Health.* London: The Stationery Office.

19 Royal College of Physicians of London. 1992. *Smoking and the Young.* London: The Stationery Office.

20 Townsend J, Roderick P, Cooper J. 1994. Cigarette smoking by socioeconomic group, sex and age: effects of price, income, and health publicity. *British Medical Journal;* 309: 923-927.

21 Department of Health Economics and Operational Research Division. 1992. *Effect of Tobacco Advertising on Tobacco Consumption: A Discussion Reviewing the Evidence.* (The 'Smee Report'). London: Department of Health.

22 Goddard E. Office of Population Censuses and Surveys for the Department of Health. 1990. *Why Children Start Smoking.* London: HMSO. (For a summary with commentaries, see: Goddard E. 1992. Why children start smoking. *British Journal of Addiction;* 87: 17-25.)

23 Cunningham R, Kyle K. 1983. The case for plain packaging. *Tobacco Control;* 1995; 4: 80-86.

24 Royal College of Physicians. 1983. *Health or Smoking? Follow-up Report of the Royal College of Physicians.* London: Pitman Publishing.

25 Reid DJ. 1996. Tobacco control: Overview. *British Medical Bulletin;* 52: 108-120.

26 Chaloupka F, Saffer H. 1992. Clean indoor air laws and the demand for cigarettes. *Contemporary Policy Issues;* 10: 72-82.

27 Reid DJ, McNeill AD, Glynn TJ. 1995. Reducing the prevalence of smoking in youth in Western countries: an international review. *Tobacco Control;* 4: 266-277.

28  Sharp I (ed.) 1994. *Coronary Heart Disease: Are Women Special?* London: National Heart Forum.

29  Townsend J. 1995. The burden of smoking. In: Benzeval M, Judge K, Whitehead M (eds). *Inequalities in Health: An Agenda for Action.* London: The King's Fund.

30  Roemer R. 1993. *Legislative Action to Combat the World Tobacco Epidemic.* (Second edition.) Geneva: World Health Organization.

31  Hu T-W, Sung H-Y, Keeler TE. 1995. Reducing cigarette consumption in California: Tobacco taxes vs and anti-smoking media campaign. *American Journal of Public Health;* 85: 1218-1222.

32  Buck D, Godfrey C. 1994. *Helping smokers give up: Guidance to purchasers on cost-effectiveness.* London: Health Education Authority.

33  Cragg, Ross and Dawson Ltd. 1990. *Health Warnings on Cigarette and Tobacco Packs: Report on Research to Inform European Standardisation.* Prepared for the Health Education Authority and the Department of Health. London: Health Education Authority.

34  Silagy C, Mant D, Fowler G, Lodge M. 1994. Meta-analysis on efficacy of nicotine replacement therapies in smoking cessation. *Lancet;* 343: 139-142.

35  Reid DJ, Killoran AJ, McNeill AD, Chambers JS. 1992. Choosing the most effective health promotion options for reducing a nation's smoking prevalence. *Tobacco Control;* 1: 185-197.

36  Austoker JA, Sanders D, Fowler G. 1994. Smoking and cancer: smoking cessation. *British Medical Journal;* 308: 1478-1482.

37  Donnan PR, Watson J, Platt S, Tannahill A, Raymond M. 1994. Predictors of successful quitting: findings from a six-month evaluation of the Smokeline campaign. *Journal of Smoking Related Diseases;* 5 (suppl 1): 271-276.

38  Committee on Medical Aspects of Food Policy. 1994. *Nutritional Aspects of Cardiovascular Disease: Report of the Cardiovascular Review Group. Report on Health and Social Subjects Number 46.* London: HMSO.

39  Sharp I (ed.) 1997. *At Least Five a Day: Strategies to Increase Vegetable and Fruit Consumption.* London: The Stationery Office/National Heart Forum.

40  Ministry of Agriculture, Fisheries and Food. 1998. *National Food Survey 1997.* London: The Stationery Office.

41  Williams C, Marmot M. 1997. Changing rationales, consistent advice: dietary recommendations on vegetables and fruit. In: Rogers L, Sharp I (eds.) *Preventing Coronary Heart Disease: The Role of Antioxidants, Vegetables and Fruit.* London: The Stationery Office/ National Heart Forum.

42  Henson S, Swinbank A. 1997. *The Common Agricultural Policy, Diet and Nutrition.* London: Consumers in Europe.

43  Lang T, von Hartmann F, Leather S, Joosens L, Raw M, Andreasson S, Colliander S, Nordgerin P, Whitehead M. 1996. *Health Impact Assessment of European Union's Common Agriculture Policy.* Sweden: National Institute of Public Health.

44  Department of Health. 1996. *Eat Well II: A Progress Report for the Nutrition Task Force on the Action Plan to Achieve the Health of the Nation Targets on Diet and Nutrition.* London: Department of Health.

45  Meat and Livestock Commission. *Pig Year Book.* Milton Keynes: Meat and Livestock Commission.

46  Johansson L, Botten G, Norum K, Bjorneboe G. 1997. Food and Nutrition Policy in Norway. In: Wheelock V (ed.) *Implementing Dietary Guidelines for Healthy Eating.* London: Chapman and Hall.

47  National Forum for Coronary Heart Disease Prevention. 1988. *Coronary Heart Disease Prevention: Action in the UK 1984-1987.* London: Health Education Authority.

48  Cawdron G, Sharp I (eds.) 1994. *Food for Children: Influencing Choice and Investing in Health.* London: National Forum for Coronary Heart Disease Prevention.

49  Ellison RC, Capper AL, Goldberg RJ, Witschi JC, Stare FJ. 1989. The environmental component: changing school food service to promote cardiovascular health. *Health Education Quarterly;* 16: 285-297.

50  Ellison RC, Goldberg RJ, Witschi JC, Capper AL, Puleo EM, Stare FJ. 1990. Use of fat-modified food products to change dietary fat intake of young people. *American Journal of Public Health;* 80: 1374-1376.

51  Roe L, Hunt P, Bradshaw H, Rayner M. 1997. *Review of the Effectiveness of Health Promotion Interventions to Promote Healthy Eating*. London: Health Education Authority.

52  Young B, Webley P, Hetherington M, Zeedyk S. 1996. *The Role of Television Advertising in Children's Food Choice*. Report commissioned by the Ministry of Agriculture, Fisheries and Food under the R & D programme in Food Acceptability and Choice. London: Ministry of Agriculture, Fisheries and Food.

53  National Food Alliance. 1995. *Easy to Swallow, Hard to Stomach*. London: National Food Alliance.

54  Black A, Rayner M. 1992. *Just Read the Label: Understanding Nutritional Information in Numeric, Verbal and Graphic Formats*. London: HMSO.

55  Levy AS, Fine SB, Suchucker RE. 1992. *A Study of Nutrition Labels: Performance and Preference. FDA Study 2*. Report by the Division of Consumer Studies, Food and Drug Administration. Washington DC: FDA.

56  Dickie N. 1997. Personal communication between M Sanderson and Dr N Dickie, Nutrition Consultant, Heinz.

57  Puska P, Tuomilehto J, Nissinen A, Vartiainen E (eds.) 1995. *The North Karelia Project: 20 Year Results and Experiences*. Helsinki: Helsinki University Printing House.

58  Cox D, Mela D, Anderson A, Lean M. 1996. *Increasing Vegetable and Fruit Consumption. Final Scientific Report to the Ministry of Agriculture, Fisheries and Food*. London: MAFF.

59  Contento IR, Balch GI, Bronner YL, Lytle LA, Maloney SK, White SL, Olson CM, Swadener SS. 1995. Nutrition education for school-aged children. *Journal of Nutrition Education;* 27: 298-311.

60  Lytle L, Achterberg C. 1995. Changing the diet of America's children: What works and why? *Journal of Nutrition Education;* 27: 250-260.

61  Brunner E, White I, Thorogood M, Bristow A, Curle D, Marmot M. 1997. Can dietary interventions in the population change diet and cardiovascular risk factors? An assessment of effectiveness utilising a meta-analysis of randomised controlled trials. *American Journal of Public Health;* 87; 9: 1415-1422.

62  Buck D, Godfrey C, Killoran A, Tolley K. 1996. Reducing the burden of coronary heart disease: health promotion, its effectiveness and cost. *Health Education Research: Theory and Practice;* 11; 4: 487-499.

63  Field K, Thorogood M, Silagy C, Normand C, O'Neill C, Muir J. 1995. Strategies for reducing coronary heart disease risk factors in primary care: which is most cost-effective? *British Medical Journal;* 310: 1109-1112.

64  Allied Dunbar National Fitness Survey. 1992. *Allied Dunbar National Fitness Survey Main Findings*. London: Sports Council and Health Education Authority.

65  Physical Activity Task Force. 1995. *More People, More Active, More Often*. London: Department of Health.

66  Health Education Authority. 1997. *Young People and Physical Activity: A Literature Review*. London: Health Education Authority.

67  Whitehead M. 1995. *Health Update 5: Physical Activity*. London: Health Education Authority.

68  Berlin JA, Colditz GA. 1990. A meta-analysis of physical activity in the prevention of coronary heart disease. *American Journal of Epidemiology;* 132: 639-646.

69  Sharp I, White J, Rogers L. 1995. *Physical Activity: An Agenda for Action*. London: National Heart Forum.

70  The Ashden Trust, London First and University of Westminster. 1997. *Company Car Taxation*. London: Ashden Trust, London First and University of Westminster.

71  Rowell A, Fergusson M. 1991. *Bikes Not Fumes*. Surrey: Cyclists' Touring Club.

72  Coalter F. 1993. Sports participation: price or priorities? *Leisure Studies;* 12: 171-182.

73  Coalter F, Allison M. 1992. *Swimming: Pricing Issues. Paper for the Recreation Management Conference, Birmingham*. Edinburgh: Centre for Leisure Research.

74  King A. 1994. Are community-wide programmes likely to be effective in getting the message across? Lessons from abroad. In: Killoran A, Fentem P, Caspersen C (eds). *Moving On: International Perspectives on Promoting Physical Activity*. London: Health Education Authority.

75    Owen N. 1994. Shaping public policies and programmes to promote physical activity. In: Killoran A, Fentem P, Caspersen C (eds). *Moving On: International Perspectives on Promoting Physical Activity*. London: Health Education Authority.

76    Owen N. 1996. Strategic initiatives to promote participation in physical activity. *Health Promotion International;* 11; 3: 213-218.

77    Health Education Authority, 1995. *Front Line Market Research: Pre-test of a Promotional Booklet*. London: Health Education Authority.

78    British Medical Association. 1992. *Cycling: Towards Health and Safety*. London: British Medical Association.

79    Harrison J. 1997. *Planning and Design of Cycling Facilities. A Case Study of the City of York. Paper for PTRC conference*. Unpublished.

80    Sustrans. 1996. *Safe Routes to Schools Newsletter;* 1: 2. Bristol: Sustrans.

81    Engel U, Thomsen L. 1992. Safety effects of speed reducing measures in Danish residential areas. *Accident Analysis and Prevention;* 24; 1: 17-28.

82    Janssen S. 1991. Road safety in urban districts. *Traffic Engineering and Control;* June: 292-296.

83    Tengs TO, Adams ME, Pliskin JS, Safran DG, Siegal JE, Weistein MC, Graham JD. 1995. Five hundred life-saving interventions and their cost-effectiveness. *Risk Analysis;* 15; 3: 369-389.

84    Flora JA, Maibach EW, Maccoby N. 1989. The role of media across four levels of health promotion intervention. *Annual Review of Public Health;* 10: 181-201.

85    Linenger JM. 1991. Physical fitness gains following simple environmental change. *American Journal of Preventive Medicine;* 7: 298-310.

86    Mathew D. 1995. *More Bikes: Policy into Best Practice*. Surrey: Cyclists' Touring Club.

87    Transport 2000. 1995. *The Royal Commission on Environmental Pollution Report on Transport and the Environment: Briefing Paper*. London: Transport 2000.

88    Bicycle Association. 1996. *Cyclewise:* Issue 9. Coventry: Bicycle Association.

89    Iverson DC, Fielding MF, Crow RS, Christenson GM. 1985. The promotion of physical activity in the United States population: the status of programs in medical, worksite, community and school settings. *Public Health Reports;* 100: 212-224.

90    Aarts H, Paulussen T, Willemse G, Schaalma H, Bolman C, de Nooijer J. 1997. *Prevention of Cardiovascular Diseases: A Review of International Effect Research on the Promotion of Physical Activity Among Youth*. The Hague: Netherlands Heart Foundation.

91    Owen N, Bauman A, Booth M, Oldenburg B, Magnus P. 1995. Serial mass media campaigns to promote physical activity: Reinforcing or redundant? *American Journal of Public Health;* 85: 244-248.

92    Booth M, Bauman A, Oldenburg B, Owen N. 1992. Effects of a national mass-media campaign on physical activity participation. *Health Promotion International;* 7: 241-217.

93    Blake SM, Jeffery RW, Finnegan JR, Crow RS. 1987. Process evaluation of a community-based physical activity campaign: the Minnesota Heart Health Program experience. *Health Education Research;* 2; 2: 115-121.

94    Blair SN. 1989. Exercise and fitness in childhood: implications for a lifetime of health. In: Gisolfi CV, Lamb DR (eds.) *Perspectives in Exercise Science and Sports Medicine: Youth, Exercise and Sport;* 2: 401-430. Indianapolis (US): Benchmark Press.

95    Sports Council. 1993. *Young People and Sport: Policy and Frameworks for Action*. London: Sports Council.

96    Royal College of Physicians. 1991. *Medical Aspects of Exercise: Benefits and Risks*. London: Royal College of Physicians of London.

97    Riddoch C, Puig-Ribera A, Cooper A. 1998. *Effectiveness of Physical Activity Promotion Schemes in Primary Care: A Review*. London: Health Education Authority.

98    Hillsdon M, Thorogood M, Anstiss T, Morris J. 1995. Randomised controlled trials of physical activity promotion in free-living populations: a review. *Journal of Epidemiology and Community Health;* 49: 448-453.

99    Hillsdon M, Thorogood M. 1996. A systematic review of physical activity promotion strategies. *British Journal of Sports Medicine;* 30: 84-89.

100 Blair PED, Wood PD, Sallis JF. 1994. Workshop E: physical activity and health. *Preventive Medicine;* 23: 558-559.

101 King AC, Jeffery RW, Fridinger FW. 1993. In: *CDC Environmental and Policy Approaches to the Prevention of Cardiovascular Disease. Conference Proceedings.* Atlanta (US): Centers for Disease Control and Prevention (CDC).

102 Roberts K, Dench S, Minten J, York C. 1993. *Community Reports to Leisure Centre Provision in Belfast.* London: Sports Council.

103 Sallis JF. 1993. Epidemiology of physical activity and fitness in children and adolescents. *Critical Reviews in Food Science and Nutrition;* 33: 403-408.

104 Bly J, Jones RC, Richardson JE. 1986. Impact of worksite health promotion on health care costs and utilisation: evaluation of Johnson and Johnson's Live for Life Programme. *Journal of the American Medical Association;* 256: 3235-3240.

105 Crow R, Blackburn H, Jacobs D, Hannan P, Pirie P, Mittelmark M, Murray D, Luepker R. 1986. Population strategies to enhance physical activity: the Minnesota Heart Health Program. *Acta Medica Scandinavica:* suppl 711; 93-112.

106 Health Education Authority. 1993 *Survey of Health Promotion in the Workplace.* London: Health Education Authority.

107 Davis A. 1997. *Reaping the Benefits: A Cycling and Health Resource Pack.* Surrey: Cyclists' Touring Campaign.

108 Shephard R. 1986. *Economic Benefits on Enhanced Fitness.* Champaign, IL (US): Human Kinetics Publishers Inc.

109 Safe routes to schools project. 1989. Odense, Denmark. In: Sustrans. 1994. *Safe Routes to Schools Information Sheet.* Bristol: Sustrans.

110 Taylor D. 1996. *Streets Ahead.* London: Transport 2000.

111 Hillman M, Adams J, Whitelegg J. 1990. *One False Move: A Study of Children's Independent Mobility.* London: Policy Studies Institute.

112 Harland G. 1997. Personal communucation with A Davis, Transport Research Laboratory.

113 Dishman RK, Sallis JF. 1994. Determinants and interventions for physical activity and exercise. In: Bouchard C, Shephard RJ, Stephens T. *Physical Activity, Fitness and Health: International Proceedings and Consensus Statement 1992.* Champaign, IL (US): Human Kinetics Publishers Inc.

114 Farquhar JW, Fortmann SP, Flora JA, Taylor CB, Haskell WL, Williams PT, Maccoby N, Wood PC. 1990. Effects of community wide education on cardiovascular disease risk factors. The Stanford Five-City Project. *Journal of the American Medical Association;* 264: 359-365.

115 Health Education Authority. 1998. *Young and Active?* London: Health Education Authority.

116 Shayler M, Fergusson M, Rowell A. 1993. *Costing the Benefits: The Value of Cycling.* Surrey: Cyclists' Touring Club.

# Chapter 6

# Changing behaviour: individual interventions to reduce risk

**TASK GROUP**

**Professor Pamela Gillies** (Convenor)
*Health Education Authority*

**Ms Hilary Whent** (Project Officer)
*Health Education Authority*

**Professor Shah Ebrahim**
*Department of Primary Care and Population Sciences, Royal Free Hospital Medical School*

**Professor Godfrey Fowler**
*Department of Public Health and Primary Care, University of Oxford*

**Mr Dominic Harrison**
*North West Lancashire Health Promotion Unit*

**Dr Margaret Thorogood**
*Department of Public Health and Policy, London School of Hygiene and Tropical Medicine*

# Changing behaviour: individual interventions to reduce risk

This chapter:

- assesses the effectiveness of individual behaviour change interventions, particularly among different social groups

- reviews the current status of individual behavioural interventions in the UK

- assesses consumer attitudes to health, and

- identifies priorities for a future strategy.

## KEY THEMES

1   While behavioural factors have an effect on coronary heart disease, social and environmental factors are important, both in the epidemiology of coronary heart disease and the social epidemiology of the behaviours.

2   Historically, UK health policy has focused on treatment and disease prevention strategies, which address individual lifestyle determinants. Trends in behavioural factors in the UK show that there have been positive changes, but many trends are in the wrong direction and the prevention strategies have not reached the most disadvantaged groups in society.

3   Evidence from a whole range of settings indicates that individual interventions have limited success in achieving sustained behaviour change and that these are more likely to be taken up by more advantaged groups.

4   There are a number of reasons for this limited success:

   - problems with evaluating interventions, and unrealistic expectations

   - the fact that interventions in isolation are likely to have little impact

   - many interventions are based on inadequate theory which does not take account of the interactions between individuals within communities or the contexts in which behaviour occurs.

5   This chapter argues that, in relation to coronary heart disease and health promotion, we should supplement approaches which focus on behaviour change with those which address the wider social and environmental factors which influence people's health and the social fabric.

# UK policy and health behaviour

Several behavioural factors are important in the aetiology of coronary heart disease: cigarette smoking, diet (including diets that are high in fat, particularly saturated fat, and the protective properties of vegetables and fruit), physical activity and heavy alcohol consumption. The majority of coronary heart disease health promotion activity in the UK has focused and still focuses on bringing about change in these factors.

At a national level, in 1992, the *Health of the Nation* strategy identified coronary heart disease as a key area for action in England.[1] Similar strategies were devised for other parts of the UK. Targets were set for a reduction in coronary heart disease mortality and associated risk factors: smoking prevalence; average percentage of food energy derived from saturated fatty acids; average percentage of food energy derived from total fat; alcohol consumption; and physical activity (no specific targets set).

There have been a number of national public education campaigns focusing on these factors: for example *Look After Your Heart, No Smoking Day, Drinkwise* and *Active For Life*.

Contemporary NHS investment strategies for coronary heart disease focus on behavioural factors among adult sections of the population.[2] Primary health care plays a major role in health behaviour change strategies. In the 1990s a number of policies were introduced to facilitate this, from the introduction of fees to run health promotion clinics in 1990, to a cash-limited banding scheme which focused on risk factors for cardiovascular disease in 1993, to a more flexible scheme in 1997 overseen by local health promotion committees. Practice nurses have increased in number since the NHS reforms and have taken on new responsibilities for health promotion. Local coronary heart disease strategies have tended to include a range of public education approaches, for example *Look After Yourself* courses, prescriptions for exercise, healthy eating sessions and smoking cessation initiatives.

There has also been an emerging interest in other 'settings' for health promotion in which health issues are approached from a holistic perspective - for example health promoting schools, hospitals and workplaces.

The Labour government's Green Paper, *Our Healthier Nation*,[3] signals a commitment to taking a broader approach to public health by addressing the underlying causes of ill health. This document and the White Paper *The New NHS: Modern, Dependable*,[4] and changes in local government, now set a new framework for the development and implementation of joint health strategies and action plans. Health authorities, the new Primary Care Groups, and local authorities are expected to work in partnership to promote the health of their populations through Health Improvement Programmes. In local government a range of policies on education, environment, urban regeneration, community governance and welfare will have an impact on public health. The Health Action Zones initiative aims to bring these and other policies together in the most deprived areas of the country with the worst health record.

**Trends in coronary heart disease-related behavioural factors**

There have been some positive trends in behavioural risk factors for coronary heart disease: for example, reductions in smoking prevalence,[5] improvements in diet seen in an increase in consumption of fruit and vegetables and wholemeal bread, and a decline in saturated fat intake in the 1980s and 90s. These trends have been identified as being factors contributing to the decline in coronary heart disease rates over those two decades.[6]

Other trends are negative and raise concerns: for example, increasingly sedentary lifestyles, increases in the proportion of people who are overweight and obese,[6] no reduction in the prevalence of teenage smoking,[7] and an increase in smoking in pregnancy.[8] These trends also differ in different groups: the poorest groups are less likely to respond to health messages. Research carried out for the Health Education Authority found that the decline in smoking prevalence has not occurred in the poorest groups in society: 60% of lone parents smoke, and the cost of smoking further adds to their hardship.[9] Dietary patterns in low income households are characterised by less dietary variety and lower intakes of many nutrients compared with others in the population.[10] The lowest income groups have the highest consumption of fat.[6]

## How effective are interventions to change individual behaviour?

It is difficult to achieve sustained behaviour change through interventions aimed at individuals. In general, evaluations of interventions have shown, at best, modest effects. On balance, these interventions are most effective with better motivated and advantaged people.[11]

The OXCHECK Study and the British Family Heart Study in primary care found that health checks and nurse counselling about behaviour change produced changes in cardiovascular risk that were small,[12, 13] and neither study achieved changes in smoking prevalence. The greatest changes were observed in the high risk groups, who also received the most intense interventions. Recent studies of the cost-effectiveness of these two trials found that the small changes were achieved with modest cost and concluded that nurse-conducted health checks can be more cost-effective than other health service interventions.[14, 15]

Systematic reviews of evaluations of single factor interventions in primary health care have found evidence of effectiveness. Brief interventions such as GP advice to stop smoking are effective in getting about 2% of smokers to quit for at least a year.[16] Brief interventions with heavy alcohol consumers result in a short-term 24% reduction in self-reported alcohol consumption.[17] A meta-analysis of dietary interventions (ie provision of advice and/or support material) found that it was possible to reduce blood pressure in people with mildly raised blood pressure levels and estimated that a reduction of about 1.2mmHg in diastolic pressure could be achieved by such advice and maintained over 9 to 18 months.[18] Likewise, it found that it is possible to reduce serum cholesterol in people with mildly raised serum cholesterol levels by 0.2mmol/l over a similar period. The combined effect of these changes in serum cholesterol and blood pressure, if maintained, could result in an estimated fall in coronary heart disease incidence of 14%.[18] A review of the effectiveness of physical activity intervention studies[19] among the general public found some evidence that previously sedentary adults could increase their activity levels and sustain that increase, through interventions which promoted activity and which could fit into an individual's daily routine.

A number of relatively small trials of multiple and single risk factor interventions among people who already have clinical disease such as high blood pressure, angina, heart attack or diabetes, have shown substantial benefits.[20-22] In the workplace and in primary care, these multiple risk factor interventions have only small, and statistically insignificant, effects on risk factors and overall coronary heart disease mortality.[23] Compared with the general population, people with disease are much more likely to change their behaviour in response to the type of health promotion interventions currently available, and thereby reduce their risk of fatal coronary heart disease events.[24, 16, 25]

Evaluations of interventions based in the workplace show mixed results. The UK arm of the WHO Factories Study achieved a 4% reduction in the net risk factor score through dietary advice, stopping smoking, weight reduction and exercise initiatives, and treatment of high blood pressure.[26] Workplace fitness programmes have had low participation rates and high drop-out rates and have found that participants tend to be those who are already physically active.[27] A systematic review of workplace-based healthy eating interventions over 10 years found that three of the four good quality workplace studies showed a positive effect on blood cholesterol (of 2.5%-10%) or dietary fat intake (of 1%-16% of energy).[25] One review concluded that it is possible to bring about change in coronary heart disease risk factors with workplace interventions that tend to be "more intensive, involve a menu of intervention types and take account of assessment of the social organisation of the workplace".[28]

School-based approaches have shown either modest effects or disappointing results in terms of behavioural outcomes. A review of interventions to encourage healthy eating, using mainly educational approaches, found a number of studies which reported reductions in dietary fat intake of the order of 2%-6% of energy intake in the intervention groups. Six studies which focused on nutrients other than fat showed no overall effect on intake of dietary fibre or fruit and vegetables.[25] Others have concluded that school-based health education alone is not effective in persuading young people not to smoke; at best such interventions can delay onset of smoking by about five or six years.[29, 30]

There is some evidence that more advantaged people take up these interventions more avidly.[31] For example, people in non-manual occupations are more likely to attend health checks than those in manual jobs.[32] Children from more advantaged backgrounds are more likely to respond to school-based initiatives.[33]

## Community-based initiatives

A number of trials have tested public health interventions involving entire communities, aimed at changing behaviour relating to coronary heart disease. These have used approaches which inform the population of the dangers of certain practices, and behaviour change initiatives. In some cases they have introduced social policies and social structures designed to facilitate a climate of change. Studies such as the Stanford Five-City project, the Minnesota Heart Health Program, the 26-workplace Take Heart Trial and the 22-city COMMIT trials (which focused on smoking), have shown at best modest effects in relation to the effort expended, and a lack of sustainability.

In the United States, the Stanford Five-City project yielded significant net reductions in cholesterol and blood pressure in the cohort and cross-sectional samples, but smoking was only reduced in the cohort.[34-36] Methodological flaws have been identified, in that treatment and control towns were not randomly assigned, and differed in baseline characteristics.[24] The Minnesota and Pawtucket heart health programmes did not show any statistically significant intervention effects for any risk factors.[37, 38] The 22-city COMMIT study was a well designed community intervention trial for smoking cessation aimed at increasing quit rates among cigarette smokers, particularly heavy smokers, over a four-year period. The intervention had a modest impact on light to moderate smokers but there was no increase in quit rates of heavy smokers.[39] The North Karelia study showed substantial changes in coronary heart disease risk factors and mortality. However they were similar both in North Karelia and in comparison regions and it is therefore difficult to attribute the changes to the intervention.[24]

## Why do these interventions show only modest success in changing behaviour?

### Problems with evaluation and methodology

The difficulties of evaluating health promotion interventions are well documented.[40] Susser[33] proposed a number of reasons for the disappointing results observed from many community trials. The interventions might be inappropriate in form or manner or content. They might be too brief in duration or insufficiently intense: "the task [of achieving behaviour change] is both difficult and slow". The comparison groups might be contaminated by exposures similar to those intended for the intervention groups. Time trends could either nullify the effort to produce them by controlled intervention, or render true effects of intervention undetectable.

### Individual interventions need to be within comprehensive strategies

A number of commentators have suggested that behavioural interventions aimed at individuals in particular settings would have greater impact if they were not isolated interventions, but rather part of comprehensive strategies which should include national and local public policy measures, such as fiscal and legislative measures and those which create supportive environments for change. The experience of most workers and researchers in the field convinces them that health promotion is most effective when interventions in several areas are combined in a concerted programme, and reinforce each other.[41, 42]

For example, teenage smoking is best addressed by combining health education in schools with: national action to control tobacco advertising and promotion and to maintain high cigarette prices; enforcement of the law on tobacco sales to children; restrictions on smoking in public places; and support for adults who wish to quit. It has been argued that the schools smoking component of the Minnesota Heart Health Program was effective because it was tobacco-specific and embedded in a general community-wide initiative.[30] A meta-analysis of community heart health programmes found that those which included a substantial component of environmental change had a greater effect on smoking and diastolic blood pressure.[43] Evaluating this synergistic effect of a range of interventions remains a technical challenge. (See also chapter 5.)

**Interventions are not always based on adequate theory**

It is difficult to determine the theoretical basis underpinning some intervention studies, but many have used psychological theories which focus on the individual and examine either simple or unsophisticated processes which impinge on individual 'cognitions'. These theories assume that, if information about risk factors is communicated, people will adjust their behaviour to avoid or minimise them in a rational manner. There is enthusiasm for some of the more sophisticated psychological theories such as the Health Belief Model, the Theory of Reasoned Action/Planned Behaviour, Social Learning Theory, and the Transtheoretical Model of Change (the 'Stages of Change' model). The latter model, developed by Prochaska and DiClemente,[44] has been widely adopted in UK heath promotion and primary care. This model describes a process by which people move from contemplating behaviour change, to attempting change, maintaining change and leaving the intervention cycle, or of failing to sustain change and thereby remaining in the intervention cycle.

While these models are useful in helping to explain behaviour (particularly one-off behaviours such as attending health screening) and in identifying points of intervention, they are subject to major criticism. They are unable to capture lay perspectives on, and meanings attached to, health-related behaviour and its persistence or maintenance.[45, 46] They inappropriately assume human behaviour to be rational.[47] They are also unhelpful in explaining behaviours which are determined by habit and contextual factors, and undertaken at a routine, non-cognitive level.

Furthermore, in many models the individual is seen as the unit of analysis or intervention while the wider environment is disregarded. The models ignore the connections between individuals - both the interpersonal and social relations in which they act and the broader social structures which govern social practice.[35, 38, 45] The tendency to focus on individual risk factors (such as smoking or diet) fails to address more holistic interpretations.

The production of more sociologically and politically comprehensive and integrated models is urgently required and these should be rigorously tested. New models should ideally fully contextualise human behaviour and draw upon a range of disciplinary perspectives, including sociology, anthropology, psychology, cultural studies and economics,[48] and locate behaviour in its interpersonal, cultural and structural context.[46]

## Limitations of behavioural approaches

Considerable evidence points to the role of wider social and environmental factors in the aetiology of coronary heart disease. Findings from the Whitehall study of civil servants indicate that differences by employment grade in smoking, blood pressure, obesity and exercise accounted for about half the grade differences in mortality.[49] Similarly, a prospective study in Alameda County in the United States, which controlled for behavioural factors such as smoking, drinking and exercise, reported that the poorest groups had death rates 1.5 times those of the richest.[50] There is emerging evidence that retardation of growth during critical periods of development in foetal life and infancy may be linked to the development of cardiovascular disease in adult life.[51, 52] A number of studies have found a role for psychosocial factors in coronary heart disease risk: for example, work stress,[53] feelings of control over one's destiny,[54] and marital status and change in marital status.[55] Others[56-58] have shown that inequality in the distribution of income at a population level contributes to poor health outcomes including the occurrence of cardiovascular disease, and that the degree of cohesiveness of a society and the extent to which individuals feel part of and have ownership of the social group in which they live or work, have implications for individual health.

The implications of these social and environmental factors have only recently begun to be explored within UK health policy.[59] The Minister of State for Public Health has indicated an approach which addresses determinants of health beyond the individual. The public health Green Paper *Our Healthier Nation*[3] published in 1998, signals a commitment to improving health through public policy, community and local action, as well as personal responsibility. There are a number of examples at a local level of health promotion policy development and practice which take account of wide determinants of health and health behaviour. These move away from the focus of stimulating or facilitating individual behaviour change within the health services, to managing social systems such as the workplace, schools and communities.[2, 60-62]

Individually focused approaches in health promotion need to be complemented with models which explain the wider social context within which health is experienced and health behaviours understood. One tool which may help advance our understanding of the social factors in a community which influence health is the concept of social capital. Social capital is a resource for health promotion. It is produced by the interactions and reciprocal activities between individuals and the state and local community. The resource flows through social relationships and formal and informal networks. Social capital has been described as:

> "... the features of social life - networks, norms and trust - that enable participants to act together more effectively to pursue shared objectives ... to the extent that the norms, networks and trust link substantial sectors of the community and span underlying social cleavages - to the extent that social capital is of a bridging sort - then the enhanced co-operation is likely to serve broader interests and to be widely welcomed".[63]

Putnam's 20-year study in Italy explored the link between communities with strong civic ties and regional government performance. He concluded that the difference in performance can be largely attributed to the strength of the civic community. He found that the characteristics of regions of high civic communities were that: there are many clubs and societies; citizens in the regions read about community affairs in daily newspapers; there is a high degree of trust, acceptance of equality, and solidarity; and civic engagement, cooperation and honesty are valued.[64] In contrast, 'uncivic' regions present the antithesis of the above. They are hierarchical; responsibility is not shared; networks, both formal and informal, are sparse; and there is little political participation from the masses. Laws are broken and corruption is widespread.

Kawachi et al[57] and Wilkinson[58] suggest that the extent of social capital in a community (however it is measured) is likely to affect health. Kawachi et al[57] in the United States have shown that aspects of social capital may indeed link smaller income differences to lower mortality rates - the results suggest that where income differences are smaller, people experience their social environment as less hostile and more hospitable. A reduction in investment in social capital appears to be one of the pathways through which growing income inequality exerts its effect on population-level mortality. In terms of health promotion interventions it has been hypothesised that social capital may be built through community interventions.[65]

An international review of approaches to improving health through community partnerships found that the recurring themes of good social relationships, social and civic activities were seen to be fundamental to influencing the health behaviour of individuals, the health status of populations and the broader social and environmental contexts of health.[66] Research carried out by the Health Education Authority in collaboration with the London School of Economics has explored notions of social capital and health in two communities in England. This work will help identify appropriate social indicators for health promotion at a community level and identify new community-based methods for promoting health. However, the production of social cohesion and social networks and 'health' through social capital should not be viewed as a convenient way to ameliorate problems, the provenance of which lies in deeper structural conditions within society.

## Conclusion

Individually-based approaches to behaviour change for coronary heart disease prevention have resulted in modest success with general populations and are more successful with people at high risk. However, future strategies for coronary heart disease prevention need to be complemented with social models of health which take account of factors which go beyond individuals and encompass the interactions between them and with the wider community and social structures. Interventions based on these models need to be rigorously tested.

### References

1    Department of Health, 1992. *The Health of the Nation. A Strategy for Health in England*. London: HMSO.

2    Harrison D. 1996. *Purchasing Effective Health Promotion*. Paper given at the Health Promotion Managers' Conference, Durham University, January 1996. (Unpublished.)

3    Department of Health. 1998. *Our Healthier Nation: A Contract for Health. A Consultation Paper*. London: The Stationery Office.

4    Department of Health. 1997. *The New NHS: Modern, Dependable*. London: The Stationery Office.

5    Office of Population Censuses and Surveys. 1996. *Living in Britain*. London: HMSO.

6    Charlton J, Murphy M, Khaw K-T, Ebrahim S, Davey-Smith G. Cardiovascular diseases. In: Murphy M, Charlton J (eds.), Office for National Statistics. 1997. *Health of Adult Britain 1841-1994, Volume 2:* pages 60-81. London: The Stationery Office.

7    Owen L, Bolling K. 1995. *Tracking Teenage Smoking*. London: Health Education Authority.

8    Bolling K, Owen L. 1996. *Smoking and Pregnancy*. London: Health Education Authority.

9    Marsh A, McKay S. 1994. *Poor Smokers*. London: Policy Studies Institute.

10   Dowler E, Calvert C. 1995. *Nutrition and Diet in Lone-parent Families in London*. London: Family Policy Studies Centre.

11   Wakefield M, Gillies P, Graham H, Madeley R, Symonds M. 1993. Characteristics associated with smoking cessation during pregnancy among working class women. *Addiction*: 88; 10: 1423-1430.

12   Imperial Cancer Research Fund OXCHECK Study Group. 1995. Effectiveness of health checks conducted by nurses in primary care: final results from the OXCHECK Study. *British Medical Journal*; 310: 1099-1104.

13    Wood D. 1995. The British Family Heart Study. In Sharp I (ed.) 1995. *Preventing Coronary Heart Disease in Primary Care: The Way Forward.* London: HMSO/National Heart Forum.

14    Langham S, Thorogood M, Normand C, Muir J, Jones L, Fowler G. 1996. Cost and cost effectiveness of health checks conducted by nurses in primary care: the OXCHECK study, *British Medical Journal;* 312; 7041: 1274-1278.

15    Wonderling D, McDermott C, Buxton M, Kinmouth AL, Pyke S, Thompson S, Wood D. 1996. Costs and cost effectiveness of cardiovascular screening and intervention: the British Family Heart Study. *British Medical Journal;* 312; 7041: 1269-1273.

16    Law M, Tang JL. 1995. An analysis of the effectiveness of interventions intended to help people stop smoking. *Archives of Internal Medicine;* 155: 1933-1941.

17    Effective Health Care. 1994. *Brief Interventions and Alcohol Use.* Leeds: Nuffield Institute for Health.

18    Brunner E, White I, Thorogood M, Bristow A, Curle D, Marmot M. 1997. Can dietary interventions in the population change diet and cardiovascular risk factors? An assessment of effectiveness utilising meta-analysis of randomized controlled trials. *American Journal of Public Health:* 87; 9: 1415-1422.

19    Hillsdon M, Thorogood M. 1996. A systematic review of exercise promotion strategies. *British Journal of Sports Medicine;* 30: 84-89.

20    Oldridge NB, Guyatt GH, Fisher ME, Rimm AA. 1988. Cardiac rehabilitation after myocardial infarction. Combined experience of randomized clinical trials. *Journal of the American Medical Association;* 260: 945-950.

21    Mullen PD, Mains DA, Velez R. 1992. A meta-analysis of controlled trials of cardiac education. *Patient Education Counselling;* 19: 143-162.

22    O'Connor GT, Buring JE, Yusuf S, Goldhaber SZ, Olmstead EM, Paffenbarger RS Jr, Hennekens CH. 1989. An overview of randomized trials of rehabilitation with exercise after myocardial infarction. *Circulation;* 80; 2: 234-244.

23    Ebrahim S, Davey Smith G. 1997. Systematic review of randomised controlled trials of multiple risk factor interventions for preventing coronary heart disease. *British Medical Journal;* 314; 7095: 1666-1674.

24    Ebrahim S, Davey Smith G. 1996. *Health Promotion in Older People for the Prevention of Coronary Heart Disease and Stroke.* London: Health Education Authority.

25    Roe L, Hunt P, Bradshaw H, Rayner M. 1997. *Review of the Effectiveness of Health Promotion Interventions to Promote Healthy Eating. A Review Commissioned by the Health Education Authority.* London: Health Education Authority.

26    World Health Organization European Collaborative Group. 1986. European Collaborative Trial of Multifactorial Prevention of Coronary Heart Disease: final report on the 6-year results. *Lancet;* 1: 869-872.

27    Health Education Authority. 1995. *Physical Activity. Health Update.* London: Health Education Authority.

28    Dugdill L, Springett I. 1994. Workplace evaluation. *Health Education Journal;* 53: 337-347.

29    Gordon I, Whitear B, Guthrie D. 1997. Stopping them starting: evaluation of a community-based project to discourage teenage smoking in Cardiff. *Health Education Journal;* 56: 42-50.

30    Stead M, Hastings G, Tudor-Smith C. 1996. Preventing adolescent smoking: a review of options. *Health Education Journal;* 55: 31-54.

31    Gunning-Schepers L, Gepkens A. 1996. Reviews of interventions to reduce social inequalities in health: research and policy implications. *Health Education Journal;* 55: 226-238.

32    Thorogood M, Coulter A, Jones L, Yudkin P, Muir J, Mant D. 1993. Factors affecting response to an invitation to attend for a health check. *Journal of Epidemiology and Community Health;* 47: 224-228.

33    Susser E. 1995. Editorial: The tribulations of trials - intervention in communities. *American Journal of Public Health;* 85; 2: 156-158.

34    Farquhar J, Fortmann SP, Flora JA, Barr Taylor C, Haskell WL, Williams PT, Maccoby N, Wood PD. 1990. Effects of community-wide education on cardiovascular disease risk factors. The Stanford Five-City Project. *Journal of the American Medical Association;* 264; 3: 359-365.

35    Fortmann SP, Flora JA, Winkleby MA, Schooler C, Taylor CB, Farquhar JW. 1995. Community intervention trials: reflections on the Stanford Five-City Project experience. *American Journal of Epidemiology*; 142: 576-586.

36    Winkleby MA, Taylor CB, Jatulis D, Fortmann SP. 1996. The long-term effects of a cardiovascular disease prevention trial: the Stanford Five-City Project. *American Journal of Public Health*; 86; 12: 1773-1779.

37    Carleton RA, Lasater TM, Assaf AR, Feldman HA, McKinlay S. 1995. The Pawtucket Heart Health Program: community changes in cardiovascular risk factors and projected disease risk. *American Journal of Public Health*; 85; 6: 777-785.

38    Luepker RV, Murray DM, Jacobs DR Jr, Mittelmark MB, Bracht N, Carlaw R, Crow R, Elmer P, Finnegan J, Folsom AR et al. 1994. Community education for cardiovascular disease prevention: risk factor changes in the Minnesota Health Program. *American Journal of Public Health*; 84: 1383-1393.

39    The COMMIT Research Group. 1995. Community intervention trial for smoking cessation (COMMIT). I: Cohort results from a four-year community intervention. *American Journal of Public Health*; 85; 2: 159-160.

40    McPherson K. A population approach to interventions in primary care: assessing the evidence. In: Sharp I (ed.) 1995. *Preventing Coronary Heart Disease in Primary Care: The Way Forward.* London: HMSO/National Heart Forum.

41    Chapman S. 1993. Unravelling gossamer with boxing gloves: problems in explaining the decline in smoking. *British Medical Journal*: 307; 6901: 429-432.

42    Sharp I (ed.) 1995. *Preventing Coronary Heart Disease in Primary Care: The Way Forward.* London: HMSO/National Heart Forum.

43    Sellers D, Crawford SL, Bullock K, McKinlay JB. 1997. Understanding the variability in the effectiveness of community heart health programs: a meta-analysis. *Social Science and Medicine*; 44; 9: 1325-1339.

44    Prochaska JO, DiClemente CD. 1983. Stages and processes of self-change of smoking: toward an integrative model of change. *Journal of Consulting and Clinical Psychology*; 51: 390-395.

45    Kippax S, Crawford J. Flaws in the theory of reasoned action. In: Terry DJ, Gallois C, McCamish M. 1993. *The Theory of Reasoned Action. Its Application to AIDS - Preventive Behaviour. International Series in Experimental Social Psychology.* Oxford: Pergamon Press.

46    Rogers A. 1997. *Inequalities in Health and Health Promotion: Insights from the Qualitative Research Literature.* London: Health Education Authority.

47    Hunt S, Martin C. 1988. Health-related behavioural change - a test of a new model. *Psychology and Health*; 2: 209-230.

48    Platt S. 1997. *Lifestyle and Social Context.* Joint MRC/ESRC meeting on health behavioural interventions.

49    Marmot M, Rose G, Shipley M, Hamilton PJS. 1978. Employment grade and coronary heart disease in British civil servants. *Journal of Epidemiology and Community Health*; 32: 244-249.

50    Haan M, Kaplan GA, Camacho T. 1987. Poverty and health: prospective evidence from the Alameda County Study. *American Journal of Epidemiology*; 125; 6: 989-998.

51    Barker DJP (ed.) 1992. *Foetal and Infant Origins of Adult Disease.* London: British Medical Journal Books.

52    Barker DJ, Osmond C, Simmonds SJ, Wield GA. 1993. The relation of small head circumference and thinness at birth to death from cardiovascular disease in adult life. *British Medical Journal*; 306: 422-426.

53    Karasek R, Theorell T. 1990. *Healthy Work: Stress, Productivity and the Reconstruction of Working Life.* New York: Basic Books.

54    Syme SL. Control and health: a personal perspective. In: Steptoe A, Appels A (eds.) 1989. *Stress, Personal Control and Health.* New York: Wiley.

55    Ebrahim S, Wannamethee G, McCallum A, Walker M, Shaper AG. 1995. Marital status, change in marital status and mortality in middle-aged British men. *American Journal of Epidemiology*; 142: 834-842.

56    Kennedy BP, Kawachi I, Prothrow-Stith D. 1996. Income distribution and mortality: cross-sectional ecological study of the Robin Hood index in the United States. *British Medical Journal*; 312: 1004-1007.

57    Kawachi I, Colditz GA, Ascherio A, Rimm EB, Giovannucci E, Stampfer MJ, Willett WC. 1996. A prospective study of social networks in relation to total mortality and cardiovascular disease in men in the USA. *Journal of Epidemiology and Community Health*; 50: 245-251.

58    Wilkinson R. 1996. *Unhealthy Societies: The Afflictions of Inequality.* London: Routledge.

59    Department of Health. 1995. *Variations in Health: What Can the Department of Health and the NHS Do?* London: The Stationery Office.

60    Grossman R, Scala K. 1993. *Health Promotion and Organizational Development - Developing Settings for Health. European Health Promotion Series. No 2.* Vienna: World Health Organization (Europe)/IFF.

61    Baric L. 1994. *Health Promotion and Health Education in Practice. Module 2. The Organizational Model.* Altrincham: Barns Publications.

62    Theaker T, Thompson J. 1995. *The Settings-based Approach to Health Promotion - An International Working Conference in Collaboration with WHO-Europe. Conference Report.* London: National Health Service Executive/Health Education Authority.

63    Putnam R. 1995. Tuning in, tuning out: the strange disappearance of social capital in America. *Political Science and Politics;* December: 664-683.

64    Putnam R, Leonardi R, Nanetti RY. 1993. *Making Democracy Work: Civic Traditions in Modern Italy.* Princeton (NJ), USA: Princeton University Press.

65    Higgins D, Gillies P, Fielding K, Tross S, Rietmeijer C. 1996. *Social Capital among Community Volunteers: Its Relationship to Community Level HIV Prevention Programs. Conference Abstract.* International Conference of HIV/AIDS, Vancouver.

66    Gillies PA. 1997. *The Effectiveness of Alliances of Partnerships for Health Promotion. A Global Review of Progress and Potential Consideration of the Relationship to Building Social Capital for Health.* Conference Working Paper, 4th International Conference on Health Promotion, World Health Organization, Geneva.

# Chapter 7

# Medical interventions in the prevention of coronary heart disease

**TASK GROUP**

**Professor Desmond Julian** (Convenor)
*Chairman, National Heart Forum, 1993-98*

**Professor Simon Thompson**
*Royal Postgraduate Medical School, Hammersmith Hospital, London*

**Professor Michael Drummond**
*Centre for Health Economics, University of York*

**Professor Rory Collins**
*British Heart Foundation Clinical Trial Service Unit, Oxford*

# Medical interventions in the prevention of coronary heart disease

This chapter:

- assesses the effectiveness of known therapies for coronary heart disease prevention

- considers the appropriateness and cost-effectiveness of such interventions for different groups (for example, high risk groups and primary prevention)

- assesses the economic implications of such therapies

- considers likely developments in therapies and their potential impact, and

- assesses the implications for a future national coronary heart disease prevention strategy.

## KEY THEMES

1   Both lifestyle modifications and medical therapies have played important roles in the decline of coronary heart disease mortality.

2   A high proportion of all deaths occur in those with diagnosed coronary heart disease, hypertension (high blood pressure), and diabetes. Preventive measures, whether pharmacological or not, are likely to be relatively cost-effective in these populations.

3   Highly effective drugs (such as the lipid-lowering agents and beta-blockers) which have the potential to reduce mortality substantially in the forthcoming decade, are available. Their use will be limited by economic considerations and, perhaps, by concerns over long-term safety.

4   While coronary heart disease mortality has been falling, morbidity - especially from heart failure - appears set to rise, partly because of the ageing population and partly because of the survival of those who would previously have died.

5   The management of the complications of coronary heart disease (angina and heart failure) is expensive both in terms of human resources and therapeutic measures. The economic burden of these disorders may well increase substantially in the next two decades, until and unless the primary prevention of coronary heart disease is effective.

# Introduction

The aim of this chapter is to review the potential of medical interventions in the prevention of mortality and morbidity from coronary heart disease in both the 'diseased' and 'normal' populations.

Ideally, the aim should be to prevent the development of coronary heart disease. Within a prevention strategy it is particularly important to address the issue of diet and other lifestyle factors such as smoking and physical activity. However, these aspects are addressed in chapters 5 and 6.

Coronary heart disease is often preceded by other disorders such as high blood pressure, diabetes and hyperlipidaemia for which medical management may need to be considered. Unfortunately, knowledge of the cost-benefit of therapies in these contexts is still inadequate and requires further large randomised trials with associated economic evaluations.

Better information is available in relation to patients with diagnosed heart disease, where many trials have demonstrated the substantial benefits of a variety of pharmacological approaches. A high proportion of all coronary heart disease deaths occur in such patients. In the FINMONICA study, 36% of patients dying outside hospital had had a previous heart attack, and a further 25% had experienced symptoms due to coronary heart disease.[1] A community survey in three British cities, as yet unpublished, revealed that nearly 50% of individuals who died from coronary heart disease under the age of 76 years had had a known prior history of heart disease.[2] Twenty-nine per cent had had a heart attack. A further quarter were known to have had hypertension or diabetes.

A programme that includes lifestyle modification as well as therapeutic approaches is highly effective and the potential for reducing the number of deaths from coronary heart disease in this way is substantial. Indeed, Hunink et al[3] claim that more than 70% of the recent decline in mortality from coronary heart disease in the United States occurred among patients with coronary heart disease. Similar conclusions were reached in the FINMONICA report on the decline in coronary heart disease mortality in Finland during 1983-92.[1] These authors emphasised the importance of the reduction in recurrent coronary events in those who had already had a heart attack, although they also commented on the decline in the incidence of first heart attack. It is of note that perhaps the most effective of all drug therapies - the powerful lipid-lowering agents - were not in widespread use at the time of these observations.

This chapter is mainly concerned with pharmacological approaches. However, the lifestyle and pharmacological approaches are complementary, and the cost-effectiveness of the various options must be carefully assessed in each individual case.

The chapter does not discuss the important topics of implementation or provision of services.

**Considerations in the choice of medical interventions**

Three major considerations in deciding whether an intervention is justifiable in an individual are its potential benefits, its risks and its costs. The benefits largely depend on the risk profile of the person concerned and the extent to which this can be modified by the particular therapy. Thus, even if the relative benefit of any treatment may be similar in all subjects, the absolute benefit will vary. The risk of any specific treatment is usually not closely related to the patient's risk of coronary heart disease or to its complications, so the dangers of a treatment may be much more important in those at low risk.

The prevention of coronary heart disease by drugs or medical interventions has important cost implications. About one-third of all deaths are due to this disease. As pointed out by Hunink et al:[3] "although CHD [coronary heart disease] incidence and mortality have decreased, absolute prevalence has increased, which implies a future increase in the financial burden associated with CHD and the possibility that age-adjusted CHD death rates may start to rise again as the enlarging pool of prevalent CHD cases remains at risk for CHD death".

In the UK, some 2 million individuals have experienced angina pectoris, and some 100,000 patients survive heart attack each year. Heart failure, which is usually due to coronary heart disease, is also a major cause of disability. With the ageing population, it is anticipated that the numbers of those suffering from heart failure will escalate rapidly in future years, as they have in the United States and Australia.[4]

Studies of the cost-effectiveness of therapies in this field have largely concentrated on cost per life year saved, but this should be net of any savings in health care costs because of reduced hospitalisations and other medical procedures. Comparisons between therapies, in cost per life year saved or quality adjusted life year (QALY) are sometimes made. In Canada, it has been suggested that a price of up to $100,000 per QALY might be worth paying[5] but no equivalent figure exists for the UK. Such a figure might be acceptable in the individual, but with a disorder that affects a high proportion of the population, the issue of overall affordability may become paramount.

**Screening for risk factors and disease**

The concept of screening in the primary care setting for risk factors, such as family history of heart disease, or high blood pressure, is widely accepted although the effectiveness of so doing is open to question. In the UK, screening for lipids and other risk factors is at present controversial because cholesterol alone is a poor predictor of outcome and many patients with coronary heart disease have 'average' cholesterol values, and because of uncertainty of the cost-effectiveness of strategies to correct them. This situation is changing, and the wisdom of screening specific targeted populations will need to be kept under regular review in the next decade as clinical trials provide further information.

There is a need both for the more efficient identification and assessment of patients with cardiovascular disease and for better implementation of proven therapeutic approaches, as was demonstrated by the ASPIRE study.[6] This may improve as the pressures to practise evidence-based medicine increase.

# Therapeutic interventions

### Smoking cessation

Observational studies show that those who quit smoking after heart attack have a mortality in the succeeding years less than half that of those who continue to smoke.[7] This is, therefore, potentially the most beneficial of all secondary prevention measures. Health professionals can play a vital role in helping smokers to quit[8] (see chapters 5 and 6).

Newer techniques for smoking cessation, such as the use of nicotine patches,[9] may have a significant impact over the next decade.

### Lipid-modifying therapies

Many epidemiological studies have provided unequivocal evidence of the importance of lipid abnormalities as a risk factor for coronary heart disease. More recently clinical trials have established the effectiveness and apparent safety of lowering raised lipid levels.

Epidemiological studies indicate that prolonged differences of about 1mmol/l in total or low density lipoprotein (LDL) blood cholesterol correspond to about 50% less coronary heart disease, and differences of about 2mmol/l correspond to about 75% less coronary heart disease, irrespective of the initial cholesterol level, down to at least 3.4mmol/l.[10] Consequently, the absolute size of the reduction in coronary heart disease produced by lowering blood cholesterol may be determined more by the combination of the absolute reduction in cholesterol and an individual's risk of coronary heart disease than by their presenting cholesterol level. Expressed in a different way, the decision to institute measures to lower cholesterol should not be tied to a specific blood cholesterol level but would take into account the presence of other risk factors, such as diabetes, high blood pressure or diagnosed coronary heart disease.

It is generally agreed that dietary measures should be tried before drug treatment is considered. There has been some scepticism about the effectiveness of dietary measures, but an analysis of metabolic studies in hospital wards indicates that replacing 60% of saturated fats by other fats and avoiding 60% of dietary cholesterol would reduce total blood cholesterol by 0.8mmol/l.[11] But even intensive dietary therapy (for example, the National Cholesterol Education Program Step 2 diet) has much less effect on cholesterol than drug therapy when agents such as statins are given: for example a 5% fall as opposed to 27%.[12] Furthermore, long-term compliance with strict dietary regimens is poor. Consequently, diet alone is not likely to be sufficient in patients at high risk of coronary heart disease and its complications.

Clinical trials of cholesterol-lowering drug therapy indicate that most of the epidemiologically-predicted reduction in risk emerges within a few years.[13] Moreover, the results of systematic reviews support the notion that the proportional reduction in coronary heart disease depends upon the absolute reduction in cholesterol, while the absolute reduction in risk depends largely upon the absolute risk of coronary heart disease in the individual treated. Recently, in the Scandinavian Simvastatin Survival Study (4S),[14] among more than 4,000 patients at very high risk (mostly post-heart attack) an average 1.7mmol/l reduction in cholesterol produced a reduction of about one-third in major coronary events (19% in treated patients vs 28% in the control group: about 90 fewer events per 1,000 patients treated for five years). Even though treatment reduced cholesterol by only just over 1mmol/l in the Cholesterol and Recurrent Events (CARE) study of post-heart attack patients,[15] coronary heart disease events were reduced by about one-quarter (10% vs 13% among the controls: about 30 fewer events per 1,000 treated for five years). This was despite the entry cholesterol levels in CARE being lower than those in 4S. (In CARE, the average cholesterol level was 5.5mmol/l and all subjects had levels below 6.5mmol/l. In 4S, average cholesterol was 6.75mmol/l, and all subjects had a level between 5.5-8.0mmol/l.) In addition, total mortality was significantly reduced by about one-third in 4S, and the need for interventions (coronary artery bypass graft and coronary angioplasty) was substantially reduced in both trials. Similar beneficial results would probably be seen in high risk patients with lower lipid levels. By contrast, in the West of Scotland Prevention Study (WOSCOPS)[16] among about 6,000 lower risk individuals (people with some coronary risk factors but, generally, no previously diagnosed vascular disease) with elevated cholesterol levels, an average cholesterol reduction of about 1mmol/l produced a similar proportional reduction of coronary heart disease risk, but the absolute difference was smaller (4.7% vs 7.0%: about 23 fewer events per 1,000 treated for five years).

Further clinical trials of cholesterol-lowering with statins (as studied in the three trials mentioned above) and with the newer fibrates[17] will help to identify which individuals are most likely to benefit from lipid-modifying therapy. Such studies will also provide more reliable safety data. For, although recently reported studies have not indicated any increases of non-coronary heart disease deaths or cancer with lipid-lowering therapy, even in aggregate these studies were not large enough to rule out modest excesses in long-term use.

It is probable that the indications for lipid-modifying therapy will be widened but the extent to which they are used may depend upon their estimated cost-effectiveness in different settings (which may change as the drug patents expire and generics become available).

Pharoah and Hollingworth[18] have estimated the cost-effectiveness of statin therapy in individuals with and without pre-existing coronary heart disease and point to the enormous differences in cost-effectiveness between groups at different risk. They give as examples a cost of £6,000 per life year saved in men aged 55-64 who have had a heart attack and whose cholesterol is higher than 7.2mmol/l, and £361,000 per life year saved in women aged 45-54 with angina and a cholesterol level of 5.5-6.0mmol/l. These authors assumed a drug cost of £540 per year, and did not consider the effects that treatment might have on reducing morbidity, and the consequent additional benefits in increased quality of life and reduction in health costs in the longer term.[19]

The costs of a course of statin therapy are very dependent upon the cost of the drug, and further costs are generated because of the need for biochemical tests. When calculating the costs it is also important to take into account the savings resulting from reduced hospitalisation. Applying the 4S data to the situation in the United States, Pedersen et al[20] concluded that the cost per patient over a five-year period would be reduced from $4,400 to $778. However, this figure should be treated with caution as a number of factors, differing from place to place, can affect estimates of cost-effectiveness (for example the much lower costs of hospitalisation in the UK).

It is reasonable to conclude that lipid-modifying therapy could have a substantial effect on overall community mortality - perhaps reducing deaths from coronary heart disease in those under 75 by 10,000-15,000 per year - but this would be at considerable expense. If the guidelines of the American College of Cardiology and of the European Society of Cardiology were to be implemented, this would involve the prescription of lipid-lowering agents to most of the 1-2 million individuals with known coronary heart disease under the age of 75. Currently, the cost of this treatment might be more than £500 million per year, but these costs can be expected to fall substantially as patents expire. On the other hand, it may well be that the numbers of people who could benefit from lipid-lowering therapy will expand.

### Fibrinolytic therapy

Fibrinolytic drugs have been shown to be highly effective in reducing mortality among people with acute heart attack, and their benefit is maintained over several years. Much of the potential for mortality reduction has probably already been achieved, but there is still room for improvement in accelerating the delivery of this therapy, and in treating women and elderly people.

### Aspirin and other antiplatelet agents

Aspirin and other antiplatelet drugs produce a significant reduction in the incidence of death and heart attack in patients with angina or heart attack.[21] The evidence for this is so convincing that authoritative guidelines recommend aspirin as routine therapy for such patients in the absence of contraindications. Aspirin also reduces the risk of cardiovascular events, including both heart attack and stroke, in patients with peripheral vascular disease, diabetes, and previous cerebrovascular disease. Newer antiplatelet agents may have the potential to increase the effect of aspirin, but they will be substantially more expensive and are unlikely to have much additional impact on community mortality.

The case for using aspirin to reduce the risk of coronary heart disease among people without diagnosed heart disease is more questionable. In the US Physicians' Health Study,[22] the proportional reduction in the incidence of heart attack in those taking aspirin was similar to that in high risk populations but the absolute reduction was very small. Moreover, overall mortality was not reduced and there was a slight excess of haemorrhagic strokes. Aspirin cannot, therefore, be recommended for primary prevention in low risk individuals, although there may be subgroups without coronary heart disease at high risk for whom the benefits outweigh the risks.

### Anticoagulants

Anticoagulants, such as warfarin, have been shown to reduce mortality and further heart attacks in patients who have had a heart attack but who are not taking aspirin. However, with conventional dosage regimens, the risks are such that anticoagulants can be used for only a relatively small proportion of people. However, low dose warfarin with or without aspirin may have a role in high risk individuals. The effects of aspirin and warfarin are approximately additive in reducing coronary heart disease.[23] Some new preparations, such as low molecular weight heparin, may have wider applicability but are unlikely to have a major impact in the community.

**ACE inhibitors**
ACE inhibitors have been shown to reduce mortality and morbidity in patients with heart failure, as well as those who have impaired left ventricular function in the absence of heart failure.[24, 25] Hart, Rhodes and McMurray[26] estimated that the incremental cost over and above conventional therapy was £2,305 per life year saved.

Studies in and after heart attack have also demonstrated the value of ACE inhibitors in this context. Long-term ACE inhibitor therapy is indicated for that one quarter of all heart attack survivors who have either had heart failure in the acute event or who have severe residual muscle damage. In the AIREX study of ramipril after heart attack, five-year mortality was reduced by 36%, with 114 additional survivors per 1,000 patients treated.[27]

Angiotensin II receptor blockers show promise of being better tolerated and more effective than ACE inhibitors[28] but large randomised trials are needed to establish this.

**Beta-blocking drugs**
Clinical trials have established the effectiveness of the long-term administration of beta-blockade in preventing further heart attack and death by about 25% in patients who have already had a heart attack.[29] Their effectiveness in preventing death in patients with angina and high blood pressure is less certain, but it is probable that they also improve prognosis in these contexts.

**Control of diabetes**
A substantial proportion (perhaps 10%-20%) of patients with coronary heart disease have diabetes as a risk factor. Lipid-modifying drugs and aspirin have been shown to improve the prognosis for diabetic patients with coronary heart disease.

**Anti-hypertensive therapy (blood pressure lowering therapy)**
Epidemiological studies show that there is a continuous relationship between the risk of cardiovascular disease and blood pressure throughout the Western 'normal' range of blood pressure levels. Typically a prolonged 5-6mmHg difference in usual diastolic pressure is associated with differences of about 35%-40% in the risk of stroke and 20%-25% in the risk of coronary heart disease.[30] Hence, effective non-pharmacological measures to reduce population levels of blood pressure would be expected to produce substantial reductions in cardiovascular disease. Although there has previously been controversy, it is now clear that realistic reductions in dietary salt consumption could produce worthwhile reductions in cardiovascular risk.[31] A diet low in fat and high in fruit and vegetables also has beneficial effects on blood pressure[32], as do increased physical activity, weight reduction in the obese, and avoiding excessive alcohol consumption.

The overall results of anti-hypertensive drug trials, which have generally involved diuretics and beta-blockers, indicate that a 5-6mmHg reduction in diastolic blood pressure maintained for a few years produces a reduction of about 16% in coronary heart disease (about one half to two-thirds of the likely eventual effect). As in the epidemiological studies, the proportional reductions in vascular risk were also similar in high and low risk individuals. Hence, the benefits of anti-hypertensive drug therapy are likely to be greatest in individuals who are at greatest absolute risk (for example the elderly, and those with occlusive vascular disease, such as prior heart attack, or cerebrovascular or peripheral vascular disease), irrespective of their blood pressure levels. Among such patients, greater blood pressure reductions with more intensive regimens may produce even greater benefits, and this is being studied in current trials.

### Heart failure

Heart failure affects some 1 million people, is usually due to coronary heart disease and/or high blood pressure, and is increasing in prevalence. It will cause a massive and increasing burden on the health services in the next decade. It can probably be prevented by the strategies that reduce the risk of heart attack, and also by the more effective management of acute heart attacks. However, the prevention of death in patients with angina or heart attack may result in the survival of patients with impaired cardiac function. There is accumulating evidence that many patients are not receiving the benefits of modern therapies for this condition and the high morbidity found in general practice may, to a considerable extent, be attributed to this.

### Hormone replacement therapy

It has been claimed, on the basis of observational studies, that hormone replacement therapy (HRT) can reduce the incidence of coronary events in post-menopausal women by 50%. However, these results are confounded by the fact that there are major differences between those who take HRT and those who do not. Optimism about the effectiveness of HRT has been seriously diminished by the Hormone Estrogen/Progestin Replacement Study which showed no benefit of this therapy in women with coronary heart disease.[33]

It is not clear whether any benefits from HRT are additive to those of other therapies, such as lipid-lowering and antiplatelet therapy, although a recent study has shown that the combination of oestrogen replacement therapy with a statin has a much more powerful effect on lipids than does either therapy alone.[34] Large clinical trials which are now being undertaken in the United States and the UK should eventually define the benefits and risks of the various preparations, although it may be more than a decade before the full results become available.

### Antioxidant therapy and the 'Mediterranean diet'

There is increasing scientific and epidemiological evidence supporting the view that antioxidants can prevent coronary atherosclerosis and its complications. Clinical trials, to date, have not produced convincing evidence of benefit from supplementary vitamins.[35] Further trials, now in progress, should determine whether, for example, vitamin supplementation, for example with vitamins C and E, can reduce coronary events in those at high risk.

Encouraging data have been provided from three studies of patients with coronary heart disease in which an increase in the use of omega-3 fatty acids and other aspects of the 'Mediterranean' diet were tested.[36-38] Larger and better designed trials are needed to establish whether such dietary modifications are as effective as has been claimed.

### Genetic factors

Single gene disorders (such as familial hypercholesterolaemia) are responsible for a small number of cases of coronary heart disease, but they are important because they may cause disease at a young age. It seems likely, however, that most coronary heart disease represents a complex interaction of environmental factors with many genes which each produce small differences in risk (ie a polygenic disorder), and studies are currently ongoing to identify such genetic risk factors. A good example of this is hyperhomocysteinaemia, in which those who have a genetic abnormality are more likely to develop coronary heart disease if their diet is deficient in folate and vitamin $B_{12}$.

As with the identification of environmental risk factors (such as smoking, high blood pressure and cholesterol), the identification of genetic markers and their reliable association with cardiovascular risk and with other risk factors will help in determining an individual's absolute risk of cardiovascular disease and so should guide therapy. Moreover, the elucidation of the genetic basis of coronary heart disease may lead to the development of new drugs and, in the longer term, of gene therapy.

### Angioplasty and coronary bypass surgery

Increasing numbers of coronary artery procedures are likely over the next 10 years. There is no evidence from countries in which these techniques are widely used that a plateau has yet been reached. This is related to the fact that age is no longer regarded as a contraindication in an ageing population. The main effect of these interventions is to reduce morbidity. The impact on overall mortality will probably be slight.

### Combination of therapies

Several of the therapies described above have a substantial impact (of the order of 25%) on coronary events. It is not clear whether the benefits of the different therapies are additive because most trials have not been large enough to answer this question, although meta-analyses in some cases have suggested they may be. Similarly, it is uncertain whether there are adverse interactions between the various agents.

## Overall community impact of medical interventions

Medical advances, such as the use of aspirin and thrombolysis for heart attack, and that of beta-blockers in chronic coronary heart disease, have already had a substantial impact on mortality. Aspirin, lipid-lowering agents and ACE inhibitors all have the potential to reduce community mortality and morbidity, but there is much evidence that these agents are not being used as widely or as effectively as they might, and further beneficial effects are to be anticipated as the management of patients at high risk of coronary heart disease improves.

If these and newer agents are shown to be both effective and safe, one must anticipate that they will be used in lower risk individuals, which would mean that the economic implications would become a major consideration. Furthermore, this might require a change in the attitude to screening for risk factors, such as cholesterol, fibrinogen and genetic markers.

An additional issue results from the fact that some of these therapies may reduce death but increase the prevalence of angina and heart disease in the community.

Evidence from the *Morbidity Statistics from General Practice*[39] indicates that there has been more than a 50% increase in reported angina over the last 10 years. The ageing of the population will also result in a great increase in disability due to coronary heart disease in the community,[4] with the attendant need for medical treatment.

## Conclusion

The application of current knowledge of lifestyle factors and drug therapy could lead to a substantial reduction in the morbidity and mortality of coronary heart disease. The former requires a combination of strategies aimed both at the individual and at the public level. Clinical trials have shown that, targeted at appropriate patients, drug therapy could have major effects on coronary mortality and morbidity, but well thought out guidelines are often not being implemented. New forms of treatment are on the horizon, but clinical trials will be needed to establish their place in therapy. Economic considerations will be a powerful limiting factor in the use of drugs.

## References

1   Salomaa V, Miettinen H, Kuuslasmaa K et al. 1996. Decline in coronary heart disease mortality in Finland during 1983 to 1992: roles of incidence, recurrence, and case-fatality. *Circulation*; 94: 3130-3137.

2   Norris RM on behalf of the UK Heart Attack Study Investigators. 1999. *Sudden Cardiac Death and Myocardial Infarction in Three British Health Districts: the UK Heart Attack Study.* London: British Heart Foundation.

3   Hunink MGM, Goldman L, Tosteson ANA et al. 1997. *Journal of the American Medical Association*; 277: 535-542.

4   Kelly DT. 1997. Our future society: A global challenge. *Circulation*; 95: 2459-2464.

5   Laupacis A, Feeny D, Detsky AS, Tugwell PX. 1992. How attractive does a new technology have to be to warrant adoption and utilization? Tentative guidelines for using clinical and economic evaluations. *Canadian Medical Association Journal*; 146: 473-481.

6   Bowker TJ, Clayton TC, Ingham J et al. 1996. A British Cardiac Society survey of the potential for the secondary prevention of coronary disease: ASPIRE. *Heart*; 75: 334-342.

7   Åberg A, Bergstrand R, Johansson S et al. 1983. Cessation of smoking after myocardial infarction. Effects on mortality after 10 years. *British Heart Journal*; 49: 416-422.

8   Silagy C, Mant D, Fowler G, Lodge M. 1994. Meta-analysis on efficacy of nicotine replacement therapy for smoking cessation. *Lancet*; 343: 139-142.

9   Taylor CB, Houston-Miller N, Killen JD, DeBusk RF. 1990. Smoking cessation after acute myocardial infarction: effect of a nurse-managed intervention. *Annals of Internal Medicine*; 113: 118-132.

10  Stamler J, Vaccaro O, Neaton JD et al. For the Multiple Risk Factor Intervention Trial Research Group. 1993. Diabetes, other risk factors and 12-year cardiovascular mortality for men screened in the Multiple Risk Factor Intervention Trial. *Diabetes Care*; 16: 434-444.

11  Clarke R, Frost C, Collins R, Appleton P, Peto R. 1997. Dietary lipids and blood cholesterol: quantitative meta-analysis of metabolic ward studies. *British Medical Journal*; 314: 112-117.

12  Hunninghake DB, Stein EA, Dujovne CA et al. 1993. The efficacy of intensive dietary therapy alone or combined with lovastatin in outpatients with hypercholesterolemia. *New England Journal of Medicine*; 328: 1213-1219.

13  Law MR, Wald NJ, Thompson SG. 1994. By how much and how quickly does reduction in serum cholesterol concentration lower risk of ischaemic heart disease? *British Medical Journal*; 308: 367-372.

14    Scandinavian Simvastatin Survival Study Group. 1994. Randomised trial of cholesterol lowering in 4,444 patients with coronary heart disease: the Scandinavian Simvastatin Survival Study (4S). *Lancet*; 344: 1383-1389.

15    Sacks FM, Pfeffer MA, Moyé LA et al. 1996. The effect of pravastatin on coronary events after myocardial infarction in patients with average cholesterol levels. *New England Journal of Medicine*; 335: 1001-1009.

16    Shepherd J, Cobbe SM, Ford I et al. 1995. Prevention of coronary heart disease with pravastatin in men with hypercholesterolemia. *New England Journal of Medicine*; 333: 1301-1307.

17    Ericsson G-G, Hamsten A, Nilsson J, Grip L, Svane B, de Faire U. 1996. Angiographic assessment of effects of bezafibrate on progression of coronary artery disease in young male postinfarction patients. *Lancet*; 996; 7: 849-853.

18    Pharoah PDP, Hollingworth H. 1996. Cost-effectiveness of lowering cholesterol concentration with statins in patients with and without pre-existing coronary heart disease: life table method applied to a health authority population. *British Medical Journal*; 312: 1443-1448.

19    Shepherd J. 1996. Cost effectiveness of lowering cholesterol. *British Medical Journal*; 313: 1142.

20    Pedersen TR, Kjekshus J, Berg K et al. 1996. Cholesterol lowering and the use of health care resources. *Circulation*; 93: 1796-1802.

21    Antiplatelet Trialists' Collaboration. 1994. Collaborative overview of randomised trials of antiplatelet therapy. I: Prevention of death, myocardial infarction, and stroke by prolonged antiplatelet therapy in various categories of patients. *British Medical Journal*; 308: 81-106.

22    Steering Committee of the Physicians' Health Study Research Group. 1989. Final report on the aspirin component of the ongoing physicians' health study. *New England Journal of Medicine*; 321: 129-135.

23    Meade TW, Brennan PJ, Wiles HC, Zuhrie SR. 1998. Thrombosis prevention trial: randomised trial of low-intensity oral anticoagulation with warfarin and low-dose aspirin in the primary prevention of ischaemic heart disease in men at increased risk. *Lancet*; 351: 233-241.

24    Pfeffer MA, Braunwald E, Moyé LA, Basta L, Brown EJ, Cuddy TE et al. 1992. Effect of captopril on mortality and morbidity in patients with left ventricular dysfunction after myocardial infarction. *New England Journal of Medicine*; 327: 669-677.

25    The AIRE Study Investigators. 1993. Effect of ramipril on mortality and morbidity of survivors of acute myocardial infarction with clinical evidence of cardiac failure. *Lancet*; 342: 821-828.

26    Hart W, Rhode G, McMurray J. 1995. The cost effectiveness of enalapril in the treatment of chronic heart failure. *British Journal of Medical Economics*; 6: 91-98.

27    Hall AS et al. 1997. Follow-up study of patients randomly allocated ramipril or placebo for heart failure after myocardial infarction. AIRE extension study (AIREX) Study. *Lancet*; 349: 1493-1497.

28    Pitt B, Segal R, Martinez FA et al. 1997. Randomised trial of losartan versus captopril in patients over 65 with heart failure (Evaluation of Losartan in the Elderly Study, ELITE). *Lancet*; 349: 747-752.

29    The Beta-Blocker Pooling Project Research Group. 1988. The Beta-Blocker Pooling Project (BBPP): subgroup findings from randomized trials in post infarction patients. *European Heart Journal*; 9: 8-16.

30    Collins R, Peto R. Antihypertensive drug therapy: Effects on stroke and coronary heart disease. In: Swales JD. 1994. *Textbook of Hypertension*: 1156-1164. London: Blackwell.

31    Law MR, Frost CD, Wald MJ. 1991. By how much does dietary sodium reduction lower blood pressure? *British Medical Journal*; 302: 819-824.

32    Appel LJ et al. 1997. A clinical trial of the effects of dietary patterns on blood pressure. *New England Journal of Medicine*; 338: 1117-1124.

33    Hulley S, Grady D, Bush T, Furberg C, Herrington D, Riggs B, Vittinghoff E. 1998. Randomized trial of estrogen plus progestin for secondary prevention of coronary heart disease in postmenopausal women. Heart and Estrogen/progestin Replacement Study (HERS) Research Group. *Journal of the American Medical Association*; 280: 605-613.

34    Davidson MH et al. 1997. A comparison of estrogen replacement, pravastatin, and combined therapy for the management of hyperlipidemia in postmenopausal women. *Archives of Internal Medicine*; 157: 1186-1172.

35  Omenn GS, Goodman GE, Thornquist MD et al. 1996. Effect of a combination of beta carotene and vitamin A on lung cancer and cardiovascular disease. *New England Journal of Medicine*; 334: 1150-1155.

36  Burr ML, Fehily AM, Gilbert JF et al. 1989. The effects of changes in fat, fish and fibre intakes on death and myocardial infarction: diet and reinfarction trial. *Lancet*; ii: 757-781.

37  Singh RB, Rastogi SS, Verma T et al. 1992. Randomised controlled trial; of cardioprotective diet in patients with acute myocardial infarction: results of one year follow-up. *British Medical Journal*; 304: 1015-1019.

38  De Lorgeril M, Renaud S, Mamelle N et al. 1994. Mediterranean alpha-linolenic acid-rich diet in secondary prevention of coronary heart disease. *Lancet*; 343: 1454-1459.

39  *Morbidity Statistics from General Practice. Fourth National Study 1991-2:* page 73. London: HMSO, 1995.

# Chapter 8

# Social, political and economic trends: the implications for coronary heart disease prevention

**TASK GROUP**

**Professor Michael Marmot** (Convenor)
*International Centre for Health and Society, University College London*

**Mr Adrian Field** (Project Officer)
*National Heart Forum*

**Mr Ian Christie**
*The Henley Centre for Forecasting*

**Mr Andrew Dilnot**
*Institute for Fiscal Studies*

**Dr Michael Wilkinson**
*Coronary Prevention Group*

**Professor Richard Wilkinson**
*Trafford Centre for Medical Research, University of Sussex*

# Social, political and economic trends: the implications for coronary heart disease prevention

This chapter:

- assesses trends in the social structure of the UK population and the implications for coronary heart disease

- assesses the key driving forces in the public policy environment

- considers economic and political scenarios for the future, and their impact on consumer attitudes, services and health, and

- suggests ways of tackling these issues in a national coronary heart disease prevention strategy.

## KEY THEMES

1   Approaches to coronary heart disease prevention encompass not only individual action, but also the wider social and economic environment. Policy decisions across a range of sectors have a significant impact on coronary heart disease prevention.

2   Since the 1980s, there has been a major shift towards a market-oriented ethos in the economy and society, with an accompanying emphasis on the minimal state, individualism and self-responsibility. The election of the Labour government in 1997 may lead to greater recognition of the importance of public policy and its role in effecting health gain.

3   Reflecting a trend across Western society, the UK population is ageing. The number of people aged over current retirement ages is projected to increase by more than half by 2034, to comprise around 24% of the population. This has major implications for future trends in coronary heart disease morbidity and mortality.

4   The gap between rich and poor increased markedly in the 1980s, although it has narrowed since then. With the growing inequality in income levels, poverty in Britain also grew significantly. European Union data indicate that Britain has a higher rate of children living in relative poverty than any other nation in the European Union, estimated at one in three.

5   A broad-based approach to tackling coronary heart disease is needed, which encompasses not only individual lifestyles, but also the structural or environmental conditions that can give rise to the disease.

# Introduction

This chapter examines trends in the public policy environment, the changing social structure of the UK population, and the likely economic and political scenarios for the future. Within this global context, the implications that current trends have for a coronary heart disease prevention strategy will be assessed, along with the responses that they demand.

Coronary heart disease prevention encompasses actions and policies at the individual, community and national levels. Central to reducing the prevalence of the leading single cause of death in the UK is a public policy environment that recognises and addresses the diversity of factors that impact upon coronary heart disease.

## The economic and political environment in the UK

### The changing policy environment

From 1979 to 1997, there was undoubtedly a shift towards neo-liberalism, with an emphasis on freedom, choice, the free market, deregulation, the minimal state and the primacy of the individual. Accompanying this approach was neo-conservatism, promoting authority, tradition, stability, order, the family and morality. Although potentially contradictory and unstable, their combination was the hallmark of Conservative government from 1979, delivered in an explicitly populist style.[1]

Important components of the approach taken by the Conservative administration were a reliance on 'supply-side' policies aimed at restoring an 'enterprise culture', deregulation by removing regulatory restriction on enterprise and competition, privatisation of state-owned assets, making labour markets more 'flexible', promoting capital ownership, and reducing taxation.[2]

Another dominant theme of the political and economic culture since the late 1970s has been the transfer of responsibility for welfare away from the state and back to individuals and families. To some extent, this was marked by the transfer of welfare activities such as pensions and housing into the private sector.[3]

The market-oriented ideology has not been confined to the UK; it gained credence, in varying degrees, throughout the international economy.[4] Accompanying the market ethos has been an increasing globalisation of the economy, where the transfer of industrial competition and consumption patterns is occurring around the world. Capital is increasingly globalised and unencumbered by national regulations, aided through liberalised global trade agreements.[5]

The policy environment of the UK has also been affected by developments in the European Union (EU). Although a source of much division and debate, the trend since the early 1970s has been the move towards integration of European nations, including the UK. While attention is frequently drawn to the effect that decisions in Brussels have on the UK policy and regulatory environment, the UK's involvement in the EU has also meant its contribution to such fundamental debates as the level of intervention in the workings of the market.[6] The Common Agricultural Policy, and its social, economic and environmental impacts, is an area that has been of some contention in the European sphere.

In the health and education arenas in the UK, the focus of Conservative reforms was to separate the purchasers from the providers of public services, with the intention of placing the demands of consumers at the forefront. The reforms also saw the introduction of private sector practices and personnel into the public services, underlining a conviction that competitive models would deliver more efficiency.[3] The move of the state from provider to facilitator further highlights the ideology of moving individuals from dependence on the state to self-responsibility.[1]

In 1992, public health was explicitly incorporated into health policy in England, although Scotland and Wales had a rather better record. The White Paper, *The Health of the Nation*, provided a focus on causes of substantial mortality and morbidity along with relevant health-related behaviours. Coronary heart disease and stroke were notable inclusions in the strategy. Targets, explicitly quantifiable and achievable, became the key instrument for recording the strategy's achievement. Although generally perceived as a positive development, particularly in the health promotion arena, the *Health of the Nation* strategy avoided the more difficult, intersectoral concerns, such as health inequalities.[7]

**The future policy environment**

Emerging since the 1980s has been a policy environment dominated by a market-oriented ethos, accompanied by fiscal austerity, deregulation, and an emphasis on individual responsibility. It is highly likely that these forces will continue to dominate in the years to come. However, the election of the Labour government in 1997 may lead to a lessening of the ideological commitment to the market culture, accompanied as it as by an acknowledgement of the importance of the public domain as well as the private sphere. The appointment of a Minister for Public Health is a recognition of the impact that other policy areas have on health, and there have been developments which are intended to address social inequalities in health. These changes in focus may make an important difference to the policy environment. However, balanced against these changes are the tight fiscal constraints.

The new directions in public health policy were clearly signalled in the public health Green Paper, *Our Healthier Nation*, published in early 1998.[8] The strategy identified coronary heart disease as a priority area (although concerns were raised about the adequacy of the targets). It also focused on tackling health inequalities and addressing the overall determinants of health and, through a 'contract' for health, set out possible action at national, local and individual levels. The shared responsibility for health that this approach encompasses could mark a major departure from strategies based on individual action. The Green Paper in England, as well as the parallel papers from Scotland, Wales and Northern Ireland, also placed a strong emphasis on community participation and involvement in public health, which could also emerge as an important policy direction.

In the broader social policy arena, constraints on public spending are likely to have a strong impact on income security provision, and may be coupled with policies intended to promote further training and employment. For example, in 1997 lone parent benefits were reduced as part of a package of measures intended to provide greater incentives for lone parents to enter work.

The role of international arrangements and organisations, such as the EU and the World Trade Organization, in the UK policy environment will continue to expand,

and may have implications for public health and well-being. The government's commitment to the Social Chapter in the Treaty on European Union has prompted differing views on its impact on employment in the UK. Public health protection, through prevention of diseases, is enshrined under Article 129 of the Treaty on European Union.[9] This was strengthened by Article 152 of the Amsterdam Treaty in 1997,[10] and may provide a basis for strengthening public health policy in the EU.

One example of public health policy action that has occurred through the EU was when European Health Ministers, with the active support of the UK government, agreed in December 1997 to phase in a ban on tobacco advertising and sponsorship, although debate raged over the scope of the ban.

Debate has also focused on the World Trade Organization and the impact that it may have on the ability of national governments to regulate areas such as the labour market and environmental protection. In the next five to ten years, the World Trade Organization may come under increased pressure to amend the GATT agreement to incorporate provisions focusing on the quality of the working environment.

## Social change

In conjunction with changes in the economic environment, significant social change took place, some of which was a continuation of the reappraisal of social norms occurring since 1945, the changing economic conditions (partly initiated through the oil shocks of the 1970s), and other changes which occurred as a response or consequence of the new ethic that became dominant in Britain.

### Age structure

The composition of the UK population is very different to that of the immediate post-war years, and even in comparison to the 1970s. The UK's ageing population is a clear indicator of the changing social environment, and carries with it significant economic and health implications. Over the period since 1961, there has been a steady decline in the proportion of the population aged under 16, and an increase in the population aged 65 and over. This is shown in Figure 1, which also gives a projection of these trends through to 2031.

The UK population is expected to increase from 58.4 million in 1994 to 61.2 million in 2023. Within the population, age groups are expected to change in different ways. The working age population is projected to grow gradually until 2011 and then decline. The number of people aged over current retirement ages is projected to increase by more than half by 2034, to comprise around 24% of the population.[10, 12]

The changing age structure of the population carries important economic implications for the fiscal priorities of governments. An increase in the proportion of the elderly population can produce higher demands on health and welfare provision, and place further pressure on other forms of government spending. The policy response, both in the UK and internationally, has been an increasing emphasis on individual provision of retirement income.

**Figure I** *Proportions of age groups within the UK population, 1961-2031*

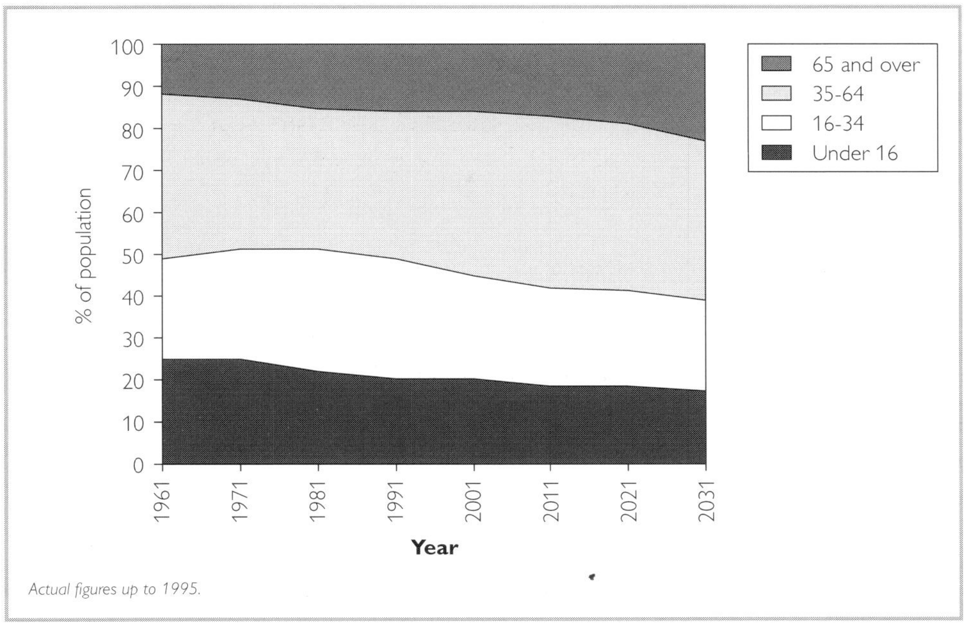

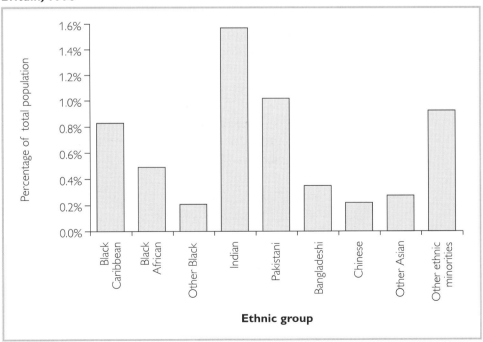

Source: See reference I I.

## Ethnic diversity

In the post-war years, the UK has built up a culturally diverse population. Around 3.3 million people belong to an ethnic minority group - just under 6% of the population. The current scope of ethnic diversity is illustrated in Figure 2.[11]

**Figure 2** *Ethnic minority groups as a proportion of the total population of Britain, 1996*

Source: See reference I I.

There is considerable diversity in terms of social advantage and disadvantage between ethnic groups, across a range of social indicators including employment status, household income and housing quality. Research has shown that Pakistanis and Bangladeshis are consistently at a disadvantage with respect to White people, and often with respect to other minorities. People of Caribbean and Indian origin are often found to experience disadvantage, but this is usually less serious than for Pakistanis and Bangladeshis. Chinese and African Asian groups have, in broad terms, reached a level of parity with the White population. There are also some important disparities between ethnic minorities as a whole and Whites.[13]

### Household composition

An important demographic change has been the rise in the number of lone parent families, which has had implications, not only for overall levels of poverty, but also for the feminisation of poverty. Lone parents headed 23% of all families with dependent children in Britain in 1994, nearly three times the proportion in 1971.

Perhaps indicative of the changing patterns of wealth, the number of owner-occupied dwellings has grown substantially since the 1960s. Local authority/new town housing increased in the 1970s but has steadily decreased since the 1980s, since the 'right to buy' legislation was enacted in 1980. By 1995-96, 68% of tenures were household-owned.[11]

### Labour market

The labour market has undergone fundamental changes since the 1970s. One of the most marked changes has been the growing participation of women in the labour force, particularly in relation to part-time work. In 1996, women made up 44% of the labour force, compared with 38% in 1971.[11]

Another outward sign of the new environment was the dramatic increase in unemployment that occurred in the early 1980s. The level of unemployment peaked at 3.3 million in 1986 and 2.9 million in 1993[14] (see Figure 3). Falls in unemployment were not accompanied by equal increases in employment. Over this period, there was a rapid increase in the numbers of men economically inactive due to disability or permanent sickness.[15] Since 1993, unemployment has entered a downward phase.[11] By March 1997, unemployment had fallen to 8.3% of the male workforce and 3.2% of the female workforce, with a total of 1.7 million people unemployed.[16]

**Figure 3**   *National claimant unemployment, 1971-1997*

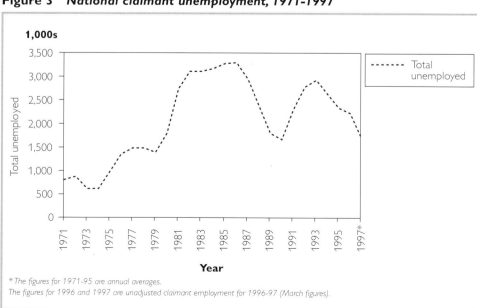

\* The figures for 1971-95 are annual averages.
The figures for 1996 and 1997 are unadjusted claimant employment for 1996-97 (March figures).

Source: See reference 14.

*Looking to the Future: Making Coronary Heart Disease an Epidemic of the Past*

Over the decade between 1986 and 1996, part-time work became more common for both men and women. Over this period, the number of women in part-time employment in the UK increased by 18% to 5.3 million; among men, the number almost doubled, but only to 1.2 million. In spring 1996, 45% of female employees, but only 8% of male employees, were working part-time.[10] Although the Office for National Statistics expects employment to increase by 1.4 million by 2006, other forecasts suggest that the number of full-time employees is not projected to change significantly between 1996 and 2006, while the number of part-time employees is expected to grow by over a tenth and self-employment by almost a quarter.[12]

### Income distribution

A social indicator with important health implications is the disparity between the richest and poorest sectors of the population. Although income distribution is by no means the only measure of wealth and poverty, it provides a useful indicator of the way social patterns have changed in the UK.

Despite evidence that the overall wealth of people in the UK has increased since the 1980s, the distribution of that income changed markedly. The gap between high incomes and low incomes grew rapidly in the UK in the 1980s, with an increasing proportion earning less than average income levels (see Figure 4). From 1977 to 1990 there was an almost continuous measurable rise in income inequality.[17] However, the proportions illustrated in Figure 4 have in recent years levelled off and were falling by 1994. Furthermore, although it is tempting to view the inequalities in income distribution as static, it is important to note that people are constantly moving within the income distribution.[11]

**Figure 4    *Proportion of UK population below 40%, 50% and 60% of mean income, before housing costs, 1961-1991***

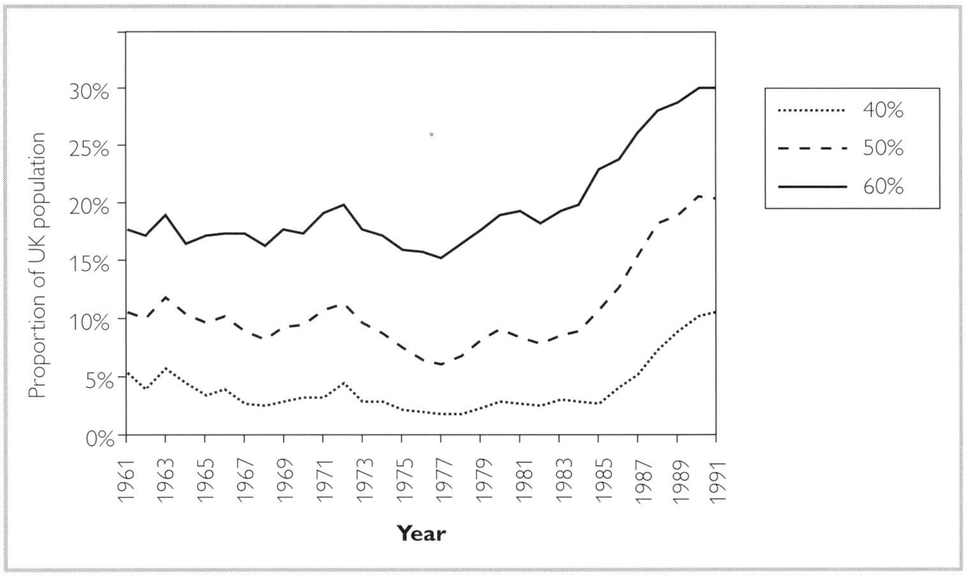

Source: See reference 17.

Nevertheless, the sheer scale of the changes in income distribution is alarming. In 1979, the number of people living below 50% of average income (the 'unofficial poverty line') was 5 million. This figure had increased to 14.1 million by 1992-93.[18] Furthermore, it is estimated that one in three children in Britain live in relative poverty - a higher proportion that any other nation in the EU.[19] Of frequent concern in relation to the gap between rich and poor is the potential for social polarisation between winners and losers, and accompanying alienation, with serious health consequences.[20]

Single people with children have been consistently over-represented among the bottom income quintile, and to a lesser extent, so too have pensioners. Ethnic minority groups are also over-represented among low income households in Britain.[11]

The Joseph Rowntree Foundation has put forward three broad reasons for the rise in income inequality in the 1980s:

- the growing income gap between those in work and those out of work (particularly when benefits were rising in line with prices, but real earnings were rising faster than prices)

- the growing numbers without income from work (as a result of both unemployment and demographic factors), and

- the widening of the distribution of incomes within the 'in-work' group.[21]

The Foundation found no sign of a 'trickle down' effect, where the increased earnings in the highest income groups raise the living standards in the lowest income groups in the population.[22] With the wide difference between incomes of those in and out of employment, and the increasing trends towards safety net provision of social security, the income penalty of becoming unemployed is likely to be significantly greater than it has been before.

### Education

More people are participating in education than they were in the 1960s and 70s. There has been a general increase in examination attainment since the 1970s, and the proportion of those who leave school without some formal qualifications has decreased. In 1995, there were around twice as many enrolments by men for undergraduate courses in the UK compared with 1971, and over four times as many enrolments by women.[11]

Of concern are those without education qualifications. Although more are gaining qualifications, it is clear from the analysis of income data that relative income levels are linked to educational achievement. Education qualifications facilitate entry into employment, and the acquisition of skills through employment. With a more demanding and flexible labour market, the stigma of leaving school without qualifications is very much greater than 20 or 30 years ago.

### Patterns of consumer spending

The changing labour market has not been the only indicator of change since the 1980s. Over the period 1978-92, there were significant changes in patterns of consumer expenditure. The average share of total non-housing expenditure allocated to necessities (food, fuel and clothing) fell from 41% to 30%. Although richer households spent less on necessities than average, and poorer households spent more, the proportion of expenditure on necessities fell for both (from 31% to 20% for the top 10% of households, and from 52% to 40% for the bottom 10%). The corresponding share increases were in luxury goods such as entertainment and the 'other' category, which was mostly services.[23] Although these figures suggest the attraction of a greater range of luxuries and services, the data may be affected by compositional change in income groups.

The seemingly constant technological changes and innovations since the 1970s, particularly in information technology, may also bring changes in means of consumption, at least for those who can afford them. European usage of the Internet is expected to double every year until 2001, by which time it will connect an estimated 100 million people.[24] The growth of the Internet and the forthcoming introduction of digital television may see the spread of home-based shopping and offer access to a diverse range of services.

**Lifestyles**

A growing trend in the lifestyles of people in the UK is the high premium attached to time. The pressures on individuals' and families' time appear to be increasing, with competing and more demanding requirements in the workplace. In the employment sphere, people in the UK tend to work longer hours and take fewer holidays than their European counterparts.[25] Analyses indicate that the people for whom the stress from time pressure is most acute are those with two jobs, and working women with children.[26] The way in which time is managed has also changed significantly, with new working patterns, multi-tasking, late night shopping and home-working.[27]

Against the backdrop of the individualist society that has developed since the 1970s, there is an emerging picture of people finding ways of making their individualism and their individual consumer choice fit into a much bigger picture of community. This pattern of 'downshifting', involving trading money and status for time and quality of life, is seen as a trend that is at a very early stage, but has potential for growth.[26]

Another indication of the changing lifestyles of people in the UK can be drawn from transport data. While greater distances are travelled by car, the average distance walked per person each year fell by one-fifth between 1975-76 and 1993-95, to 321 kilometres a year. This fall was the largest for children aged 5 to 15 where the distance walked per child fell by over a quarter.[11] Much of the decline can be attributed to parents' concern about safety concerning traffic and other dangers.[28]

Road traffic levels have been rising sharply since 1951 and are projected to increase well into the next century, to the extent that by the year 2025, road traffic levels are forecast to rise by at least 55% from 1995 levels.[11] This clearly has implications for walking and cycling. It is likely that over the next 20 years there will be more determined measures to reduce or restrict private transport usage, which could be assisted by ongoing developments in information technology and the Internet.

## Implications for coronary heart disease

The effect that social, political and economic trends can have on coronary heart disease can be expressed through many of the risk factors that give rise to the disease. Since the 1970s the inequalities in coronary heart disease mortality between the richest and poorest social classes have widened[29] (see Figure 2 in Chapter 3).

This widening gap provides a clear illustration of how measures of health status can change rapidly over a short period of time, and begs questions about the social and economic conditions behind the changes. Underpinning the links between social, political and economic trends, and coronary heart disease, is the policy environment. Policy decisions can impact significantly on the risk factors for coronary heart disease.

### Age structure

The ageing population raises concerns about the quality of life for older people. As people age, they are more likely to suffer from chronic diseases. Increasing longevity may be accompanied by the burden of disability through chronic diseases and consequent suffering and loss of enjoyment of life. When the baby boomer population reaches the age of 65 in the 21st century, a huge increase in cardiovascular disease (at least in absolute terms) can be expected.[30] The importance of coronary heart disease prevention, from a morbidity rather than mortality perspective, will therefore assume greater importance. As a World Health Organization report states: "increased longevity without quality of life is an empty prize. Health expectancy is more important than life expectancy."[31]

### Ethnic diversity

The changing ethnic composition of the UK population has its own pertinent health issues, with coronary heart disease rates varying between ethnic groups. For example, South Asians living in the UK have a higher death rate from coronary heart disease than the indigenous population. The rate is at least 36% higher for men and 46% higher for women and may be greater, and the ethnic differences in death rates from coronary heart disease appear to be increasing.[32] Moreover, the health differences between ethnic groups 'follow socioeconomic contours.' The difference in health status appears to be less connected to the cultural practices of each group than to disparities in employment, income and standards of living.[13]

### Material deprivation

There is no doubt that the material effects of deprivation have an effect on health. A telling example, with strong implications for coronary heart disease, is modern malnutrition - the re-birth of food poverty in Britain. Although low income families spend a higher proportion of their income on food (including a greater proportion spent on fresh fruit and vegetables) than average or high income families, low income families are frequently unable to purchase an adequate diet. The years from 1990 to 1994 saw a widening 'food gap' between the highest and lowest income groups (the top and bottom 20%), with declining fruit consumption among the poorest, and the opposite trend among the richest. A food gap also emerged with regard to fat consumption. The income-nutrition problem is compounded by the trend among food retailers to site supermarkets away from city centres. Lower income people living in city centres consequently have reduced access to cheaper food.[33]

Material deprivation, poor life chances, and the pressures of not having enough resources to provide a reasonable quality of life can also be also expressed through patterns of smoking. Although over the past two decades the prevalence of smoking has declined among higher income groups, it has not declined among the lowest income quarter. It has been argued that the very high level of smoking among low income families is primarily a response to poverty. Its expense deepens their poverty

*Looking to the Future: Making Coronary Heart Disease an Epidemic of the Past*

and effectively blocks a way out. People tend to give up smoking for reasons connected to optimism about themselves, their families and their lives.[34]

Of wider concern are the pockets of deprivation, characterised by concentrated patterns of high unemployment, low relative income, low education levels, lower quality housing and poorer health, including prevalence of coronary heart disease. Often such pockets of deprivation are marked by higher concentrations of black and ethnic minorities and single parent households. These patterns also raise concerns of social cohesion in disjointed and isolated communities, and the psychosocial impact of the lack of social support.

## Income distribution

Health may also depend, not on the level of aggregate wealth of a society, but on the distribution of wealth within that society. Studies have found that the relationship between income distribution and health appears to be highly significant, even after controlling for average incomes, absolute levels of poverty, maternal literacy, education, racial differences, smoking and various national measures of the public or private provision of medical services. Societies which are both egalitarian and healthy are also markedly more socially cohesive than others. With increased inequality, such societies show markedly higher rates of death from most causes, as well as alcohol-related deaths, homicide, violence, crime and probably drug use.[35]

## Education

Educational achievement, with its flow-on into employment, and the material and psychosocial rewards that can accompany it, can be considered a passport to health. Evidence, particularly from the United States, points to important health gains in adult life which are linked to educational and social interventions in childhood. Programmes in the post-neonatal, pre-school and school-age periods, often involving both parents and children, are believed to have positive effects on cognitive and social-emotional development. These in turn can improve long-term outcomes in health, well-being and competence throughout the life cycle.[36]

In the UK, an observational study found that both education and social class can serve as indices of life course socioeconomic experience, and both are strongly associated with mortality in middle-aged men. Cardiovascular disease is the cause of death which is most strongly associated with a low level of education, which could reflect that education is an indicator of socioeconomic circumstances in childhood. Education is likely to be important for the opportunities it creates for improved material conditions of life, rather than for specific effects of education itself.[37]

There is also evidence that men and women with low educational qualifications and attainment are the least likely to respond to health education messages, such as those relating to smoking and diet. This may be due to a variety of factors, such as the association of poor education with low income and consequent access to a healthy diet, lack of knowledge about diet, or peer group influences.[38]

## Labour market

Changes in the labour market and workplace practices may have important psychosocial influences on coronary heart disease. These influences may also be expressed through the modern social hierarchies of everyday life. The Whitehall studies have demonstrated strong coronary heart disease mortality in intermediate grades and low grades of civil service hierarchies, compared to the high grades. The results of these studies provide evidence that the risk of cardiovascular disease in affluent societies rises sharply with decreasing occupational status, even among office-based workers who are not in absolute poverty as usually understood.[35]

In addition to the impact of hierarchies, low job control in the work environment is also seen to contribute to the development of coronary heart disease among British male and female civil servants.[40] The increasing competitiveness in the economy and the more flexible labour market has an impact on the workloads and time pressures on individuals within organisations. This can have an effect on levels of stress and tension within workplaces, with accompanying health effects. These effects may be counteracted where employees are feeling needed, effective and useful, and where work becomes much more an expression of abilities, value and worth.

The stress issue links with the increased participation of women in the labour force. Although the increased presence of women in work is not reflected in increased rates of coronary heart disease (coronary heart disease rates for women have in fact been declining) this does not deny the problem of the double burden that women in the workforce tend to carry, as opposed to men. In addition to the demands of work, women also shoulder home and family responsibilities, and this has costs that are manifested in stress hormones and relate to disease risk. It may also have implications for patterns of food preparation and type of food consumed.

Job insecurity is another important factor in the psychosocial pathways of coronary heart disease. The Whitehall II study found that self-reported health status measures for middle-aged civil servants anticipating job change or job loss showed significant deterioration, relative to a group remaining in secure employment. The relative change in health status could not be accounted for by changes in health-related behaviours.[41] Other research suggests that the emergence of insecurity about income and prospects is a growing source of stress in the working lives of certain groups within the labour market.[26] There is however some controversy over the degree to which job insecurity has increased in recent years, despite the common fears and perceptions of changes in the labour market.[42]

### Social support

A poor social network with few relations and/or a low level of social support is associated with a high risk of cardiovascular disease, as well as total mortality. A good social network not only has beneficial effects in itself, but may also be crucial to changing health behaviour patterns, such as smoking.[43] A sense of control and availability of social support are both important in determining health inequalities and health differences between whole societies. The subjective quality of life is not simply determined by the material environment, but very powerfully by the social environment.

### Lifestyles

Transport patterns and environmental pollution can directly impact upon the uptake of physical activity - for leisure or transport - which directly impacts upon coronary heart disease. Fear of accidents on roads, broken pavements, as well as traffic fumes and pollution, have been identified as barriers to physical activity.[28] The pressure of time also heavily impacts on the ability of people to take part in physical activity.[26]

The growth of new media carries a host of possibilities, including its potential to impart health knowledge, connect communities, and also to promote and provide a wide range of goods and services (both healthy and unhealthy).

## Further research

This chapter has outlined the key social, political and economic issues and their links with coronary heart disease, but there are a number of avenues for new research that need to be explored. They include:

- the potential growth of coronary heart disease morbidity in older people, and the means to reduce it

- pathways of income distribution among older people, and their links with rates of coronary heart disease

- the particular coronary heart disease risk factors and health needs of specific ethnic groups

- the health impact of the process of change to the more competitive social and economic environment, and the impact of management practices

- the possible role of the Internet and the other new media as mediators in building links between communities, and

- the development of indicators of social cohesion and involvement in social networks, as markers of quality of life.

Although further research will improve the knowledge base for developing effective policies, this chapter has shown that there is already a sizeable body of evidence that should give sufficient impetus for policy action that targets not only health behaviours, but also the environmental factors that can reduce coronary risk.

## Conclusion

Social, political and economic trends clearly have important implications for developing coronary heart disease prevention strategies. Such strategies will need to be broad-based, and directed not only at the traditional modifiable risk factors, such as nutrition, physical inactivity and smoking, but also at promoting access to lifestyles that can reduce the incidence of coronary heart disease and improve health. This approach should include policies that encompass such issues as:

- childhood development

- education and skills training

- employment and the workplace

- quality of the physical environment

- community development, and

- income distribution.

Health is a pivotal area of policy, so assessment of the health impact of all policy proposals must be integrated within the policy-making process. Essential to the success of reducing coronary heart disease is the commitment to improved health by all the key agencies of government, in partnership with local government and the health professions, and with the research, industrial, consumer and voluntary sectors.

Although the market-oriented approach to the economy is likely to continue, the experience of the UK is that markets will function according to the regulatory environment that is set. Therefore, setting standards for health can directly impact upon healthier lifestyles, and healthier lives. Those with responsibility for health, at all levels, and in both the public and private spheres, need to be challenged to act within an ethos of public responsibility.

Coronary heart disease is a vital marker of health status, with a substantial body of research behind it, and sharing factors in common with many other diseases. However, coronary heart disease is preventable, and policy has an important role in averting the levels of death and disability that coronary heart disease can cause. Coronary heart disease therefore is an important indicator of the success of public health policy, not just in terms of modifying individual lifestyles, but also in modifying the structural conditions that can give rise to the disease.

### References

1    Atkinson R, Savage SP. The Conservatives and public policy. In: Savage SP, Atkinson R, Robins L. 1994. *Public Policy in Britain*. London: MacMillan.

2    Dunn M, Smith S. Economic policy under the Conservatives. In: Savage SP, Atkinson R, Robins L. 1994. *Public Policy in Britain*. London: MacMillan.

3    Pierson C. Social policy under Thatcher and Major. In: Ludlam S, Smith MJ (eds.) 1996. *Contemporary British Conservatism*. London: MacMillan.

4    Hutton W. 1996. *The State We're In*. London: Vintage.

5    Labonté R. 1997. Healthy Public Policy and the World Trade Organization: A Proposal for an International Health Presence in Future World Trade Talks. Internet: *http://www.ens.gu.edu.au/eberhard/WTO.htm*

6    George S, Sowemimo M. 1996. Conservative foreign policy towards the European Union. In: Ludlam S, Smith MJ (eds.) 1996. *Contemporary British Conservatism*. London: MacMillan.

7    Kendall I, Moon G. Health policy and the Conservatives. In: Savage SP, Atkinson R, Robins L. 1994. *Public Policy in Britain*. London: MacMillan.

8    Department of Health. 1998. *Our Healthier Nation: A Contract for Health*. London: The Stationery Office.

9    *Article 129 of the Treaty on European Union*. Internet: *http://europa.eu.int/en/comm/dg05/health/ph/art129.htm*

10   *Brussels Brief*. 20 June 1997. Internet: *http://www.stanbrook.com/brief/inserts/amster.html*

11   Church J (ed.) 1997. *Social Trends 27*. London: The Stationery Office.

12   Harris T. Projections: a look into the future. In: Church J (ed.) 1997. *Social Trends 27*. London: The Stationery Office.

13   Modood T. Conclusion: Ethnic Diversity and Disadvantage. In: Modood T, Berthoud R, Lakey J, Nazroo J, Smith P, Virdee S, Beishon S. 1997. *Ethnic Minorities in Britain: Diversity and Disadvantage*. London: Policy Studies Institute.

14   There have been changes to the definition of 'unemployed' on many occasions over the last 20 years. Source of data: Office for National Statistics Labour Market data.

15   Bartley M, Owen C. 1996. Relation between socioeconomic status, employment, and health during economic change, 1973-93. *British Medical Journal;* 313: 445-449.

16   Office for National Statistics. 1997. *Labour Market Statistics to March 1997*. London: Office for National Statistics.

17   Goodman A, Webb S. 1994. *For Richer, For Poorer: The Changing Distribution of Income in the United Kingdom, 1961-91*. London: Institute for Fiscal Studies.

18   Elliot L, Brindle D. 1997. Unequal 'not unfair' in Tory equation. *The Guardian;* 28 April 1997: 13.

19   Brindle D. 1997. Children in poverty: Britain tops the European league. *The Guardian;* 28 April 1997: 1

20   Wilkinson M. 1996. Our at-risk society: exclusion as a threat to health and democracy. *The Journal of Contemporary Health.* Summer 1996; 4: 62-64.

21   Joseph Rowntree Foundation. 1995. *Joseph Rowntree Foundation Inquiry into Income and Wealth, Volume 2*. York: Joseph Rowntree Foundation.

22   Joseph Rowntree Foundation. 1995. *Joseph Rowntree Foundation Inquiry into Income and Wealth, Volume 1*. York: Joseph Rowntree Foundation.

23   Crawford I. 1994. *UK Household Cost of Living Indices: 1979 -1992*. London: Institute for Fiscal Studies.

24   Gregston B. 1996. The European picture. The NET is conquering the old world. Internet: *http://www.iworld.com.* Reprint from *Internet World;* 7: 12.

25   Tyrell B. 1995. Time in our lives: facts and analysis on the 90s. In: Demos. The Time Squeeze. *Demos.* Quarterly issue 5.

26   The Henley Centre. 1996. *Planning for Social Change 1996/97*. London: The Henley Centre.

27   Leather S. 1997. *What is happening to home cooking?* Paper presented to the Royal Society. Unpublished.

28   Sharp I, White J, Rogers L. 1995. *Physical Activity: An Agenda for Action*. London: National Heart Forum.

29   Drever F, Whitehead M, Roden M. 1996. Current patterns and trends in male mortality by social class (based on occupation). *Population Trends.* Winter 1996; 86: 15-20.

30   Kelly DT. 1997. Our future society: A global challenge. *Circulation;* 95: 2459-2464.

31   World Health Organization. 1997. *The World Health Report 1997: Conquering suffering, enriching humanity.* Geneva: World Health Organization.

32   Boaz A, Kaduskar S, Rayner M. 1996. *Coronary Heart Disease Statistics*. London: British Heart Foundation.

33   Leather S. 1996. *The Making of Modern Malnutrition*. London: The Caroline Walker Trust.

34   Marsh A, McKay S. 1994. *Poor Smokers*. London: Policy Studies Institute.

35   Wilkinson R. 1996. *Unhealthy Societies: The Afflictions of Inequality*. London: Routledge.

36   Hertzman C, Wiens M. 1996. Child development and long-term outcomes: a population health perspective and summary of successful interventions. *Social Science and Medicine.* 43; 7: 1083-1095.

37   Davey Smith G, Hart C, Hole D, MacKinnon P, Gillis C, Watt G, Blane D, Hawthorne V. 1998. Education and occupational social class: which is the more important indicator of mortality risk? *Journal of Epidemiology and Community Health;* 52: 153-160.

38   Wadsworth M. 1996. Family and education as determinants of health. In: Blane D, Brunner E, Wilkinson R. *Health and Social Organisation*. London: Routledge.

39   Marmot MG, Davey Smith G, Stansfeld S, Patel C, North F, Head J, White I, Brunner E, Feeney A. 1991. Health inequalities among British civil servants: The Whitehall II study. *The Lancet.* 337: 1387-1393.

40   Bosma H, Marmot MG, Hemingway H, Nicholson AC, Brunner E, Stansfeld SA. 1997. Low job control and risk of coronary heart disease in Whitehall II (prospective cohort) study. *British Medical Journal;* 314: 558-565.

41   Ferrie J, Shipley MJ, Marmot MG, Stansfeld S, Davey Smith G. 1995. Health effects of anticipation of job change and non-employment: longitudinal data from the Whitehall II study. *British Medical Journal;* 311: 1264-1269.

42   Burgess S, Rees H. 1996. Job tenure in Britain 1975-92. *The Economic Journal;* 106: 334-344.

43   Kristensen TS, Kornitzer M, Alfredsson L. 1998. *Cardiovascular Diseases, Social Factors, Stress and Work*. Brussels: European Heart Network.

# Implications and priorities

*This chapter is based on the workshops and discussions at the Coronary Heart Disease Prevention: Looking to the Future conference.*

One of the main reasons for the slower decline in coronary heart disease rates in the UK than in other similar developed countries has been the failure to adopt a genuine and strategic population approach to tackling the disease and its risk factors. A comprehensive programme to reduce coronary risk could make a measurable difference, but to do so, needs to be set within a broader national public health strategy and supported by a legislative framework and fiscal policies.

A broad public health perspective, tackling the fundamental determinants of ill-health, and taking account of widening social inequalities and an ageing population, is needed. Action to reduce coronary heart disease should be set within the context of other chronic diseases; there is a need to avoid developing strategies and programmes in isolation from one another. Given the major environmental and lifestyle factors involved in the causation of coronary heart disease, a wider - *Health of the People* - agenda is needed. If action to tackle the determinants of ill-health and health inequalities is comprehensive, the overall health gain will be great, influencing not just coronary heart disease but also other chronic diseases such as cancer. Action targeted specifically towards coronary heart disease should focus primarily on setting agendas, responding to the public's concern about their risk of disease, and secondary prevention.

With scientific consensus on the major causes of coronary heart disease, there is a need now to develop an effective prevention strategy which anticipates the challenges of the future. It should take account of two factors:

- inequalities in the risk of coronary heart disease - namely widening social class inequalities, and geographical, gender and ethnic differences

- the possible increase in morbidity from coronary heart disease, particularly as the population ages, and the implications for services.

## A comprehensive national strategy: what should it encompass?

Any strategy to prevent coronary heart disease needs to incorporate a balance of population, individual and medical interventions. Comprehensive population approaches, where the potential for health gain is greatest, should command the majority of resources, although individually focused interventions are particularly important for those at high risk of coronary heart disease.

Previous strategies for preventing coronary heart disease have not been particularly successful in reducing risk factors or the prevalence of the disease - largely because the approach has been piecemeal, and there has not necessarily been the political will. A national public health agenda needs to encompass comprehensive strategies on nutrition, tobacco and physical activity - as well as strategies to address social determinants and the wider environment, such as deprivation and transport. National targets are needed, including process as well as outcome targets. However, since some policies and interventions can have differential effects on different socioeconomic groups, approaches which adapt the effective elements for specific population groups will also be important.

A strategy to reduce morbidity and premature mortality will be important, and should focus on: the circumstances or health determinants which lead to ill health; health behaviours; and risk factors for coronary heart disease.

The priority should be to develop healthy environments, through policy and legislation nationally and internationally, and local and community action. A unified approach will be important, for example focusing on a diet that promotes overall health, as well as on clusters of behaviours, such as smoking, and alcohol and drug misuse among young people.

One of the most important aims of a prevention strategy must be to create a culture in which a healthy lifestyle is a socially desirable choice, and an environment which facilitates such choices. A culture shift is needed, which will take long-term planning and commitment. However, culture is becoming increasingly globalised, and it is important to tackle the issues at international as well as national and local levels. For example, trends in smoking and in food consumption among young people can be seen across national borders, largely due to the international nature of trade. The culture and fashions of the consumer society can have a significant impact upon health. Public health must anticipate international market trends and act accordingly.

Agenda-setting activities will be needed, including: advocacy and direct work with policy makers, public education and professional training and paid and unpaid media activity. It will also be important to work with industry to help ensure that commercial influences shape culture for the benefit of public health.

Health impact assessments should be routinely undertaken on policies of national government departments, and of local agencies within Health Improvement Programmes, to ensure that health is taken into account in all policies.

Although there is a need for further evidence on the effectiveness of specific interventions and policies, through long-term evaluation, the precautionary principle should always be adopted. That is, where there is doubt about the benefit of an approach or policy, the benefit of doubt should be given to the population's health. The cost is then simply that of preventive action, rather than the greater costs likely if fears are proven. Retrospective liability is often difficult to attribute.

**Action on health inequalities a priority**
Tackling health inequalities must be a priority for any future public health strategy. The failure of previous UK health strategies to address health inequalities meant that they could not tackle coronary heart disease effectively. The social class inequalities in rates of the disease - particularly the high rates in lower income groups - and the marked geographical and ethnic differences, need to be a priority. Coronary heart disease could be used as a test case for action to reduce health inequalities.

The relationship between socioeconomic inequalities and health is well established. A particular cause for concern is that income inequalities are predicted to increase. Relative poverty and the quality of life are vital public health issues, and it is important to ensure that lack of income does not become a risk factor for coronary heart disease in itself. Although the mechanisms and the extent to which low socioeconomic status impacts on health through routes other than the 'classic' risk factors and health behaviours are not fully clear, there is good reason not to neglect fundamental action on inequalities. The widening socioeconomic differences are also reflected in risk factors such as rates of smoking, obesity, some dietary factors such as vegetable and fruit consumption, and blood pressure. Links between social class and behaviour are not inherent and there is a need to address cultural factors to reduce this link.

An issue that needs to be debated is whether the most effective way to reduce health inequalities overall might be to focus on raising the health status of deprived groups. This is a particularly important issue since preventive interventions so far seem to have been successful among higher socioeconomic groups, and the impact on the lowest income groups has been minimal.

In order to tackle inequalities in health, there is a need also to address social inequalities, and to monitor the impact of policies on health inequalities. The major issues include inequality of income, opportunity, access, choice, social inclusion, health care, exposure to influences, and power. Possibilities for action include:
–   Initiatives to reduce long working hours and job insecurity, ensure adequate wages and promote healthy workplaces.  Importantly, unemployment, long working hours, low wages and short-term contracts affect ethnic minority groups disproportionately.
–   Urban regeneration and economic development, especially in the context of Agenda 21. The focus of investment should be on sustainable local service industries. Regeneration also needs to ensure the quality of public services and ensure that they do not become ghetto services.
–   Investment in a public transport infrastructure.
–   Investment in new public housing.
–   Investment in education, health promoting schools and life-long learning for adults. In particular, schools could be a focus for community regeneration.

There is a question about how such investment should be paid for. There may be scope for local taxes, hypothecation of taxes, and fiscal levers to promote healthier behaviours, by further taxing, for example, of tobacco, alcohol, petrol and cars. Scope for transferring funds from other areas of government spending, such as the NHS and defence, should be explored. The role of the private sector may be limited by vested interests, although there is likely to be some under-explored potential.

**Focus on children: a life course approach**
A strategy for coronary heart disease prevention needs to adopt a life course approach, beginning with a focus on children. Population policies, which address the environment in which children and young people grow up, will be important: many children want a healthy lifestyle, but the social and physical environment they live in works against this. Children and young people have been insufficiently involved in the development of health policies and programmes, although studies show that they are concerned about their health, and will participate if given the opportunity.

There are major differences in health behaviour and attitudes, among children and young people of different ages, so understanding and addressing the motivations of young people in different age groups will be important.

Tackling disadvantage from a young age will need to be central: one in three children in the UK are now born into poverty. For example, although there has been an increase in smoking among young people, those in higher socioeconomic groups are more likely to give up earlier. The factors that lead from experimentation to addiction among young people, and how this can be prevented, need to be better researched, to inform action.

Children and young people who do well educationally are more likely to transfer what they know to what they do. The national healthy schools initiative should form a framework for a comprehensive approach to healthy lifestyles among both pupils and teachers, although measures will also need to reach beyond schools into the community. Health should become an important element in the curriculum.

## An ageing population

A key concern for any strategy to prevent coronary heart disease is the ageing population, and the implications for levels of morbidity and for support from health and social services, as well as carers. In particular, a fundamental shift in the provision of social support will be needed. Caring for the elderly by family members is becoming less feasible in both economic and social terms, and it is important that decisions about future provision for an ageing population, including fiscal policies and tax incentives, are taken now. A national investigation into options for long-term care packages, and to ensure adequate pensions in retirement, is needed; the twin trends of a shrinking workforce and an ageing population mean that current arrangements will be inadequate. Creating social cohesion will also be important, both in the care of the elderly and in tackling health inequalities, and this might be aided with fiscal policies.

## Ethnic groups

Coronary heart disease is a major cause of death in all ethnic groups living in the UK, although rates vary between different ethnic groups, and tackling this should be a priority. The established causes of coronary heart disease account for the large majority of events. The higher risk among Asians from the Indian subcontinent and the lower risk of coronary heart disease among Caribbeans mainly reflect differences in the relative contribution of the causal factors. Blood cholesterol levels among Asians are similar to those of the whole population, but additional risk is associated with a high prevalence of diabetes and possibly with lower physical activity levels.

There has been a decline in excess deaths from coronary heart disease among Asians and a reduction in the relative immunity to coronary heart disease of Caribbeans, supporting the environmental hypothesis. Furthermore, Jamaicans living in the UK have a higher risk than those living in Jamaica. Although causes are broadly the same, there may be differences in the degree to which various mechanisms are affected, which has implications for intervention strategies. In particular, health messages need to be appropriate and sensitive to the cultural patterns of different ethnic communities.

# Creating new public health structures

### A national voice for public health

In the UK, there is currently no national, overarching body for public health. Public health has been fragmented, without a coherent strategy, cohesive intellectual base or strategic research framework, and with no clear relationship between the national and local public health structures. With its own Minister, however, public health should become more central to health policy, and it is important that appropriate and supportive structures are put in place. In particular, there is a need for change at a statutory level, and for a broad public health framework to coordinate policy.

A new national public health agency should be established.[1] It should be concerned with policy, and have the power of intellectual analysis to deal with current and future public health challenges. The systematic creation of opportunities to debate issues and to think beyond current paradigms will be important, and this might be achieved either through existing structures, or through new think tanks, or an intersectoral public health forum.

A coherent and comprehensive vision for public health is now needed. The important role of public health may be to provide the health justification, and to stimulate action. 'Health impact' might become an overarching and uniting theme. In particular, the public health sector needs to increase its effectiveness in taking research findings to decision makers and influencing agendas - to bridge the gap between knowledge and action - perhaps following the successful example set by the environment movement.

At the same time, cross-governmental action is needed, including policy analysis and assessment of the health impact of policies. Health impact assessments should be an integral part of policy making, with a rolling programme to audit all policies and recommend changes accordingly. Ensuring robust and coherent structures and processes for an integrated public health audit function, such as a standing Royal Commission or the National Audit Office, will be vital. Health audits should be of a quality and status that cannot be ignored.

Cooperation between agencies, and 'joined up working', will be vital for success, as real health improvements will be achieved beyond the health sector. In particular, greater alliance working, and 'alliances of alliances' across different sectors, will be important. It will be vital to involve agencies for whom health is not a primary goal. For example, in the case of tackling health inequalities and physical inactivity, the greatest improvements may be made by those working to reduce poverty or improve social welfare for children, or those working to a transport or environment goal. The role of government, non-government agencies and industry, in public health, needs to be thought through.

### A community-based approach

The health status of those living in communities with social support tends to be better than that of those without such support and living alone. There is therefore a strong need to foster healthy communities, and to develop an approach driven by communities if substantial changes in health-related behaviour are now to be achieved. Such an approach could ensure that the needs of specific communities are appropriately addressed.

A priority should be the establishment of 'citizens' health panels' or 'community health action teams', using a community development approach.[2] A primary feature should be local ownership and participation. The teams could be linked in with Healthy Living Centres and with Health Improvement Programmes. One of their first tasks should be to produce, with assistance, community health profiles which could be put on the agendas of relevant local and health authorities, with a requirement on those authorities to respond and be held accountable for action.

A minimum criterion should be substantial community participation in identifying priorities and action. Such teams should be centred on communities which view themselves as such, and characterised by an approach which encourages communities to set their own agenda, and to determine their aims and objectives. There should be dialogue between communities and professionals, appropriate support, and transparency in operations. Local priorities will need to be accepted, even if they do not include coronary heart disease prevention as such.

There are many examples of successful community-based projects driven by the enthusiasm and commitment of local people, including quit-smoking groups organised by and for low income women, and projects for Asian groups to encourage physical activity and to lower saturated fat consumption. Although the effectiveness of these projects was not scientifically evaluated, their achievements, while small scale, are apparent, and a diffusion effect to friends and families leads to wider involvement.

*Recruitment and support*
Recruitment to such panels should use well-tested recruitment approaches, perhaps with time-limited membership to avoid stagnation and narrow ownership. Efforts should be made to make the panels truly representative, including men and women, older people, and children and young people. In particular, mechanisms to incorporate local children's views are needed; children's citizens' juries have been successful in other areas, and could be extended to health. Community health action teams should be intersectoral, and also include representatives of voluntary, private and statutory sectors.

The 'citizens' panels' or 'community health action teams' should be supported by community health or development workers, with a ratio determined by health needs. In the most deprived quarter of the population, this might be one worker per 10,000 population; elsewhere, it might be one per 30,000 population. Management arrangements should be flexible, and staff might be deployed from health or local authorities, possibly through joint arrangements. However, staff should be accountable to the local community, with protective contracts which give freedom to speak or act within this framework. Appropriate other professional support would also be needed, to ensure links with existing services.

*A national framework*
There is a need for a national, formal mechanism or structure to provide an underpinning strategy for a network of community health initiatives. This could also provide a framework for the evaluation of local initiatives, and dissemination of information on effectiveness, to inform policy and development. It is particularly important that existing initiatives are built on, and that new initiatives learn from

past experience, so a mechanism to gather and share information is needed. Government should have a facilitating role, and ensure financial support and resources.

*Funding and sustainability*
The cost of setting up such citizens' health panels is estimated at about £50 million a year. Funding might come from top-slicing of health authority and local authority funds. Further funding opportunities for local initiatives and community projects may include Lottery funding, regeneration funding and European funding.

The sustainability of community initiatives is a key issue, and there is a need to ensure continued funding for valuable initiatives, and to avoid raising expectations unrealistically.

*Evaluation*
Initially, community health action teams should be established as pilot projects, to ensure the effective and staged development of a national network. A national evaluation plan will need to be part of this. Evaluation plans also need to be built into initiatives, to measure progress towards the aims and objectives identified by the community. Evaluating the effectiveness of community projects is an urgent task, although it is clear that traditional epidemiological approaches based on a biomedical model, such as randomised control trials, are not necessarily appropriate. New evaluation methods and approaches, which take into account the process as well as outcome, such as benefits of establishing local ownership and control, are needed. Lessons could also be drawn from previous initiatives through the use of 'grey' literature, personal contacts, databases and directories.

**Building local alliances and social capital**
New alliances between health authorities and local authorities, particularly through Health Improvement Programmes, will be needed to support community health action teams and community initiatives to improve health. Community development approaches could also be promoted through local commissioning by Primary Care Groups. As part of this, the concept of social capital needs to be developed. It is likely to take time to put structures in place to create such social capital, and further discussion is needed in order to create well-designed programmes. Government could also have a role in developing fiscal and other policies to create healthy communities and build social capital.

In particular, local authorities will have a central role in improving facilities for health locally and in promoting community development initiatives through economic regeneration. Health impact should be a consideration integral to planning, and health improvement could be in the criteria for local development programmes. For example, new schools should demonstrate links with cycle routes and how their sports facilities would be used by local residents. Urban regeneration, including upgrading and replenishing public housing, is also important, particularly because many social and ethnic groups who are at high risk of ill-health live in such housing. Urban regeneration and housing should be a national priority, with funding available locally.

Directors of public health should have a role in auditing local policies to create healthy communities, and joint appointments between health authorities and local authorities should be considered. Setting targets, and particularly joint targets between health and local authorities, may be an important means of generating activity. These should include both long and short-term targets, measuring health outcomes as well as indicators of progress.

### Health professionals and clinical interventions

Health professionals have an important role in a prevention strategy, but this needs to be set in a context that recognises the structural nature of the wider determinants of health. The establishment of Primary Care Groups and the development of Health Improvement Programmes are likely to demand a re-evaluation of the public health roles and responsibilities of different health professionals.

A priority for the health service, and particularly the primary care team, should be identifying, advising and treating people at high risk of coronary disease, that is, those with established risk factors, as well as those with existing coronary heart disease. The evidence for the effectiveness of medical interventions among those with established disease is strong, and in recent years, the use of such therapeutic preventive interventions has increased greatly. The importance of assessing overall risk, taking into account multiple risk factors, is now well established. With new technology, 'at risk' registers might be established by Primary Care Groups.

Training, and protocols and guidelines, will be important in ensuring that health professionals always give clear and effective preventive messages, such as dietary advice. National protocols, perhaps developed through the National Institute for Clinical Excellence and monitored through the Commission for Health Improvement, in conjunction with professional bodies, are needed. Although guidelines for therapeutic regimes may have been widely disseminated, there is a need for training, and for monitoring of their implementation. Training of nurses in appropriate care for hypertension and diabetes, for example, using approved guidelines, could lead to more success with treatment.

Furthermore, health professionals dealing with children and young people should take all opportunities to communicate relevant health messages, and training is needed to ensure that this is done effectively as well as accurately and consistently.

A particular issue for ethnic minorities is the high use of traditional herbal remedies. It is important that health professionals ask about the use of non-prescription and herbal remedies, as there may be important implications for interaction with standard drug regimes, and compliance with prescriptions.

## Components of a new, comprehensive strategy

### Diet and nutrition

Diet is one of the fundamental causes of coronary heart disease and of the high levels of the disease in the UK, and should be a central focus for a coronary heart disease prevention strategy. The COMA reports on diet and cardiovascular disease provide important consensus and a basis for policy and action. A strategic, sustained and comprehensive national strategy to improve the UK's diet should be a priority. So far, the UK has not had a national food strategy, but the Food Standards Agency provides an opportunity.

*Partnerships with industry*

A partnership with industry to improve the nutritional quality of food should be a priority, particularly since much food is now processed or pre-prepared. Government, health professionals and consumer groups will need to work more closely with the food industry in order to improve choice, availability of, and access to 'healthier' foods, such as vegetables and fruit, particularly for low income groups.

Food choices can be changed, through availability and marketing, and health messages can be an effective marketing tool. The increasing popularity of skimmed and semi-skimmed milks, for example, and polyunsaturated margarines, illustrates this. There is a strong case for the health sector and the food industry to collaborate on other similar initiatives. Food manufacturers and retailers, including caterers, could also offer incentives to healthy eating, such as a piece of fruit or salad served with every burger.

In addition, food needs to be 're-modelled' for health ends. In particular, the hidden fat and salt in foods need to be reduced in mainstream products.

*Food availability and accessibility*

Making healthy diets, and particularly vegetables and fruit, both accessible and affordable should be a priority. Food accessibility - including price as well as physical availability - is a key concern.

At an international level, the Common Agricultural Policy (CAP) needs reform. Directed towards the production and subsidy of agricultural produce, rather than the diets and health of populations across Europe, it fails to meet many people's food needs adequately. The transformation of the CAP into a 'Common Food Policy' is essential to encourage competitive pricing for healthier foods, and should include the transfer or diminution of subsidies for full-fat dairy products in favour of fruit and vegetables.

Other factors that need to be addressed to improve accessibility, particularly among low income groups, include:

- The income of low income families, who spend the greatest proportion - about one third - of their income on food. It is estimated that this would increase to over 50% if they were purchasing a healthy diet.

- The disparities in price and range of foods offered by supermarkets and local corner shops in deprived areas. In particular, fresh vegetables and fruit command some of the highest profit margins in larger retailers and this needs to be tackled.

- Transport issues, particularly as food retailing becomes less local. This is particularly important for bulkier and heavier items such as vegetables and fruit.

- Retailers' knowledge of the sources of 'healthier' foods, which might be increased through retailers' education initiatives.

- Initiatives to enable low income families to experiment with 'new' foods and new recipes. Fear of food waste is an important deterrent to experimentation.

*Food messages and marketing*

A key concern that needs to be addressed is the dissonance on diet - although the experts may agree about dietary messages, the public report confusion, and media reporting may contribute to this confusion. Consumer advice on diet needs to be clear and consistent, particularly with regard to new evidence on for example, the benefits of the Mediterranean diet and oily fish. A dialogue between health professionals, consumer groups and the food industry could lead to better and more valuable nutrition messages. There may be a need to focus on two fundamental and simple dietary messages:

- reduce fat

- eat more vegetables and fruit.

There is also a need for selective messages for specific population groups. The increasing complexity and plethora of foods means that messages need to be clear and simple. Unfortunately, it is often foods of the poorest nutritional quality that are most heavily marketed.

Clear, comprehensive and meaningful nutritional labelling and education should also be a priority. Although the concept of a simple labelling system is now generally accepted in principle, information on packaging still does not enable consumers to choose easily between products.

*Schools*

Children's diets give major cause for concern, and improving the quality of food at school should be a priority. The reintroduction of minimum nutritional standards for school meals presents an important opportunity to improve the content of school meals, and health. Minimum standards should cover all school food provision, and these should be complemented by teaching food buying and cooking skills as part of the school curriculum.

## Obesity and overweight

The huge increase in overweight and obesity, which shows no signs of abating, is a major issue for coronary heart disease prevention. Obesity - that is, body mass index over $30kg/m^2$ - doubled during the 1980s. Furthermore, there is a strong social class divide in levels of obesity in the UK among women, and the prevalence of obesity is now almost twice as high among women in social class V than among those in social class I. New strategies which tackle obesity by focusing on diet and physical activity are needed.

## Smoking

The UK's successes in smoking control among adults are overshadowed by failures among children and young people, particularly girls, and by the widening social class divide in cigarette smoking. A comprehensive national tobacco control strategy is a priority for coronary heart disease prevention, and the White Paper on tobacco, *Smoking Kills*, presents the framework for effective action.

The health message on smoking is well known, but is not necessarily acted on, and it is important that any tobacco policies are backed up by consistent messages from government. The government's commitment to a comprehensive ban on tobacco advertising and sponsorship throughout Europe, is therefore a welcome development. Other tobacco control policies should include:

- regular increases in tobacco tax above the rate of inflation

- a ban on cigarette sales to under-18 year olds - backed up by effective prosecutions - which could be particularly important in reducing smoking among children

- new initiatives to help smokers quit, including nicotine replacement provided free or at reduced cost to smokers on low incomes who attend cessation clinics or self-help groups to stop smoking.

It is important to set tobacco control policies in a global context, and for the UK to work at an international level, and press for action within Europe and globally. One focus might be on the profitability of tobacco: an international agreement, and perhaps a price limitation scheme, could lead to better control of tobacco profits and distribution. The European Union, World Health Organization, World Trade Organization, and the Office for European Cooperation and Development, for example, might cooperate on this.

International comparisons of smoking policies and their effectiveness are also needed. An international review of smoking among children should be a priority, to highlight the extent of the problem and action that is being taken by different countries to address it.

**Physical activity**
A comprehensive national strategy to increase physical activity across the whole population is long overdue.  Although there have been some increases in leisure time activity, physical activity is gradually being eroded from daily life, and a strategy is needed to create a culture which promotes and enables physical activity throughout life.  Much of the change will need to be environmental. The strategy should:

- promote physical activity among all age and gender groups

- focus on activity as part of daily life, such as walking or cycling

- promote a wide range of activities to appeal to different tastes

- address the issue of location of facilities to ensure accessibility by all social groups

- address cost issues to ensure affordability

- ensure provision of information to promote wide awareness of the available facilities and options.

To support this, a comprehensive transport strategy, led by government, with incentives to encourage activity, such as walking and cycling, is also needed. Transport policy has hitherto run counter to the goal of increasing physical activity. The transport system is a key barrier to change and to improvements in health, and a better public transport system, which encourages less car use and greater activity, must be a priority.  Several cities are already experimenting with such an approach, and urban regeneration plans also present an opportunity to construct such systems. Tackling the road lobby, which can be a major barrier to public health interests through its promotion of private transport, will be an important facet of such an approach. There is a need for health and transport agencies to work together.

A focus on children and young people in such a strategy should be a priority, with policies which encourage activity both in and out of school. Cycling to school, for example, depends critically on safe routes for children in the local environment. Setting a minimum time for physical activity in the school curriculum is important, but it is essential to provide opportunities that promote continued activity throughout life - recognising the different preferences of boys and girls. Other options could include walking games or clubs for getting to school, after-school clubs and disco fitness classes, which could bring together different generations.

**Creating public awareness**

There is also a need to raise public awareness of the risk of coronary heart disease in new and imaginative ways. Campaigns could draw from cancer awareness campaigns, and highlight illness and disability as well as the risk of death. They should address two public misconceptions:

–   that the experts disagree and that health messages are conflicting.

–   that coronary heart disease is a 'quick killer': it is important that the public and professionals are aware of the disability that coronary heart disease can cause.

It is also important to focus on positive health messages that stimulate action, rather than simply negative messages.

Both paid and unpaid media activity can be effective. Messages could be tailored to the specific needs of different age, socioeconomic and ethnic groups, by using appropriate media channels. The Internet will become increasingly important, particularly for children and young people, and imaginative use of interactive technology may act as an effective means of education. Specific radio stations or cable television may be appropriate for different ethnic communities. However, the increasing globalisation and privatisation of the mass media, which enhances the power of multinational advertisers, may conflict with health promotion - an issue that needs to be addressed.

Media messages, including advocacy, can also provide an effective backdrop for local work, such as support for adult smoking cessation initiatives through a telephone helpline.

# Research and evaluation

A comprehensive, and adequately resourced, research strategy to support the national public health strategies must be a priority, and an essential element of this must be to ensure coordination of research and the dissemination of information. Both government and the voluntary sector have an important role in funding public health research, including epidemiology and intervention studies, to ensure its independence, and central funding of the research programme needs to be restored appropriately to ensure its viability.

*Trends and epidemiology*

There is a need for reliable data on incidence and prevalence of coronary heart disease, to form a basis for policy. In particular, better morbidity statistics and trend data are needed to ascertain whether the quality as well as the quantity of life is increasing - that is, whether the extra years of life are years of disability or of health - and the implications for services. There is also a need for research data on sex differences in coronary heart disease morbidity, and on morbidity among ethnic minorities. Exploration of improved ways of measuring health and the quality of life may also be needed, incorporating self-esteem and health aspirations, for example.

Further research is also needed to understand why greater health improvements have been achieved in some regions and countries, and to ascertain which factors - including interventions - have contributed to the success. For example, international comparisons of smoking policies and their effectiveness, particularly among children, should be a priority.

*Ethnicity*
Data currently available on ethnic trends in coronary heart disease are inadequate. Ethnic origin is not currently recorded on death certificates; most analyses use country of birth as a proxy for ethnic origin, but clearly this excludes information on second generation migrants, an increasingly important group.  In the 1991 census, in which ethnic origin is recorded, half of those of Caribbean origin were born in England or Wales. Evidence on coronary heart disease trends in younger and second generation migrants is particularly important. Ethnic minorities are increasingly in high risk age categories.

While ethnic monitoring addresses some of these issues, it is currently confined to hospital inpatients, and there is a need to broaden monitoring to primary and community care. Ethnic classifications also need to be reviewed as some categories assume an inappropriate homogeneity. In particular, national surveys need to use appropriate weighting methods in sampling the ethnicity of populations.

Furthermore, there is a need to improve information about health lifestyles, including diet and physical activity patterns, among ethnic minorities.

*Assessing the impact of policies*
Developing new methodology for health impact assessments should be a priority, to improve analysis and monitoring of the impact of policies on health, and on rates of coronary heart disease. Trends in coronary heart disease and its risk factors need to be assessed against the implementation of the public health strategy, and wider social and environmental policies, at national and local levels.

*Understanding health behaviour change*
Current understanding of motivation and choice in relation to health behaviours is limited. In particular, there is a need for research on the barriers to behaviour change and how to overcome these, and to explore why some groups are less likely to respond to health messages. For example, how to tackle smoking among low income women who continue to smoke despite awareness of the health risks; and why patients with established coronary heart disease show poor compliance with free exercise programmes, despite having a strong incentive to participate.

There is also a need for information on how children's beliefs, attitudes and motivations can change in relation to health and health behaviours, and how health messages can be successfully targeted to children and young people.

Further research, particularly on determinants of mass behaviour change, and on the effectiveness of specific behaviour change techniques and motivators for individual interventions, is needed to inform the development of effective interventions. For example, can GPs be as effective with simple dietary messages, such as 'eat at least five portions of vegetables and fruit a day' as they are in encouraging people to stop smoking?

There is also a need to develop indicators, and collect data, on attitudes to health, and to measure how health beliefs, aspirations and motivations change.

*Models to evaluate the effectiveness of interventions*
Public health and population prevention strategies have suffered from having inappropriate models of evaluation: new research strategies and evaluation methods are needed. Many prevention interventions do not fit easily into current models for assessing efficacy. In particular, better measurements of effectiveness are needed to measure the impact of interventions tackling the wider determinants of health - including the impact of healthy environments and community development approaches. Randomised controlled trials (RCTs) - the 'gold standard' in measuring effectiveness - have not provided evidence on what works in population and individual interventions, partly because of the difficulties in implementing cross-population trials and achieving true control groups. RCTs may need to be adapted, or interpreted more 'intelligently' if they are to be useful in assessing health promotion interventions. Training on appropriate evaluation for health promotion interventions is also needed, for researchers as well as practitioners.

However, it is important that the absence of evidence of effectiveness does not act as a barrier to introducing policy - for example, smoking programmes were initiated on evidence of the disease that tobacco causes, before RCTs showed results. Most projects or initiatives have some effect, and although this may be small or unexpected, it may still be important. Furthermore, the impact of a whole public health strategy is likely to add up to more than the measured sum of individual projects.

*Disseminating research findings*
Disseminating research findings, and ensuring that they are accessible to policy makers and practitioners, and non-government audiences beyond academia, must be a priority. The increased use of information technology offers potential for the analysis and dissemination of research. The National Heart Forum and its member organisations have an important role in distilling and accrediting such information, for wider dissemination. At a national level, there is also a need to share knowledge about the effectiveness and impact of community-based projects. Furthermore, it is important that industry makes available data that could be used to promote health.

**References**

1    National Heart Forum. 1998. *Public Participation for Public Health: Proposals for Local Health Action*. London: National Heart Forum.

2    National Heart Forum. 1999. *Strengthening Public Health: Proposals for National Public Health Structures*. London: National Heart Forum.

# List of participants

*The following people participated in the National Heart Forum conference on Coronary Heart Disease Prevention: Looking to the Future, held in 1997.*

| | |
|---|---|
| Mrs Veena Bahl | *Head of Ethnic Unit, Department of Health* |
| Dr John Brown | *Senior Counsellor, Burson-Marsteller Ltd* |
| Dr Eric Brunner | *Senior Research Fellow, Department of Epidemiology and Public Health, University College London* |
| Mr Michael Burden | *Pharmaceutical Consultant, Royal Pharmaceutical Society of Great Britain* |
| Mr Anthony Byrne | *Healthcare Consultant* |
| Mr Geoffrey Cannon | *Director of Science, World Cancer Research Fund* |
| Dr Angela Coulter | *Executive Director of Policy and Development, King's Fund* |
| Dr Kennedy Cruickshank | *Senior Lecturer, Clinical Epidemiology Unit* |
| Baroness Cumberlege | *House of Lords* |
| Ms Marlene D'Aguilar | *Health Promotion Adviser, City and East London Health Authority* |
| Mr Adrian Davis | *Project Coordinator, Bike For Your Life* |
| Dr Barbara Davis | *Senior Medical Officer, The Scottish Office, Department of Health* |
| Ms Susann Dinan | *Clinical Exercise Therapist, Royal Free Hospital* |
| Mr Andrew Dougal | *Chief Executive, Northern Ireland Chest, Heart and Stroke Association* |
| Ms Pauline Doyle | *Policy Communications Officer, National Heart Forum* |
| Ms Karen Dunnell | *Director, Demography and Health Division, Office for National Statistics* |
| Professor Shah Ebrahim | *Professor of Clinical Epidemiology, Department of Primary Care and Population Studies, Royal Free Hospital Medical School* |
| Mr Adrian Field | *Policy Development Officer, National Heart Forum* |
| Mrs Marcia Fry | *Branch Head, Health Promotion Division, Department of Health* |
| Dr Brian Gaffney | *Chief Executive, Health Promotion Agency for Northern Ireland* |
| Professor Pamela Gillies | *Research Director, Health Education Authority* |
| Professor Raanan Gillon | *Editor, Journal of Medical Ethics* |
| Ms Louise Gitter | *Principal Researcher, Health Which?, Consumers' Association* |
| Dr Fiona Godlee | *Deputy Editor, British Medical Journal* |
| Ms Shirley Goodwin | *Associate Director of Commissioning, Hillingdon Health Authority* |
| Ms Seeromanie Harding | *Senior Research Analyst, Office for National Statistics* |
| Dr Nicholas Hicks | *Consultant Public Health Physician, Faculty of Public Health Medicine* |
| Mr Melvyn Hillsdon | *Research Fellow, Department of Public Health and Policy, London School of Hygiene and Tropical Medicine* |

| | |
|---|---|
| Ms Paula Hunt | *Food for Health Network* |
| Mr Will Hutton | *Editor, The Observer* |
| Professor Philip James | *Director, Rowett Research Institute* |
| Dr Martin Jarvis | *Reader in Health Psychology, ICRF Health Behaviour Unit* |
| Dr Susan Jebb | *Head of Obesity, MRC Dunn Clinical Nutrition Centre* |
| Ms Tessa Jowell MP | *Minister of State for Public Health* |
| Professor Desmond Julian | *Chairman, National Heart Forum* |
| Dr John Kemm | *Director of Public Health, Health Promotion Wales* |
| Dr Brian Kirby | *Chairman, Coronary Prevention Group* |
| Dr Janet Lambert | *Nutrition Manager, Mars Confectionery Ltd* |
| Professor Tim Lang | *Centre for Food Policy, Thames Valley University* |
| Ms Suzi Leather | *Food policy consultant* |
| Ms Rosie Leyden | *Wordworks* |
| Mr Paul Lincoln | *Business Team Manager, Health Education Authority* |
| Ms Jeanette Longfield | *Coordinator, National Food Alliance* |
| Dr Aidan Macfarlane | *Director, National Student and Adolescent Health Unit* |
| Professor Michael Marmot | *Director, International Centre for Health and Society, University College London* |
| Dr Sue Martin | *Environmental Health Section Head, Department of Health* |
| Dr Alan Maryon Davis | *Consultant and Senior Lecturer in Public Health Medicine, Royal Institute of Public Health and Hygiene* |
| Professor Klim McPherson | *Health Promotion Sciences, London School of Hygiene and Tropical Medicine* |
| Dr Dawn Milner | *Senior Medical Officer, Department of Health* |
| Dr Kevin Moreton | *Scientific Administration Officer,* |
| Dr Duncan Nicholson | *Cambridge Health Futures* |
| Dr Noel Olsen | *Chairman, Public Health Medicine Consultative Committee, British Medical Association* |
| Professor Sir Michael Peckham | *Director, School of Public Policy, University College London* |
| Professor Brian Pentecost | *Medical Director, British Heart Foundation* |
| Dr Vivienne Press | *Assistant Medical Director, British Heart Foundation* |
| Dr Mike Rayner | *Head, British Heart Foundation Health Promotion Research Group* |
| Lord Rea | *Chairman, Parliamentary Food and Health Forum* |
| Ms Maria Reader | *Policy Officer - Leisure, Local Government Association* |
| Mr Donald Reid | *Director, Association for Public Health* |
| Dr Alistair Robertson | *Director of Technical Operations, Safeway Stores PLC* |
| Dr John Robson | *Healthy Eastenders Project* |
| Dr Michele Sadler | *Senior Nutrition Scientist, British Nutrition Foundation* |
| Ms Maggie Sanderson | *British Dietetic Association and Principal Lecturer in Dietetics, University of North London* |
| Ms Monika Schwartz | *Coordinator, Healthy Islington* |
| Ms Seroj Shah | *Health Visitor, Lambeth Healthcare NHS Trust* |
| Professor Gerry Shaper | *Vice-Chairman, National Heart Forum* |
| Ms Imogen Sharp | *Director, National Heart Forum* |
| Ms Olivia Simmonds | *Health Promotion Facilitator, Ealing, Hammersmith and Hounslow Health Authority* |
| Professor Peter Sleight | *Professor Emeritus of Cardiovascular Medicine, Nuffield Department of Clinical Medicine, University of Oxford* |
| Professor Andrew Tannahill | *Chief Executive, Health Education Board for Scotland* |

*Looking to the Future: Making Coronary Heart Disease an Epidemic of the Past*

| Dr Margaret Thorogood | *Reader in Public Health and Preventative Medicine, Department of Public Health and Policy, London School of Hygiene and Tropical Medicine* |
| Mr W G Walker | *Chairman, Van den Bergh Foods* |
| Dr Virginia Warren | *Consultant in Public Health Medicine, BUPA* |
| Dr Steven Watkins | *Director of Public Health, Stockport Health Authority* |
| Ms Hilary Whent | *Senior Researcher, Health Education Authority* |
| Dr Michael Wilkinson | *Director, Coronary Prevention Group* |
| Dr Keith Williams | *Director of Public Health, Coventry Health Authority* |
| Professor David Wood | *Professor of Clinical Epidemiology, National Heart and Lung Institute* |
| Mr John Wood | *Head of Scientific and Regulatory Affairs Division, Food and Drink Federation* |
| Ms Anne Woodham | *Chair, Guild of Health Writers* |
| Ms Lynn Young | *Community Health Adviser, Royal College of Nursing* |

## Conference administration

| Ms Jacquie Allix | *Administrative Assistant, National Heart Forum* |
| Ms Gill Cawdron | *Administrative Manager, National Heart Forum* |
| Ms Tuesday Udell | *Student Placement, National Heart Forum* |
| Mr Chris Wyborn | *Administrative Assistant, National Heart Forum* |
| Ms Rosemary McMahon | *Conference Consultant, Professional Briefings* |
| Ms Karen Stone | *Conference Consultant, Professional Briefings* |

# List of commentators

*The following people commented on Task Group papers as they were being prepared.*

| | |
|---|---|
| Dr Keith Ball | *Patron* |
| Ms Jill Barlow | *Chartered Institute of Environmental Health* |
| Mrs Beryl Bevan | *Ealing, Hammersmith & Hounslow Health Authority* |
| Dr Kathie Binysh | *Ealing, Hammersmith & Hounslow Health Authority* |
| Dr Henry Blackburn | *University of Minnesota* |
| Dr Eric Brunner | *University College London* |
| Dr Jacky Chambers | *Birmingham Health Authority* |
| Professor Sir Richard Doll | *Patron* |
| Professor Len Doyal | *University College London* |
| Professor Shah Ebrahim | *Royal Free Hospital School of Medicine* |
| Professor Aaron Folsom | *University of Minnesota* |
| Professor John Goodwin | *Patron* |
| Dr Jeffrey Graham | *Department of Health* |
| Dr Sian Griffiths | *Oxfordshire Health Authority* |
| Professor R F Grimble | *University of Southampton* |
| Dr Spencer Hagard | *London Health Economics Consortium* |
| Dr Adrianne Hardman | *Loughborough University* |
| Sir Raymond Hoffenberg | *Patron* |
| Dr Susan Jebb | *Medical Research Council Dunn Clinical Nutrition Centre* |
| Dr Michael Joffe | *St Mary's Hospital Medical School* |
| Dr John Kemm | *Health Promotion Wales* |
| Dr Brian Kirby | *University of Exeter* |
| Professor Lewis Kuller | *University of Pittsburgh* |
| Ms Suzi Leather | *Individual Member, National Heart Forum* |
| Professor Tony McMichael | *London School of Hygiene and Tropical Medicine* |
| Professor Jim Mann | *University of Otago, New Zealand* |
| Professor Michael Marmot | *International Centre for Health and Society* |
| Professor Jerry Morris | *Patron* |
| Dr John Noakes | *Simpson House Medical Centre* |
| Professor Michael Oliver | *National Heart and Lung Institute* |
| Professor Brian Pentecost | *British Heart Foundation* |
| Dr Mike Rayner | *British Heart Foundation Health Promotion Research Group* |
| Dr Theo Schofield | *Royal College of General Practitioners* |
| Professor Gerry Shaper | *Vice-Chairman, National Heart Forum* |
| Professor Desmond Sheridan | *St Mary's Hospital Medical School* |
| Ms Olivia Simmonds | *Ealing, Hammersmith & Hounslow Health Authority* |
| Mr David Taylor | *GJW Government Relations Ltd* |
| Professor Dag Thelle | *University of Oslo* |
| Dr Margaret Thorogood | *London School of Hygiene and Tropical Medicine* |
| Ms K F Twine | *British Dietetic Association* |
| Professor Walter Willett | *Harvard School of Public Health* |
| Ms Lynn Young | *Royal College of Nursing* |